KT-513-332

## Ten Great Brand Champion Questions

1. What is your brand equity? How do you know? What can you do to be sure?

2. Do you have a strong positioning statement that everyone can repeat quickly and easily, one that captures the very essence of what the brand really means?

3. How far can you stretch the brand equity to maximize its potential without hurting its current success?

4. What are you doing to make your brand more important to the customer?

5. How do you continue to develop the brand equity? Name three decisions that were directly and knowingly impacted by a respect for the brand equity.

6. What are you doing to use technology to the brand's advantage?

7. What can the Internet really do for your brand, and what can your brand do for the Internet? What is your Internet strategy?

8. Do you think the other associates in your company really understand what the brand is about?

9. Who is your real competition? Who else? What else?

10. What brand, company, or change could be lurking in the shadows that is capable of disrupting our happy lives as brand managers?

## Your Everyday Pricing Guide: The Master Formulas

Memorize this easy master formula:

**(Selling price – Cost) ÷ Selling price = Gross margin %**

For example: ($1.00 – $.30) ÷ $1.00 = 70%

**To find the selling price** when you know the cost and the margin desired (margin desired is 70 percent, so the inverse is 30 percent, which is .30):

**Cost ÷ Inverse of margin desired = Selling price**

For example: $.30 ÷ .30 = $1.00

**To find the cost level** that you can afford when you know what percent margin is required:

**Selling price × Inverse of margin = Cost**

For example: $1.00 × .30 = $.30

alpha
books

*tear here*

## The Heads Up! School of Management

This could happen to you any time now. Be prepared!

The president of the company is walking down the hall right toward you and wants to know your thoughts on …

1. Do you really believe that customer service should be a core strategy for us? What would we do differently if it were?

2. How should we measure success around here?

3. Tell me something, just between us: Why would anyone honestly care about which brand of XXX they buy? I know your brand is a good one, but why should anyone buy it at this price? In this package?

4. What do you think a mission statement should do?

5. Do you think a vision statement is a good idea?

6. Do you think our market research really teaches us anything we didn't already know?

7. Do you think we really understand the equity of our brand names?

8. Has your competition changed much in the last five years?

9. What keeps you awake at night?

10. What would happen to the brand if a bus hit you? Not that we want that to happen, mind you ….

In Print £9-99 2310 Aug 2002 JG
latest edition 04/03/15 £2.59
95070

M L C
LIBRARY

658-62NIC
642c

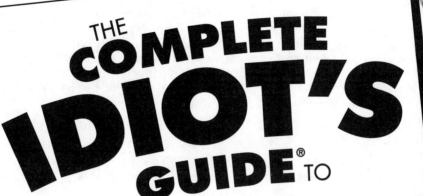

# THE COMPLETE IDIOT'S GUIDE® TO

# Brand Management

## by Patricia F. Nicolino

**alpha books**

Macmillan USA, Inc.
201 West 103rd Street
Indianapolis, IN 46290

A Pearson Education Company

THE LIBRARY
MEAT AND LIVESTOCK COMMISSION
PO BOX 44
WINTERHILL HOUSE
SNOWDON DRIVE
MILTON KEYNES
MK6 1AX

AHDB LIBRARY
02476 478839
CC.NO. 2310    PO NO DONATION
RICE: £9-99    DATE:
LASS.NO. 658-8NIC  05/03/15

# Copyright © 2001 by Patricia F. Nicolino

All rights reserved. No part of this book shall be reproduced, stored in a retrieval system, or transmitted by any means, electronic, mechanical, photocopying, recording, or otherwise, without written permission from the publisher. No patent liability is assumed with respect to the use of the information contained herein. Although every precaution has been taken in the preparation of this book, the publisher and author assume no responsibility for errors or omissions. Neither is any liability assumed for damages resulting from the use of information contained herein. For information, address Alpha Books, 201 West 103rd Street, Indianapolis, IN 46290.

THE COMPLETE IDIOT'S GUIDE TO and Design are registered trademarks of Macmillan USA, Inc.

International Standard Book Number: 0-02-863992-8
Library of Congress Catalog Card Number: Available upon request.

03  02  01     8  7  6  5  4  3  2  1

Interpretation of the printing code: The rightmost number of the first series of numbers is the year of the book's printing; the rightmost number of the second series of numbers is the number of the book's printing. For example, a printing code of 01-1 shows that the first printing occurred in 2001.

*Printed in the United States of America*

**Note:** This publication contains the opinions and ideas of its author. It is intended to provide helpful and informative material on the subject matter covered. It is sold with the understanding that the author and publisher are not engaged in rendering professional services in the book. If the reader requires personal assistance or advice, a competent professional should be consulted.

The author and publisher specifically disclaim any responsibility for any liability, loss, or risk, personal or otherwise, which is incurred as a consequence, directly or indirectly, of the use and application of any of the contents of this book.

**Publisher**
*Marie Butler-Knight*

**Product Manager**
*Phil Kitchel*

**Managing Editor**
*Cari Luna*

**Acquisitions Editor**
*Mike Sanders*

**Development Editor**
*Nancy D. Warner*

**Senior Production Editor**
*Christy Wagner*

**Copy Editor**
*Krista Hansing*

**Illustrator**
*Chris Sabatino*

**Cover Designers**
*Mike Freeland*
*Kevin Spear*

**Book Designers**
*Scott Cook and Amy Adams of DesignLab*

**Indexer**
*Brad Herriman*

**Layout/Proofreading**
*Darin Crone*
*John Etchison*

# Contents at a Glance

# Contents

## 10 The Powerful Duo: Brand Name + Positioning Statement 115

## 11 Branding Inspiration: Information and Education Go Branded 127

## Part 5: Taking Ownership: The General Management Part of Brand Management     245

### 20 Analysis Without Paralysis: Learning to Love Those Numbers     247

### 21 How Will You Measure Success?     259

**xvii**

# Appendixes

# Foreword

Pat Nicolino first approached us to seek Internet and Digital Media information that would help her readers understand just how rapidly this important new medium was evolving. Pat wanted to know about both the lifestyle and business implications of the dynamic online world. What started as a straightforward information request developed into an exciting opportunity for us here at Media Metrix, Inc.

As we began to work with Pat, her enthusiasm for this book and for understanding how our company operates encouraged us to spend time explaining how we run our business and the intricate Web of decisions we make everyday. When she approached us with the concept of doing a case study on our brand equity and business development, we were flattered and very excited. It is an honor to be part of a book that will, no doubt, be an outstanding contribution to the ongoing studies on brand management.

With hundreds of businesses struggling to gain recognition in a crowded marketplace, a company's brand equity plays a big role in its success. Although Media Metrix is a relatively young company, we have always placed a high premium on building a strong brand. We live with a keen awareness that our brand equity is built each day. Our commitment to the equity of Media Metrix's image and reputation is reflected in every decision we make. This is why we have a deep appreciation for the mental and physical energy, and the tough discipline it takes to build a successful company in such a volatile business environment. We tip our hats to each and every one of you who comes to this book seeking knowledge and inspiration.

To help you on your way, we are very pleased to impart some competitive business intelligence with you. At the back of this book, you will find a special bonus section on Internet Movers and Shakers—the 10 most-visited Web sites in 20 categories, ranging in topic from business news/research to sports. We urge you to use this data as a research tool; visit the sites and study why they are so successful. May your research invigorate you with creative ideas for your own Internet strategy.

As I write this, Media Metrix and Jupiter Communications, the leading provider of research on global Internet commerce, are about to merge. Recognizing both companies' strong brands, we decided to name the new company Jupiter Media Metrix—a brand that represents a company that is more than the sum of its parts. Evidently, brand management is an exciting field that will continue to evolve. We hope that you will join us in this ongoing evolution.

Mary Ann Packo, President, Media Metrix, Inc.

# Introduction

This book will launch you into one of the most engaging, exciting business journeys of your life. Brand management is a much more complicated and sophisticated process than it may sound at first. It is also one of the easiest philosophies to embrace because it makes so much sense. It is a little like some of the people in our lives: easy to love, challenging to live with.

Welcome to the exciting world of brand management. Today the vitality, image, and trust associated with a brand name is more important than ever.

Brand managers have been in demand for decades now, and those who are strong, disciplined thinkers, who can move quickly, and absorb ideas deeply, will find extraordinary career opportunities. The rapid pace of change in today's world is creating a profound need for people who appreciate the past, understand the present philosophies and disciplines of brand management, and are confident enough to evolve new ways of doing business for the future.

As our lives get busier, we turn to the things we know, the things that we are comfortable with, and the things that simplify instead of add stress to our day. Now that millions of us use the Internet for research and shopping, we find a new array of names with *.com* on the end of them. Some are familiar; most are not. Over time, we will adopt a number of them as favorites, just as we have done with clothing, food, and electronic equipment.

This desire for trusted favorites and familiar names creates wonderful opportunities for people like you who are interested in the business side of branding.

## How This Book Is Organized

The book is divided into five parts and is organized as though you were stepping into a company with a brand management structure. We will move from building your background knowledge on what it is all about, all the way through making you the senior executive who gets to ask the tough questions.

**Part 1, "The Power of Brand Management,"** looks at the impact of living in a branded world, where strong brand names are at once taken for granted and highly sought after. We will look at the confusion that has developed around what the term "brand management" really means and be sure that you feel comfortable using it in the right context. This part ends with a look at how the Internet and e-commerce are changing the way we look at brands today.

**Part 2, "Thinking Like a Brand Champion,"** jumps right in with some classics such as the Five P's and some newer thinking, the Four T's. The emphasis all the way through this part is on helping you learn to think like a brand champion, which I believe is the ticket to success in this business. We will put a lot of emphasis on defining and building your brand equity, an emphasis that will stay front and center throughout the rest of the book. The dual approach of a brand champion mind-set and a commitment to brand equity building are the cornerstones of success. These two themes take center stage in this part.

**Part 3, "You've Earned It: The Fun, Creative, Inspirational Part,"** steps back just a little bit from the intensity of the first two parts and talks about the elements of brand management that are considered to be the most fun. And they are. We will look at brand names and what roles they play. We will talk about defending and protecting your brand, including some guidance on getting yourself up to date on trademark issues. We will go on a couple of field trips together and visit three companies with completely different stories and histories, and see how they view their own success today. We will go on a little intellectual field trip as well and ask "What if ...?" as we look at some very new ideas.

**Part 4, "Building Your Brand Perspective,"** contains two main themes—a brand champion attitude and a clear, strong commitment to brand equity building—that are now transformed into the brand perspective. We will take the time to look at five critical disciplines that all affect your brand and yet are not always in your direct control. In each of these five chapters, we do a review of the basics that you need to understand and load up that understanding with the brand perspective.

**Part 5, "Taking Ownership: The General Management Part of Brand Management,"** brings us to the end of our journey, where we will step back once again and look over the landscape we have marched through. Our final mission is to prepare you for more senior, more strategic positions. Key questions to think about include how you measure success, how you will motivate your associates, and how you will help them develop the skills that they need are addressed. What will it take just to pull the best value out of all the data you have? These questions are central to the senior manager's job.

# Some Things to Help Out Along the Way

We will use four sidebars throughout the text to add some extra thoughts, provide another example, or even challenge your assumptions.

### Heads Up

These are the red flags or the "don't miss this" points in the book, where you can find tips and warnings and insight on what lies ahead.

### Mentoring Memo

This is where it is just us talking and the office door is closed. Advice, things to consider, encouragement and people issues are all up for grabs.

### Talk the Talk

You will find lots of the expressions we use explained here. Some of them are jargon, and many of them are words that you know but may not be familiar with in this context.

### Big Brand Insight

This is some comment on the subject under discussion, from the perspective of an established, successful brand. This will give you a longer-term view than you may have right now or a different twist on an idea.

# Acknowledgments

I feel very fortunate to be able to say that I genuinely like my life, and that is because both the personal and professional parts of it are terrific. I owe enormous debts of gratitude to so many people who have shaped my experience and cheered on my growth.

The first round of thanks has got to go to my family, for whom the summer of 2000 will live in memory as the time when no one saw me, but there were rumors that I was alive and well and chained to my computer. My husband is my best friend and, for sure, one of the finest biotech and pharmaceutical consultants around. My daughter is an Internet operations engineer, and I am so proud of her, I could burst.

I want to give special acknowledgment to the many people and companies who contributed directly to this book. Many articles and quotes are incorporated here out of the generosity of the copyright holders. The three companies profiled in depth deserve special thanks for their cooperation and the input provided by key individuals: Dan Dillon, Jeff Hartman, Kathleen Mirani, and Charlotte Rist at Welch's; Mary Ann Packo, Doug McFarland, Max Kalehoff, and Catherine Yao at Media Metrix; and Jake Karger and Maria Toufas at KISS 108-FM. This project would not have been as much fun and as interesting without you.

The people at Macmillan have been a delight to work with. Special thanks to Mike Sanders, Nancy Warner, Christy Wagner, and Krista Hansing for their enthusiasm and dedication at every stage of this project. My literary agent, Andree Abecassis, of the Ann Elmo Agency, is an inspiration and a joy.

To all of my co-workers, clients, and students over the years, thank you for my real education. I hope I did you proud with all I shared here. But now that you have the book, will you still show up for the seminars?

## Special Thanks to the Technical Reviewer

*The Complete Idiot's Guide to Brand Management* was reviewed by an expert who double-checked the accuracy of what you'll learn here, to help us ensure that this book gives you everything you need to know about brand management. Special thanks are extended to Bill Fucito.

Bill Fucito has a BA and MBA from Duke University in business; experience in consumer packaged goods marketing for 20 years; and has worked with and managed the following major brands: Fasteeth Denture Adhesive, Clearasil Acne Treatment, Weight Watcher's Bakery/Licensed brands, Welch's Frozen Concentrate Juices, and Cadbury Cookies.

## Trademarks

All terms mentioned in this book that are known to be or are suspected of being trademarks or service marks have been appropriately capitalized. Alpha Books and Macmillan USA, Inc., cannot attest to the accuracy of this information. Use of a term in this book should not be regarded as affecting the validity of any trademark or service mark.

# Part 1
# The Power of Brand Management

*Brands are exciting businesses to work on. They have a life of their own and yet always reflect the attitudes, strengths, and skills of their managers. It is as though they absorb the best and worst of what we offer, and that is enough to give any good brand manager—indeed, anyone in the company whose work impacts the brand—good reason to pause.*

*This part gives you a lot to think about. It explains why the term "brand management" is used so many different ways. It shows you how the philosophy came to life in the way companies were organized. It describes how marketing is part of brand management, but only one part; they are not the same thing at all. This part even talks about the dark side of brand management and how the intense focus on the brand can lead people to miss the big picture.*

# Living in a Branded World

This morning a child was born in a big downtown hospital near you. This little bundle of joy already owns 10 babyGap® outfits and has a Fidelity® Magellan® mutual fund that his grandfather started for him eight months ago. His name will soon find its way into the first of dozens of marketing databases so that he can get free samples of diapers, lotions, and formulas—and, of course, applications for college savings accounts. We know he will distinguish himself in a way that his own parents never did: He and his generation will be the full flowering of the Brand Called You phenomenon. This child has his own portfolio, wardrobe, and stash of marketing goodies, not to mention that he has—no, excuse me, he *is*—a brand unto himself. Not bad for a kid who doesn't even know his own name yet.

We do live in a branded world. There is no doubt about it. We all make product decisions every day. We probably all have certain types of products of which we like only one or two brands, while we buy other things based on what is on sale on a given day. This inclination to buy branded products is rooted in two basic things: recollection and satisfaction. We remember which one we like by brand name.

The concept of branding is so powerful that we now extend it to human beings as well. Have you heard people talk yet about the idea of the Brand Called You? That's right: People are now thinking that you had better become the brand manager of you, and soon. Say what? This brand thing is getting very close to home.

# What Is a Brand Anyhow?

Let's start right in with a short definition of what a brand actually is:

> A brand is an *identifiable entity* that makes specific promises of value.

That sounds kind of textbookish, so let's pull those words apart to see what they mean.

➤ **Identifiable:** You can readily separate one thing from others similar to it by some means. Quite often, this will be a word, color, or symbol (a *logo*) that you can see.

➤ **Entity:** I even checked *Merriam-Webster's® Online Collegiate Dictionary* for you on this one, and it says that an entity is "something that has separate and distinct existence."

➤ **Specific promises:** This expression may seem a little odd, but not really. A product or service makes claims about what it can deliver to you. Those claims—whether fresh breath, on-time delivery, a stress-free tax return, or a kinder, gentler dental visit—are promises.

➤ **Value:** Whatever you get has to be something that you care about to some extent. The basic logic is that if you live in an apartment in New York City, you probably assign little value to a tractor, no matter how many acres of land it can work in an eight-hour day. However, you may have a high value feeling for a dry cleaner who would deliver to your home. And the cleaner who promises to deliver between 7 and 9 o'clock at night, after you get home from work, has more value to you than one who only delivers during the day.

So when you look at these four components—identifiable, entity, specific promises, and value—what kinds of things could be a brand? There are a lot of obvious items, such as shoes and tennis racquets. There are a lot of obvious services, such as accounting, temporary job placement, house cleaning, and lawn mowing. Beyond these, there is a whole world of *branding* opportunities for tangible things like those we mentioned, and for things much more elusive—things you may have never considered before.

**Talk the Talk**

A **logo** is a symbol of some type that identifies an entity. A logo can be a graphic design, which is what most people think of, or it may be a word or set of words.

Whether you are looking for a new business idea or are reading this book to grow a business you are already in, the whole concept of branding has exciting possibilities.

Let's take a few minutes and bring the idea of branding very close to home. Branding, and the notion of managing the brand that you create, is so powerful a concept that a new generation of thinking has arisen. Today we extend brand management into managing the Brand Called You.

# New Thinking and Motivation: The Ultimate Brand Is You

I want to be sure that you are aware of a very exciting and very personal approach to looking at brands: To be successful in business today, you need to think of your career as a brand to be developed and managed. Right here, in Chapter 1, is the place to bring up this subject so that you can be thinking about it as we move along.

Have you picked up a copy of *Fast Company* magazine recently, or one of management guru Tom Peters's latest books? If you want to catch up on this idea of viewing yourself as a powerful brand, take some time to read what these two sources have to say. I want to make sure that you hear this thinking in the context of our study of brand management because it so perfectly underscores what makes a brand such a vital and exciting thing to work with.

The foundation of this new thinking is that our world of work is changing very quickly. Job security sounds like an incredibly old-fashioned notion, and much has been written about a lack of loyalty from either the individual or the organization. When you translate all of this into the very personal goal of wanting to be successful, two things emerge pretty quickly. First, a big component of being viewed as "successful" has always been how other people assess your accomplishments. The second, of

**Talk the Talk**

**Branding** is the whole business process of choosing what promises, what kind of value, and what kind of identifiable components the entity will have. In Part 4, "Building Your Brand Perspective," we will work through the process of building a brand profile, which is the heart of branding, and the kind of decisions that go into it.

**Mentoring Memo**

It is vitally important that you stay in touch with challenging business ideas such as Brand Called You. You have a tremendous variety of magazines, newspapers, Web sites, and television programs to tap into. In fact, we are going to talk later about how some of these very entities are branding themselves these days.

course, is the satisfaction and good feeling that you have, or don't have, about what you do.

The philosophy of Brand You, which is Peters's term, or the *Brand Called You,* which Fast Company uses, is to distinguish yourself by the way you approach the work. If people see that you are passionate and committed, that you are willing to challenge comfortable old answers, and that you can live with the risk of being wrong sometimes, you will stand out. You create an identifiable entity that is distinctly different from the other workers around you. People come to see that your actions and abilities are specific promises of value that they can count on. As crass as it may sound, that branding makes you as easy to pick out from a crowded employee roster as a Coke can at a dairy convention.

### Mentoring Memo

This is an interesting quote from an interview that ran in *USA Today* with Tom Peters, the author of *The Brand You 50:*

> "If I'm hiring you, I'm going to look at what you have done to stand out. Brand You isn't about self-publicity, but about accumulating a portfolio of projects worth bragging about."

© 1999, *USA Today.* Reprinted with permission.

I am putting emphasis on this concept right up front in this book for two reasons:

➤ It is the newest phase in the evolution of branding and brand management, so it is important that you know about it.

➤ It is a perfect setup to what I believe is the most fun, most challenging, and most personally satisfying opportunity for you: becoming a brand champion.

Could we really brand you? Could we ever. Let's set for ourselves the goal of making you a powerful brand at work. And just to make sure we stay focused, we will make that goal more specific: to have you recognized as the most exciting, most productive, most strategic brand champion that your company and your five biggest competitors have ever seen. That sounds good.

What's all this brand champion stuff? Just hold on for now, and dwell on the sound and the image of those words. Sounds impressive, doesn't it? A brand champion is probably pretty strategic: a good thinker overall, insightful, disciplined but not dull, and an altogether fascinating person to work with and for. Oh, yeah, that could definitely be you.

I am actually going to hold off on discussing exactly what I mean by a brand champion until we get to Part 2, "Thinking Like a Brand Champion," but I think you have already got some idea. Starting right now, and moving through the rest of this book, we will focus on making you into that person. We are going to create Brand You/brand champion. And because you are going to become a powerful brand, we need to get a real appreciation for what brands can mean in our lives.

# Stop, Look, and Listen: You Are Surrounded by Brands

Take a minute and identify all the brands you see in this paragraph:

> Dave is studying for the final exams that will bring his senior year to an end. His Sony® boombox runs nonstop, pushing out tunes from Madonna and 'N Sync. He is heavy into the MP3 thing and will probably hit Napster.com soon. This day of studying won't be so awful. He steps over his size 12 Nike® sneakers, almost trips on the Titleist® golf balls rolling out from the closet floor, and finally snags his hay fever pills. Two long sips of Pepsi® later, Dave is ready to settle in for some serious effort. Just as he opens the first book, his mother yells up to him, "David, did you take your Claritin® today?"

Now, count up how many brands you see in this paragraph. Did the ® symbol, meaning registered trademark, give them all away? Is there anything here that could be a brand according to our definition but that doesn't have any official designation that makes it stand out? Consider a few more questions:

➤ How many of these brands are products, and how many are services? What other kinds of brands can there be?

➤ What about Madonna and 'N Sync? Are they people or brands, or both?

➤ Do you know what the references to MP3 and Napster.com are all about? If not, you just gave away your age. Both of these allow consumers to access music over the Internet. They are software, Web sites, services, and products. Welcome to the new world of multidimensional brands.

➤ What is one thing we know about the attitude Dave and his mother have for a certain product?

I see nine brands when I read that paragraph, but you probably already figured that out from my questions. To me, Madonna and 'N Sync have very successfully branded

**Big Brand Insight**

Here are a few subtleties for you. Have you seen any advertising for Dave's brand of allergy medication? Pharmaceutical companies now talk with the consumer directly about their promises, not hoping or waiting for the docs to do it. Dave takes the medication, but his mother buys it. Who is the real target audience for these ads?

themselves as popular music artists. In Part 3, "You've Earned It: The Fun, Creative, Inspirational Part," we will look at lots of individuals and groups who have basically branded themselves, without ever getting that ® or ™ next to their names.

Now, what about Dave and his mom? To Dave, medicine is medicine—he is just taking what the doctor gave him. To his mother, Dave is taking a specific allergy medication that promises less drowsiness than some other brands, which is very important to her. After all, Dave is an active teenager and drives the family car a lot, so that promise has real value. She cares very much which brand of medicine Dave uses.

# Why Does Anyone Care About Brands?

Brands are like anchors. They are like street signs. They are like reliable friends. A brand gives you a way to recognize what you like, quickly. It gives you confidence, just like Dave's mother feels about that medication. Sometimes a brand becomes so personal that it is a part of your own projected image. Worn any blue jeans or T-shirts with designer symbols or the names of rock bands or retail stores on them recently?

When you ask people about their favorite brands, you hear responses such as these:

➤ I can rely on it to be good.

➤ I can trust it.

➤ It always works for me.

➤ I don't have to worry.

➤ It's so good that I don't even have to think about it.

Are these people talking about their deodorant soap, favorite blue jeans, kid brother, or puppy dog? This is getting kind of personal.

And, to add just a little more food for thought, think about the mental process behind these warm and friendly statements. To feel this way about a brand means that these people have differentiated it from lots of other choices. It really stands out in their minds.

Remember that basic definition of a brand a while back? Looking at the statements we just saw, would you say that these people are talking about an *identifiable entity?*

Do you think they get a sense of *specific promises* that have *value* to them? You bet they do. Now you are starting to get a feeling for what makes working with a brand so exciting: People often have feelings as well as thoughts about their brands.

## Do Branded Products Really Sell More?

Branded products definitely outsell private labels, yes. What makes that statement far more interesting than it looks on the surface is that private label marketers themselves are pushing the trend to buy brands. Does that make sense? Let's spend a few minutes in the one place we can all associate with, and probably the hotbed of the branded versus private label debate: the supermarket. As the trends go here, so go many other industries in the years ahead.

As you walk the aisles of most any supermarket in America, you have access to 25,000 or maybe even 50,000 different items, all under one roof. In many sections of the store, you will have the choice of several *national brands,* a few *regional brands,* and probably a *store brand,* usually referred to as a *private label* as well. So, if you want a whole range of jellies to choose from, you've got it. In other sections, there may be only two brands to choose from, and neither one is a private label.

### Talk the Talk

**National brands** are available pretty much across the country. **Regional brands** may be very small, only around your area, or quite large, such as in the whole southeastern United States, but they are not available nationally. **Store brands** or **private labels** are manufactured by an outside company and are sold to the retailer. The product arrives at the store with a label showing the store name or some brand name created just for these products.

The idea of a private label is basically to draw sales away from the bigger brands. For the most part, private labels coast along on the market demand that has been created, and paid for, by the branded companies. Often you will see the private-label item sitting right next to the leading brand with a sign that challenges you to compare the prices and promises. If you have wondered why you don't see private-label items in all categories, it is because of the basic economics of demand. If there isn't a big demand—and, therefore, big sales—it probably isn't worth the effort to create and stock a private-label product of that type. Also, if there is so little demand for that type of product, there probably isn't a big national company paying to advertise and promote it. There isn't a built-in demand to work off of.

So, the idea of having lower-cost products with the store name on the label has been around for a long time. In the United States, we even went through a phase of having very plain products, sometimes with just black-and-white labels and the word "generic" on them. The word "generic" on the label probably wasn't the best choice. If I were to ask you what that word means, you might well say "blah or nondescript." I checked *Merriam-Webster's® Online Collegiate Dictionary* to get a more eloquent definition, and it defines generic as "having no particularly distinctive quality or application." Ouch.

The whole premise behind these products was that you could save money buying them instead of the big brands. When economic times were tight, it was reasoned, people would flock to them, and a good business opportunity was just ready to take off. The private labels did okay, but not great, for many years; but the generics never seemed to get anywhere, even when the economy turned downward. What was wrong?

A fundamental part of branding was missing. If you go back to our definition of a brand, the phrase "specific promises of value" really explains it. The generics and early private labels communicated their value as lower price. For some products, that is enough of the right kind of value to be successful. But when the products in question are the food that you will feed to your family, an emotional and intellectual process kicks in. What is "good enough" is a big question.

In supermarkets, branded products have outsold private labels and generics by a wide margin for a long time. Let's take a quick look at some market share information for the supermarket industry. ACNielsen, one of the largest marketing research firms in the world, shared some numbers with me showing that in 1999, only 14 percent of supermarket sales were for private-label items.

However, don't just dismiss this subject and think that you can ignore it. Let's stay focused on the kinds of consumer products that we all know you can find in supermarkets and now dig a little further into the private label phenomenon. There are good lessons here for many other industries as well.

First of all, that 14 percent of supermarket sales in private-label products adds up to a whopping $40 billion a year. Now take a look at how that $40 billion is split across the various departments in the store.

## Private-Label Sales by Department

| Dollar Sales | 52 Weeks Ending 1/22/00 |
| --- | --- |
| Total private-label product sales | $39,939,865,371 |
| PL grocery department | 15,684,126,639 |
| PL dairy department | 13,531,143,651 |
| PL frozen foods department | 4,131,117,976 |
| PL nonfood grocery department | 3,218,205,756 |
| PL health and beauty care department | 1,410,344,561 |
| PL packaged meat department | 1,009,065,551 |
| PL deli department | 565,300,253 |
| PL general merchandise department | 309,629,198 |
| PL alcoholic beverages department | 80,931,785 |

*Source: ACNielsen, NetDispatch, © 2000, ACNielsen*

Private label is big business. When the smallest of the businesses we just looked at brings in $80 million a year, there is a lot of activity and opportunity.

But your products aren't sold in supermarkets, so should you really bother to investigate the private-label issue? Let's take a second look at it. I spent some time talking with Thomas Aquilina, a business consultant who also teaches private-label strategy at St. Joseph's College. He reviewed some findings with me from a private-label study comparing 1999 to 1991. Let me share a few of those findings with you here. You can get more information about Aquilina and this study in Appendix B, "Resources and Revelations Guide."

## Private-Label Study Comparing 1999 to 1991

| Finding | 1991 | 1999 |
| --- | --- | --- |
| Consumers with awareness of store brands | 86% | 94% |
| Consumers who buy store brands regularly | 77% | 87% |
| Consumers who say that store brands are as well packaged as national brands | 68% | 80% |
| Consumers who say that price has a major effect on buying store brands | 67% | 56% |

The first thing you notice should be that all these numbers are pretty high. The third issue, that of private-label items being well packaged, is fascinating and certainly true. Private-label items look good these days, no longer like second-class citizens. It's interesting to see that last item, where the numbers went down over time. Fewer people say that price has a major effect on whether they buy a store brand. One last thought: 1999 was a boom time for the U.S. economy, in stark contrast to the recession felt in 1991. Private label is growing without the economic impetus that originally created it. What is going on here?

# Exciting Evolution: Make That Mine

Back to our history lesson. The generics quickly faded away, but the idea of having the store name on the label held up for two good reasons. First, supermarket operators liked the idea of making better profit margins on those items. After all, they didn't need to spend money on television or coupons. Second, and far more important to a whole range of industries, a new idea was forming: Maybe having a store brand could be part of the company's overall strategy. Maybe they could provide good products, with more value pizzazz than just being cheap, and use them to build their own business. Don't you like it when you hear people having smart ideas? Me, too.

There is one more step in this evolution that you need to know about. The newest term for a privately controlled label is "own brand." I like this. The consensus from everyone I asked is that this terminology, first referred to as "own label," came over from Europe. What I like so much about it is that it underscores everything this book is all about: When you think of your brand as your own brand, you take ownership of it and treat it with respect.

**Big Brand Insight**

Go back to the table of private-label sales by department, and look again at the sales volume for private-label products. If you owned one of the top national brands in the dairy department, you would need to create a strategy to happily coexist with the store's own label, because these supermarket operators are not likely to walk away from a $15 billion success.

# The Sincerest Form of Flattery

You have to like this: Private-label products have come full circle from almost throwaway ideas to core pieces of business strategy. What started as an antibrand strategy turned 180 degrees and became a branded strategy. Private-label goods are now modeled on and managed as major advertised brands, and many are referred to as "premium private label." As a marketer of branded goods and services, you have to grin. And then you need to figure out how you are going to compete with them.

The best news for the consumer is that today there is an enormous focus on making private-label/own-brand products competitive with national brands. In fairness, some are terrific; some aren't. The great lesson for us as we study brand management is this:

What started as a way to make money off a one-dimensional idea, lower price, has itself evolved into very sophisticated branding.

I asked Tom Aquilina for his thoughts on the trend to marketing private-label items as premium products. He gave me a few more very interesting numbers about how consumers look at private labels and the new premium private labels:

81 percent of consumers perceive store brands as "brands."

57 percent of consumers say their supermarket offers a premium private label.

Of these people:

89 percent bought premium private-label items.

Of these people:

96 percent will buy premium private-label items again.

91 percent believe that premium private-label items are "better than" or "equal to" national brands.

Aquilina's observations are that retailers have made great strides in the last 15 to 20 years, and most now see their private label as a critical part of their overall brand-equity strategy. He sees these products continuing to grow, with some categories, such as health and beauty care, already posting gains of more than 25 percent. He encourages you to follow these suggestions:

➤ Assume that your purchasers will make more informed decisions and have more options to get what they want.

➤ Think about a new key position that is evolving, a private-label brand manager.

Aquilina encourages retailers who want to build their private label to become more proactive in their communications to the consumer. He also counsels them to make private labels part of a long-range growth strategy, not just a tactic for short-term sales hits.

The flip side of this for branded marketers is to assume that all of this will happen and that it will happen in lots of other industries.

Start watching the ads for the large department stores in your area, and see if you can pick out one of those own brand names used in women's or men's clothing. What about the local hardware store or home center? What about appliances and tires? See any patterns there with a brand name that you have never seen anywhere else? Ask a salesperson if the store has a brand name that it considers its own.

The best retailers today have very stringent guidelines for what kind of quality their private-label products must provide. They have package design guidelines, and they even advertise their own brands.

## The Least You Need to Know

➤ Brands have a powerful appeal because they help us make buying decisions quicker and with more confidence.

➤ Whether something is a brand that can be managed and developed is a function of whether it is an identifiable entity with specific promises of value. That may be a product, a service, or even a person.

➤ Branded products really do sell more than private labels, and they always have. However, there is a definite initiative underway to make private-label brands look and feel like big national brands.

➤ The Brand Called You concept brings the idea of branding and brand management really close to home. It says that you should distinguish yourself the same way that a strong brand does, by making and keeping specific promises of value.

# What Is Management Anyhow?

## In This Chapter

➤ The different meanings of "brand management"

➤ The relationship of marketing and brand management

➤ Learning to think from the brand perspective

➤ How being brand–centered helps keep a company focused

Brand management has a mystique about it that stretches from the hallowed halls of Harvard to the vineyards of the Napa Valley and far beyond. It is now making its leap into cyberspace, where brand identity takes on a new importance. Corporate recruiters, also known as headhunters, still seek out people with "brand experience," and they value people whose resumés indicate that they did time on a well-known brand. Why is everyone so excited about brand management, and how can we make some of this magic for you?

One of the most important things you need to take away from this book is learning to think from the brand perspective, and that involves both strategic and functional disciplines. We will spend a lot of time developing those skills for you. Maybe you want to build your own business. Maybe you work for a company that sells branded products, and you want to understand just why the management of your company does what they do. You will need to get a firm grip on three things:

➤ The basic philosophy of brand management and the organizational design that flows out of it

> The spirit of brand management that needs to be shared throughout the organization

➤ The function, or practice, of being a brand manager

It all starts with understanding what all these people are talking about: What is brand management anyhow?

# A Simple Look at Brand Management

One of the hardest things for many people when they first approach this subject is the confusing use of the term "brand management." Let's jump right into the heart of the issue and create our own working definition for brand management. The term has two parts: first the brand (also defined in Chapter 1, "Living in a Branded World"), and then the brand management process. 1) The brand is an identifiable entity that makes specific promises of value; and 2) Brand management is the process of making sure that the brand's value and promises are kept and communicated.

The term "brand management" was created around 1927 by Procter & Gamble and then was adopted and adapted by many other consumer products companies, including Nestlé, Pepsi, Nabisco, and many others. Its heritage is firmly rooted in the consumer products/supermarket sector, but it has been successfully integrated into many industries. Financial services, automobiles, electronics, and computers are some good examples.

The term "brand management" has been used to mean a number of different things:

➤ An organizational design

➤ A job in the marketing department

➤ A business philosophy and discipline

**Talk the Talk**

The **business philosophy** of brand management is all about managing each brand separately and looking to maximize the brand's value to the consumer. The **spirit** encourages respect for the value of a healthy brand. This is something that everyone in the company needs to embrace. The **practice** of brand management is the work of the managers assigned to the individual brands.

You may have heard it used all these ways, so we will address each one. But, before we go any farther, I want to alert you, as you are reading these opening chapters, to be sure that you are picking up the fact that there is a difference between the business philosophy called brand management and the job function called brand manager. As we will see, the *business philosophy* drives the organization design and feeds a *spirit* that needs to be shared throughout the organization; the functional activities, or the *practice* of managing and coordinating all the brand's needs, are usually done by a fairly small group of people.

# *Organizing a Brand Management Structure*

First we will look at two typical brand management structures on organizational charts so that you can see both the philosophy of brand management and the function of the people charged with being the brand managers. We will then talk about why brand management and marketing are so often used interchangeably, but they are not really the same.

As businesses continue to go through rapid change, there may be many different ways to organize the functional part of the job. For now, here is some good background that should help put the phrase "brand management" into perspective.

The term "brand management" was traditionally used to designate a particular organizational design and the job responsibilities that flowed from it. The brand management design was a product of large companies that needed a logical way to organize their various products. Each brand, or product line, had its own products and sales revenues and costs. Each brand would have a central group of people to coordinate the work.

Then the concept of creating two of the same type of product, with each one providing a different promise, took hold. It made sense to have one detergent mild enough for baby clothes and another tough enough to clean grass stains off an older child's pants. And what about having a soft drink in regular and diet versions? One brand or two?

## Big Brand Insight

One of the classic elements of a brand management system has been both praised and criticized: Competing brands are usually managed by separate brand groups, and many companies openly encourage them to be personally competitive. You can argue both sides of this one, but the bottom line, if you are in one of these situations, is not to get pulled into losing focus on what is in the best interests of the brand.

First we will look at two typical brand management structures on organizational charts. In the first, you will see how the philosophy of brand management is translated into action. You will see that brands are kept separate and are managed separately, even when similar brands exist inside one company. Then we will look at how the work needed for each brand is organized.

Let's take a look at a traditional organizational chart within a company with multiple brands. This is the way the brands in my division were organized when I was a new MBA hired to be the product assistant on the Clearasil® business at Richardson Merrell (later sold to Procter & Gamble) back in 1978. Just so you know, there were other brands and other divisions in the company, but I am not showing all of that here—the page isn't big enough. You won't see my job on this first chart because it looks at how the brands themselves were organized, not who works on them.

## Brand Management Organization Chart

| Skin Care | | Oral Hygiene | |
|---|---|---|---|
| **Teen Skin** | **Adult Skin** | **Denture Products** | **Mouthwash** |
| Clearasil® | Oil of Olay® | Fasteeth® | Lavoris® |
| Topex | | Fixodent® | |

What you see is a simple, very logical way to bring focus by grouping brands by function and user group. Skin care is completely separate from oral hygiene (that's the fancy industry term for taking care of teeth, whether they are yours or not). Also note that teenage problems with pimples and oily skin—and, therefore, the products to help teens—were separate from adult problems of dry skin and wrinkles. There were a lot of good reasons to have a separate focus on such different consumer problems. Also note that under the teen skin category, however, there were two different brands, and they competed for essentially the same purchasers. The two denture adhesives were different in form—one a powder, the other a cream—but both obviously targeted people with dentures.

## The Marketing Department Mirrors the Business Philosophy

Back in 1978—and still today, in many companies—if you want to see the brand management structure, you look at the organizational chart for the marketing department. Brand management "lives" in that department, and that is a reality in most companies. We were considered the keepers of the brands, and a very lively office rumor mill was regularly fed whenever brand assignments were changed or a position was added or deleted. It was assumed that each of these changes meant something strategic. Quite often, they were just the ongoing rotation of marketing people through different assignments for grooming and development. We had a lot of laughs among ourselves as each new rumor found its way back to us.

So now let's look at my own group, skin care (we are dropping the oral hygiene group off this chart completely to look more in-depth at just one side). For clarity, and to use the more up-to-date jargon, I have changed some of the actual titles to use "brand manager" rather than "product director," which is what our people at that level were called back then.

---

**Traditional Brand Management Organizational Chart**

**VP Marketing—Skin Care**

| Director of Marketing | | | Director of Marketing | | |
|---|---|---|---|---|---|
| Teen skin care | | | Adult skin care | | |
| **Product Director** | **Product Director** | **Product Director** | **Product Director** | **Product Director** | **Product Director** |
| Clearasil® | Topex® | New products | Teen skin | Oil of Olay | Olay Beauty Cream® |
| Asst. Product Director | | | Asst. Product Director | | |
| **Product Asst.** | **Product Asst.** | **Product Asst.** | **Product Asst.** | **Product Asst.** | **Product Asst.** |

---

Now you see how many people were intensely involved in managing and coordinating the business of fighting pimples and wrinkles: one VP, two directors, five brand managers, two assistant brand managers, and four of us brand assistants.

The demands of the business and the size of these brands created good reasons to have a senior management person looking at the whole skin-care picture, separate from the other group's concerns with loose dentures and bad breath. The VP job was to bring that broader perspective, and middle- and junior-level managers focused on brand groups and then individual brands.

The design created a *brand group,* with a middle manager (brand manager, in this case) in charge of each brand, with one or more assistant-level people, depending on the size and complexity of the business. There was a separate brand manager responsible for developing new products for the teen skin group. Those new items, once developed, would be assigned to an existing brand group or might become the basis for a whole new brand. All the teen skin-care brands, shown here on the left side, reported to one director of marketing, who reported up to the vice president.

**Talk the Talk**

The term **brand group** refers to those people directly involved with the day-to-day organization of the brand. Usually it means that small group that includes the brand manager plus the assistants. A director or VP would not be counted, but they would be viewed as having X number of brand groups reporting in to them.

The vice president of marketing also had another group reporting to him for adult skin care, and the Oil of Olay® brand products were managed by separate brand managers and assistants.

This organization chart looks like thousands of others, but in fact it symbolized something very different. On paper, this is the organizational chart for the marketing department's skin-care group. But, if you lined up the organizational charts for finance, research and development, and manufacturing, you would see people there who were organized along the same lines. We had accountants and scientists and people in the manufacturing group assigned to specific brand groups. Yes, there were also lots of other people in those departments whose jobs were not specific to a brand or product type. You would be amazed, however, how many people were directly responsible for ensuring that their assigned brands were produced on time, in a cost-effective manner, and on budget, and who were kept on management's mind.

# Is Brand Management the Same Thing as Marketing?

Marketing is a big part of brand management, but brand management is not just marketing. I sure didn't know that until I had been in it for a long time. I thought everyone who had a marketing job did all the financial projections, production forecasting for the manufacturing plants, legal clearances, package design, pricing analysis, advertising development, coupon costing, artwork approvals, market share analysis, selling materials, objective setting for R&D, justification for capital investments, and project management for anywhere from 5 to 15 separate "priority projects" all the time.

Boy, was I surprised when I met marketing people who worked only on advertising campaigns, selling materials and pricing, and who had no idea when R&D would be finished testing the newest formula or when engineering was going to get the equipment for the production line. I envied them their ability to focus their time and energies, and yet, I felt superior for the fact that I knew everything that was happening on my brand. Being at the hub of all the activity on the brand was often exhausting but really interesting. And what an education!

At this point, you want to start separating the classic marketing functions of advertising, promotion, brand positioning, and analysis, from the broader perspective of ensuring that every aspect and every single activity related to a brand is in that brand's best interest. The first list of activities would definitely fall under marketing; when you do all of that and add on the broader perspective, it is brand management. Look at companies where you have worked. Some of them will have marketing departments that are pretty much focused on the shorter list of activities. Others will use the marketing group as the central point of communication on everything that involves the brand. You may have worked in organizations where it isn't really clear to you where marketing fits at all.

In a classic brand management system, the marketing people will still do the advertising and promotion, but they will be involved, at least to some extent, with much, much more. They aren't qualified to do the process engineering or cost accounting, but they are always involved with and are held accountable for knowing what is happening in all those areas.

Maybe it will help you to think about a career in brand management as growing through two levels of awareness, and my own early days are a good example. The first, most basic level is almost a job description for the brand manager and brand assistants: Get all the work done. Make sure that the brand keeps moving along. When I was at those earlier levels, I was incredibly busy learning how to do all those various tasks. It took a while before I realized that I was absorbing the other, more strategic part, from the senior people around me. They knew that the real heart of brand management isn't just in doing everything for the brand—it is in doing what is really right for the brand.

We have looked at the business philosophy and organizational design, and a little bit at the function or practice of brand management. The best way for you to really profit from learning about brand management in the fast-changing world we now live in is to learn to think from the brand perspective. When you understand that, you will start to identify opportunities where you thought none existed. This gets to the heart of the true spirit of brand management.

# The Brand Perspective: Philosophy Becomes Action

Twice now I have referred to something called the brand perspective, so let's get right to it. The brand perspective means looking at each element of the work you are doing relative to what is in the best interests of the brand. When you put that into action, it can mean setting aside your own ego when disagreements flare up, and always, *always,* stepping back and asking, "What is right for the business?"

The most important thing for business people like you to know and embrace, and the heart of what modern brand management is all about, is how to bring the energy of this philosophy to life. Earlier, when we were looking at the marketing organizational chart for the skin-care group, I talked about the fact that there were lots of other people throughout the company besides marketing who were also brand-focused. Let's assume that you worked in the purchasing department while I was on the Clearasil® brand. What did the company's brand management philosophy and marketing organizational design have to do with you?

If you were the purchasing manager assigned to the teen skin category, you cared intensely about the quality, price, and delivery schedule for things like the benzoyl peroxide that would fight pimples, and you cared not one bit about the flavoring that would make the mouthwash brand a hit with garlic lovers. You didn't just order packaging and supplies.

You also knew about new products being developed, even when this was highly confidential information and restricted to only a few key people. You had input into the annual business plan, offering insights on cost increases to expect and any raw material inventory problems that you anticipated. Your title said "purchasing," but your responsibility was keeping the brand healthy. You were an important part of the total brand strategy. You were an integral part of real brand management, doing the right things to help the brand deliver on its value and promises.

You were expected to keep the brand group involved and informed, through both formal channels (planning meetings) and informal ones (pick up the phone). If you disagreed with the direction being taken on an element of the brand's management, and if it was something you had knowledge about, you had the right to speak up to your boss and mine.

Now, I need to insert a political comment here: If you didn't like the actor who starred in the television commercial for the brand, frankly, I would have suggested that you keep that little gem to yourself. If you thought that my ideas for a new package were wasteful and creating needless expense—fire away.

This concept, that people throughout the organization are key to the brand's health and success, and that everyone needs to keep the brand at the forefront of their attention, is an important part of what I call the brand perspective. This isn't about you, or me, or whose title is bigger and whose name the president knows—it's about the brand.

I have five golden guidelines for thinking from the brand perspective, and they sound so remarkably simple:

1. The brand is a real, valuable asset of the company—every bit as much as a manufacturing plant and raw materials, and quite possibly a lot more.

2. The brand is nothing more and nothing less than a set of promises—break them at your own peril.

3. The associates in the company work for the betterment of the brands—the sales and profits of your brands fund the paychecks.

4. The brand can bring a lot of accomplishment, satisfaction, and enjoyment to the associates' jobs—but only if the associates treat it right. Dying, abused, and confused brands are miserable businesses to work on.

5. When in doubt, reread numbers 1 through 4 until you get it. They are all important.

So all we need to do in the next 300 pages is help you understand and embrace these five guidelines, and we're in good shape.

I have spent more than 20 years working with the development, manufacturing, marketing, and selling of branded products, and it still saddens me to hear people who think that somehow the marketing people own the brand and everyone else just works on it. Everyone who works on it needs to feel a sense of ownership. A good brand needs to be treated like a person, not an inanimate object. The bottom line is, as the brand goes, so go your sales and profits—and, therefore, your jobs.

# The Power of Focus: Why Big Companies Like Brand Management

Big companies learned a lot of lessons as they grew, and many of those lessons revolve around communication. The bigger the organization, the harder it is to make sure that everyone knows what you talking about. Companies that have been devoted users of a brand management system find it a lot easier to keep projects and budgets and meetings on track by focusing on what each brand needs.

If your background is in engineering or accounting, you may be thinking that this isn't the best way to do things—that a manufacturing facility should be organized around processes and efficient work flows and loading docks, and let the marketing people organize themselves around the brands. Within the manufacturing facility itself, all of these things are critically important elements, and the fact is they always will be. However, when the people in manufacturing want a new production line, the people in finance will immediately ask what brand is going to be serviced so that they can look at just who is going to pay for all this investment. In the end, the answer is the brand.

Companies make investments in new plants and equipment all the time because they need the capacity to grow, but every investment eventually ends up in some brand's cost structure. Every expenditure gets allocated back to some cost center, and anything directly related to making, selling, and managing a branded product gets charged against the brand.

The first thing that a financial analyst is going to look at when evaluating a new production line, hiring more scientists in research and development, building a new warehouse facility, or even adding more financial analysts is the growth track and the profitability of the brands that will be impacted by these investments. Even general overhead costs such as electricity and telephone and computers are reduced down to an allocation that is then charged to each individual brand.

So one simple answer to why big companies like a brand management structure is this: It makes it much easier to focus resources. When you organize around brands, you know who to call and where to send the bills.

## The Least You Need to Know

➤ Brand management was developed as a philosophy of maximizing the value of each brand to the consumer and the company.

➤ Organizing a company around the brands makes all the functional groups stay focused and feel responsible.

➤ The brand management structure usually shows up most clearly in the way the brand groups are organized in the marketing department.

➤ Traditional marketing activities are part of brand management, but they're not the same thing.

➤ The whole company needs to embrace the fact that the brand is a very valuable asset.

➤ Learning to think from the brand perspective means always asking, "What is best for the brand?"

# Chapter 3

# A Short History of the Evolution of Brand Management

## In This Chapter

➤ The brand is the hub of the wheel

➤ Brand management has career mystique and big value

➤ Brand managers are carefully groomed

➤ Managers living in ivory towers hurt their brands

➤ Brands lose some of their power in industry shake-ups

Let's take a fast walk through the evolution of brand management, including the career mystique that has surrounded being a brand manager for so many years now. There is no question that brand management training has been—and still is—very valuable for a business career in almost any industry. The people referred to as brand managers are almost always the marketing people, so here we are focusing primarily on the practice or function of brand management.

We know that brand management started within what is still commonly called the consumer products industry. Over time, it garnered so much praise for turning out people with good, strong thinking skills that other industries started looking for this kind of disciplined approach to their own businesses. In the 1980s, financial services firms started to raid consumer products companies. In the 1990s, it was automotive firms, retailers, and then, at the end of the decade, Internet companies. The venture capitalists that were funding these new businesses quickly realized that the Internet world was highly dependent on brand recognition, and who were the best people to help them build a new brand? The same folks who knew how to market tuna fish and bleach and soft drinks.

surprise you to know that brand management, for all its glory and acclaim, ...nt through some very tough times in the 1990s. Years of disciplined thinking and promoting from within had created some problems with inbreeding and myopia in the consumer products world. That shortsightedness affected individuals as well as whole companies, and it threatened to seriously disrupt billions of dollars in sales. Remember that most brand managers were trained in these companies before they got pirated away to other industries, and so our story focuses on what happened first in consumer products. Many other industries have been affected since then. There are great lessons here for all of us operating in fast-paced environments.

## The Hub of the Wheel

Let's start our look at the evolution of brand management with a real "oldie but goodie" from the consumer products industry, where brand management really grew up. It seems like every brand manager I know was shown the "Hub of the Wheel" during their first week of orientation. Very simply, it was a circle with the word *brand* inside it, and then lines radiating out from that so that it resembled the spokes of a wheel. This was a graphic way of looking at all the functions involved in creating and selling a branded product.

*The "Hub of the Wheel."*

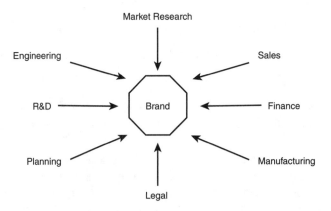

The message from that wheel design is pretty simple. The activities of the various departments within the company were tied in to specific brands and, by implication, needed to be coordinated through and communicated to the people at the heart of the brand. Simple enough, right? Makes all the sense in the world. And when we look at the job responsibilities of the brand manager teams in just a minute, it is clear that this is what was happening.

Occasionally someone would make a mistake when using this chart to explain how things needed to work. When it says *brand* in the middle, it is easy to use it to describe a philosophy (the health of the brand is central to our success) and a set of responsibilities. When that inadvertently got changed to *marketing*, it pretty much communicated "who" was supposedly the most important. It was an easy mistake to make, and it wasn't necessarily intended to do that at all. If you labeled this chart as "Communications Flow," it would work pretty well. But when you still call it the "Hub of the Wheel" and it says *marketing* in the middle, it can set up some very bad feelings. The marketing people weren't trying to be obnoxious, but when you understand how broad their influence was and how they got involved in everyone's department and formed opinions about who was competent and who wasn't, it is easy to see why people got upset with them. It is also easy to see how, over time, a lot of those marketing/brand manager types got more and more defensive and insulated.

### Heads Up

The next time you use an existing graphic, whether it is an organization chart or something like the "Hub of the Wheel," stop and ask yourself what you *could* think it is showing if you worked in another department. Quite often all you need to do is put a better, more descriptive label on the top. Sometimes, just by changing a word or two, you can avoid a serious miscommunication.

# The Mystique of a Brand Management Career

Comments like these continue to create high expectations for people trained in a good brand management discipline:

> "There are few things in life that are transforming experiences. Intuit would not be here today were it not for what I learned at Procter & Gamble."
> —Scott Cook, founder and chairman of the Executive Committee, Intuit, Inc.

> "I have that same feeling about my experience in Vietnam ... that sense of rigor and intense training."
> —Jim Mead, executive recruiter, James Mead & Co.

Both of these quotes appeared in a *Wall Street Journal* article about a reunion being held in June 2000 for 1,250 former brand people at P&G. The article even relates that these alums refer to themselves as "Proctoids," so alike and so disciplined was their training.

After I read that article, I picked up the phone and talked with Jim Mead, the executive recruiter quoted here. I wanted to get the perspective of someone who spends every day focused on finding people for senior-level positions with big companies. I asked him what he looks for when he analyzes someone's brand experience, and what he thinks of the opportunities to get good brand management experience today. I think you will find his comments insightful:

➤ Mead looks at the brands that a person has worked on as an indicator of what kinds of exposure they have had. Did the brands have a little or a lot of competition? Did they have a lot of pressure on pricing? Did the brands have distribution issues (how they physically get the product to market)?

What does this mean for you? Look at the kinds of challenges that each branded business you work on presents as an education for you.

➤ Mead points out that many of the dotcom companies that are so exciting today are headed by former P&G-type people. The venture capitalists funding the companies want someone with a keen, strategic brand focus and basically a pedigree.

What does this mean for you? There are a very limited number of jobs at P&G or Pepsi headquarters each year. However, there are a tremendous number of companies now managed by people who come out of good brand management environments. Look hard at the management team before you accept a new job if you are trying to get on-the-job training in place of an MBA and five years at a major corporation.

➤ Mead encourages people interested in applying brand management philosophies and disciplines to really study the major brands. Read everything you can. Seek out books and magazine articles that will help you understand the decisions that have been made and how they have impacted the brand's development.

**Mentoring Memo**

One of the things you can take away from Jim Mead's comments about the number of top leaders who have been groomed in brand management is this: If you work for one of these people, you can bet that he or she has a keen appreciation for people who understand and embrace the driving philosophies of brand management.

## The Big Companies Built the System

Generally speaking, the big consumer products companies recruited their entry-level brand marketing people from each year's crop of new MBAs. A master of business administration degree was pretty much mandatory to even be considered in the 1980s and 1990s. Before that, the advanced degree was very helpful, but until the mid-1970s, not that many people had one. The emphasis on having a graduate degree came about because of the heavy demands that would be made on these people for analyzing, managing multiple priorities, interfacing with people in scientific and engineering positions, and exhibiting a general mental flexibility to handle whatever demands the brand's business presented.

It was not at all uncommon for brand managers to attend meetings on production line problems, manufacturing forecasts, legal clearance for a television commercial, unexpected cost overruns on raw materials, selling materials for the sales force, and a budget review with the comptroller, all in one day. We were expected to be fluent in all the issues and jargon, polite but firm in what the brand needed, and magically composed and ready for whatever happened.

One thing that doesn't show on most brand management organizational charts, and that was not done by all companies, is a stint in the sales force. My company made it mandatory before you got promoted to assistant brand manager, and I must tell you that I still wish today that all companies did that. The thinking was that after a year of being immersed in numbers and running through long days of meetings and projects, it would be a good idea to remind us future managers that the company actually sells products to make a living.

The way my old company looked at it, all those meetings we attended were important, but if we don't or can't sell the products, it doesn't much matter how flashy the new advertising is. The brand will fail. It was very easy to lose sight of the real consumer who bought the product during that first year of boot camp–style learning. It was even easier to ignore the fact that first we had to sell the product to supermarkets, drug stores, discounters, and wholesalers, or the consumer would never have the chance to buy it.

Before we go on, you may want to refer back to the traditional brand management organizational tables in Chapter 2, "What Is Brand Management Anyhow?" for just a minute to refresh your memory on how a brand management organization is typically structured. I said it earlier, and it is generally still true today: The brand management function really lives inside marketing. This time, let's talk about what kind of responsibilities the various levels of marketing people were assigned to see how they were groomed and developed. This will give you an appreciation for how much was really learned on the job, as well as give you a first look at the broad range of issues that a brand encounters. For perspective, the typical time frame from entry as a brand assistant to making brand manager was three years.

## Building a Career Brick by Brick

Here is the typical list of responsibilities for each level in the brand group, along with an indication of how long you might spend at each of the earlier jobs.

If you study the types of projects that were typical at each of the first three levels, you will see a few things:

➤ First, you learned how to work with numbers and analysis. This was typically referred to as "grunt work," and that is a pretty good description of what it felt like many days.

➤ You got to work with sophisticated outsiders such as ad agencies only when your mental and social skills had been checked out, so that you didn't embarrass anyone.

➤ When you made it to the exalted level of brand manager—and that was a big deal indeed—you didn't have to do the grunt work anymore. However—and this is a really big however—you were held responsible for training all those assistants who now reported to you, so you never really got away from any of it.

*The feeding and grooming of a brand manager.*

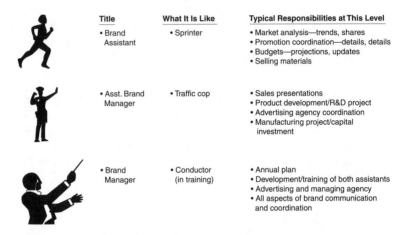

| | Title | What It Is Like | Typical Responsibilities at This Level |
|---|---|---|---|
| | • Brand Assistant | • Sprinter | • Market analysis—trends, shares<br>• Promotion coordination—details, details<br>• Budgets—projections, updates<br>• Selling materials |
| | • Asst. Brand Manager | • Traffic cop | • Sales presentations<br>• Product development/R&D project<br>• Advertising agency coordination<br>• Manufacturing project/capital investment |
| | • Brand Manager | • Conductor (in training) | • Annual plan<br>• Development/training of both assistants<br>• Advertising and managing agency<br>• All aspects of brand communication and coordination |

The whole design for the development of a brand manager was based on creating people with very strong analytical skills, sound people management skills, and the ability to be both precise and concise when they communicated. An overwhelming sense of responsibility for the welfare of the brand was ingrained into their souls, or else they never made it to that level.

## Big Brand Insight

In every company with multiple brands, there are always those that everyone wants on their resumés. Usually these are the biggest and most heavily advertised. However, it is great experience to work on smaller brands that have something else going for them. For example, getting assigned to the most profitable brand (senior management pays a lot of attention to you) or the one about to go through a major change such as package redesign is terrific exposure.

When you go through that kind of intense training, you e
You live, breathe, and eat for your brand. You talk in a kind
noxious for others to hear, and your family and best friends thi
kind of zombie. You find yourself asking your four-year-old to prio
portunities, and you reprimand your eight-year-old for not commun
for summer vacation in a succinct one-page memo. And all of this for t
paper towels or denture adhesive or mustard. No wonder people thought
weird.

## Ivory Towers and Silos Crowded Out Some Good Thinking

A common complaint that was made very often by sales and other departments was that the brand managers were all living in ivory towers. We spoke of benefits, of premium pricing strategies, of exquisite package design, and of the obvious failings of our competitive set. Say what? The sales force wanted to know what they were supposed to tell the buyer from their biggest retailer, the guy with bad breath, hemorrhoids, and an ugly predisposition to embarrassing salespeople in public just for fun. To this guy, a premium pricing strategy means that the product is way more expensive than all the others that he has to choose from. To him, your lovely package design is (expletive deleted) because it takes up too much space on the shelf. To him, your biggest competitor is a great guy who takes him out to lunch and coaches his son's baseball team. Shall we try this again?

Unfortunately, a lot of this criticism was true. Right now there are a thousand former brand managers cursing at me for saying this, but it is true. We were so busy doing the hundreds of things that we needed to do, and it became harder and harder to see over our own office walls. Too many brand managers avoided sales meetings like the plague. Way too many of them went out of their way to avoid making a sales call because the last time they did they got bloodied.

Even within our own safe haven in the marketing department, we kept our heads down and did what we were supposed to do: We gave our all to our brand, and nobody could say that we weren't dedicated. We were developing into amazingly strong analytical and strategic thinkers, but we didn't see and couldn't sense that outside our doors, the world was changing. We didn't know that for all our sophisticated skills, all the things we were analyzing were now only a part of a new changing equation.

## The Balloon Didn't Burst—It Exploded

Did you ever look back on a situation and wonder why you didn't see something coming? That is pretty much what happened to a lot of people in the consumer products industry in the 1990s. To bring this situation to life, let's pretend that it is 1991 and that you are a brand manager at a large consumer products company.

d up remarkably focused.
f shorthand that is ob-
k you may be some
ritize his play op-
cating his wishes
he love of
ve were

industry back then was to say that there were ba-
world: You are either a supplier or a seller. In this
res products, so you are a supplier. You supply
g stores, mass merchandisers, and some of those
turn, are the sellers. Everyone has been living
ts were increasing but no one felt like they could
ded to get the profit that they wanted. You
but frankly, your boat is springing leaks, and
to keep the cash flowing around.

imple. Suppliers and sellers were the yin and
groups, we spent an extraordinary amount of
to sell more products.

biggest competitor comes out with a new prod-
makes the sales pitch to Retailer A, and you find out that it is accepted. That means that this new product will start to be sold in all those Retailer A
stores. This is bad news. This will probably cut into your sales, and this is no time to
miss your forecast. You meet with the VP of sales and tell him that you are willing to
spend extra promotion money with Retailer A to make sure that you don't lose any
sales. Retailer A accepts your extra promotion money, and you feel relieved.

What you don't know yet is that your other two biggest competitors are doing the
same thing. They are worried, too. Now, all of you have spent too much money and
blown your budgets for sales that never materialize. The situation has shifted from
your brand standing out to every brand standing out, which means that no brand is
standing out. But every brand manager was left standing out in the cold. It is just status quo at a much higher cost. This happens over and over again. This is headache
number one.

Headache number two is brewing down the hall. Being the big thinker you are, you
have created special packs for those new warehouse club stores. They like big sizes
or multiple units banded together—not what your regular customers want—so their
products have different pricing. Some of your supermarket customers are asking
tough questions about why these club stores are running ads for your product at
lower prices than they can afford to do. Are you being unfair somehow? Is this legal?
The clubs are hurling insults back that they are better business people, and that's why
they can have lower prices. Your own mother admits that some days she feels like she
is running around in circles, getting exhausted trying to figure out where she should
shop to get a good deal. Ain't nobody happy.

Headache number three just landed. Your VP comes back from some industry meeting and says that your 25 biggest supermarket accounts have started talking about re-
thinking the whole business. They cannot afford to keep doing things the old way,
and everybody had better tighten their seat belts 'cause its going to be a bumpy ride.
It feels like a war is starting.

Let me release you from your misery and fast-forward a few years.

# From Soup to Nuts: Everything Changed

Over the next few years, the consumer products industry went through a total renewal. It was expensive, and it got ugly some days, but through an astonishing example of first-rate teamwork, a whole new approach to the business was born.

The project was called *Efficient Consumer Response,* or *ECR,* for short. As many of us said in our presentations during this period, "Notice that the word *consumer* is right in the middle, where it belongs." The word *efficient* kept people focused on finding ways to eliminate wasteful costs. The word *response* was again to keep people focused that all of this work was to respond to a difficult situation, and then to keep responding, to keep all eyes on making sure that the industry never lost track of giving the consumers what *they* needed ever again.

For our purposes here, the most important things for you to know are ...

> ➤ The single most important thing that happened is almost embarrassingly obvious when you hear it: Instead of two major players on the radar screen, suppliers and sellers, there were now three. It is as simple as this. In the preceding discussion, we answered the question "Who makes the world go 'round?" by saying that suppliers and sellers do, because that was the thinking back then. Now, what has changed isn't radical—the world still looks the same for the most part, but people recognized that it was only for the consumer that suppliers and sellers got together at all.

> ➤ Everyone was in financial distress, so the misery was pretty well shared. The thing that everyone in the industry could agree on is that the consumer needed to be happy or they would all be out of business.

**Talk the Ta**

**Efficient Consumer Res**
**(ECR)** is the name for what may want to think of as the re-engineering of the consumer products industry during the 1990s. It was a joint effort of many of the major retailers, brokers, technology providers, manufacturers, distribution services companies, and consulting groups in the country.

**Mentoring Memo**

I have used the consumer products industry as an example here because it is easy for all of us to associate with supermarkets and warehouse clubs and nationally advertised brands. It is very important that you research what industry initiatives are happening in whatever business you are looking at. The term *ECR* will not apply elsewhere.

**33**

d, and years of work were done that resulted in a
...ent industry.

...nd developing and implementing technology ap-
...e paperwork, make order processing flow much
...sive way to figure out which products and pro-
...nsumer.

## ...on't Even Talk Brand

...rested in brand management: Today, when
...ECR movement have a sales call, they talk
...*gory management*, not brand management. There has been a definite shift in
power from the brand side to the seller, or retailer side. The mind-set today is that the
individual brand must complement what the retailer wants to present to the consumer.

### Talk the Talk

**Category management** is a process that analyzes consumer preferences in each category of products, based on market share data, and then identifies the specific mix of
products that will satisfy both the consumer's desire for variety and the retailer's desire for
profit. It puts the emphasis at the total category level. The individual brand is downplayed
somewhat because now brands are simply components of a larger picture.

The underlying logic is that the consumers have certain categories of products that
they want. Within each of those categories (shampoo, refrigerated juices, frozen vegetables) are brands and product types that they like better than others. Finding a
good mix of products for the specific neighborhood in which the store is located
means making the consumer happy. Finding a mix that the seller can afford to sell
means making the seller happy. Having your brand part of that profitable mix makes
you, the supplier and brand manager, happy.

In a sales call today, the talk is about where the brand fits in the bigger picture of the
whole category. The talk is about how the brand adds profit and consumer appeal to

the current assortment. The suppliers/manufacturers present all kinds of analysis of how consumers respond to various pricing levels and discounts, highlighting which ones seem the most efficient. It is a whole new world, and the lessons learned here apply to just about every industry in town.

The move from brand focus to category focus has happened. The shift in mind-set is almost as simple as this: The whole business has to make sense to both the consumer and the seller. In times of rapid change, when new competitors can show up around the corner, you will need to come back over and over again to what the very essence of your brand's value really is. Does it truly have a meaningful place in the category? If you were the seller (instead of the supplier), would you push this brand? What can you do to make your brand the one that the seller has to have?

Everyone who gets involved in managing a brand gets a little myopic. This is human nature—we fall in love with our own ideas. All this change doesn't mean the end of the brand at all. It does mean that we have even greater pressure to build and manage and defend our brands with passion and zeal. I still think that the advent of ECR and category management is one of the best things to happen to the industry ever. It made a lot of smart people work harder, but those who did got very smart indeed.

---

### The Least You Need to Know

➤ Brand management started in the consumer products industry around 1930 and is now widely used in many industries.

➤ The brand should always be the central focus of the business, not any group or individual.

➤ Big companies carefully groom and develop their brand managers with increasing levels of responsibility and exposure.

➤ Brand managers are valued in the marketplace for their analytical, organizational, and strategic skills.

➤ Radical change in the consumer products industry has forced brand marketers to learn how to compete for attention.

# E-Commerce Makes Branding Hotter Than Ever

The explosion in the number of people now using the Internet has created some of the most exciting opportunities and puzzling public policy issues ever seen. It is changing our own daily lives in a confusing number of ways. For many years, a running joke in family life was that every family hoped to turn out a doctor or a lawyer. Now Grandpa is hoping for a "dotcom millionaire."

The impact of the Internet has already had enormous impact on business. Many successful companies selling products or services have seen their lives turned upside down in just a few years. New competitors have arisen from parts unknown and made some experienced executives look like they were asleep at the switch. It all happened very fast—and, in fairness to everyone, we still don't understand all of its potential.

The Internet presents an array of challenges to existing brands and to anyone wanting to create a new brand. The biggest challenge of all may be to understand what the opportunity is for you; it isn't the same for all brands and all businesses. On the plus side, it permits and actually empowers a level of communication that we didn't even dream of 10 years ago. You will need to be open-minded and inquisitive in your learning, firmly rooted in what your brand's value and promises really are, and faster than a speeding bullet in implementing smart changes.

# Three Great Reasons to Have an Internet Strategy

Can you think of any other movement or product that, within about five years of being known, managed to get 76 million Americans involved with it? When I say *involved,* I mean, on average, that we go online 13 days a month and stay there a total of 615 minutes a month. Now, in plain English, that's almost every other day that we spend an average of 48 minutes online. When I started talking with the people at Media Metrix to get these statistics for you, I was prepared to hear big numbers. But, after reading some of their Digital Media Reports with numbers like these, I began to wonder: Where do we find the time to do all this? How many people does it take to keep this new world of communication open to us? Is all of this ever going to pay out for businesses?

I am old enough to remember the great computer scare of the 1960s and early 1970s, when computers were gigantic mainframes and most of us had absolutely no idea what they did. We all heard wild and crazy projections from a few intellectual types, commonly referred to in most neighborhoods as "wackos," that these machines were going to change the world.

No one paid much attention until the news media picked up some stories that what computers did is replicate the way humans work, but do it much faster. These machines could add and subtract faster than us, could print out the answer so that you didn't even need someone to type anymore, and were secretly being designed to be robots who would someday replace human beings—and we would all be out of work. Horrors.

In the 30 years since then, those early projections have been proven right and wrong so many times that I get seasick just watching the bouncing ball. Computers did indeed change the world, and in ways that would probably overwhelm even those early pioneers. The latest incarnation of all this change, of course, is the World Wide Web, commonly referred to in most places as the Internet or just the Web. It is part of our everyday life, and the new innovations in technology that brought us truly portable personal computers (PCs) are now adding smaller and more powerful devices to our lifestyles.

It is pretty easy to conclude that the Internet is here to stay because millions of people like it, and they use it so much that we have billions of dollars of our national economy tied up in it and a couple million people working away at it every day. It is definitely here to stay.

## Reason One: People Use It and Like It

At family reunions all across America right now, strange things are happening. It is commonplace to hear a 12-year-old niece talking about how cool and easy it is to learn HTML. The dinner conversation is dominated by your aunt and your 85-year-old grandmother talking about the latest virus, and you know they don't mean the flu. Your father secretly confesses that he ordered your mother's birthday present at the last minute by going online and having it sent by express mail. Something weird has happened to your family, and to lots of others around the world.

The Internet phenomenon is explosive here in the United States, but we are only one of the many countries that have moved into this new *virtual world*.

### Talk the Talk

The expressions *virtual, virtual world,* and *virtual void* are important. **Virtual** is used to make a simple contrast of something that cannot be seen or touched but that is still there, such as a Web site. So, the **virtual world** is just the bigger universe of the Internet versus the physical world of offices and stores. The **virtual void** is a somewhat sarcastic expression for the nothingness of the Internet—you can't see it, smell it, or touch it, but it is there. Kind of like a black hole in space, I guess, or the Bermuda Triangle.

Look at the number of active Internet users estimated by Media Metrix in just these seven countries, and keep in mind that, in this case, it is only the number of people using it from home—we are not counting office users as well:

| Country | Active Internet Users (in Thousands)* |
|---|---|
| United States | 74,275 |
| Japan | 16,400 |
| United Kingdom | 9,631 |
| Germany | 8,554 |
| Canada | 8,854 |
| Australia | 5,275 |
| France | 3,721 |

*Source: Media Metrix, Multi-Country Home Usage Report, March 2000 © 2000 Media Metrix.*

*\*Because these are written in thousands that means you read them as 74,275,000 people in the United States and so on.*

Who are all these people jumping on the Internet? Another quick look at some data from Media Metrix shows that in the United States, Internet users are split evenly between male and female. The bulk of the users are between the ages of 18 and 54, which you would expect. However, what is so nice to see is that both ends of that age spectrum are pretty even: 35 percent of users are 18 to 34, and 36 percent are 35 to 54. Children ages 2 to 17 already make up 19 percent of users (for perspective, that is about 15 million kids) and, my favorite number of all, 9 percent of users, almost 7 million people, are over age 55. I like that number because it flies in the face of all the people who believe that computers are a young person's game. No way.

When you look at huge numbers like these, you know that these are everyday people, not just professionals, for whom the Internet is quickly becoming simply one more element in a busy life. One of the great questions of the last few years is whether it could become another shopping outlet, whether ordinary citizens, in great enough numbers, would be willing to pay via credit card for something that they could not see, smell, or touch. I think we have that answer. A good example is online toy sales. Based on what has happened in just the last two years, Media Metrix estimated in its Toy E-visory, Holiday 1999 report, that online toy sales will jump from only $45 million in 1998 to more than $1 billion in 2000, and upward of $2 billion two years later.

I can go on for pages with great facts and figures, but rather than do that, let me direct you to Appendix B, "Resources and Revelations Guide." It includes, courtesy of Media Metrix, more than 20 charts that will let you see just how big Internet activity has become. You can see the sales generated by a number of Internet commerce Web sites. You can analyze all kinds of opportunities, and I provide some guiding questions for you to consider on the opening page of the appendix. I am very excited about providing this level of data for you as readers of this book. Ordinarily, you and I could never afford to purchase this information. However, Media Metrix responded with great enthusiasm to my research for this book and agreed to provide this bonus section for you. Dive into it—this is great material.

**Heads Up**

Okay, somebody needs to say this: There are still a fair number of executives, not to mention your own parents, who are not passionate about computers. Some avoid them at every turn. Be gracious about your comfort level, and be savvy with these devices. Your next promotion and raise could be tied to your gracious good manners.

## *Reason Two: It Is a Big Industry Unto Itself*

Would you like to be part of an industry that added 650,000 new jobs last year? How about one that increased its revenue by 62 percent in one year? Sound like a good place to go work? Those figures, from The Internet Economy Indicators study at the University of Texas, Austin, are real eye-openers. Doesn't look like you have to worry about layoffs in this industry. Do you think that maybe you should give your kids some sage career advice and an open account at the local computer store? That may be the best thing you can do to secure a comfortable old age for yourself. And, by the way, no matter how old you are today, if you ignore this revolution, you will be old and out-of-date sooner than you think.

How big is the Internet economy? A great report from The Internet Economy Indicators indicates that it was about $524 billion in 1999 and expects it to move up to $850 billion in 2000. That makes it bigger than some of our biggest well-established businesses such as life insurance ($724 billion) and auto and truck production ($728 billion). Those are some numbers.

If you are interested in working within this mystical entity called the Internet economy, or selling your products or services into such a hot area, your first question is probably, "What exactly is the Internet economy?" This same report details it as comprising four Internet layers of businesses:

1. **Infrastructure:** Telecommunications companies, Internet service providers, Internet backbone carriers, "last mile" access companies, and manufacturers of end-user networking equipment. Examples are AT&T, AOL.com, and Mindspring.

2. **Application:** Software products and services necessary to facilitate Web transactions and transaction intermediaries, consultants, and service companies that design, build and maintain all types of Web sites. Examples are Oracle, Adobe, and Microsoft.

3. **Intermediary:** Predominantly what is called an "Internet pure-play," meaning that their Web-based businesses generate revenues not from transactions, but through advertising, membership subscription fees, and commissions. Examples are Yahoo!, E-Trade, and Travelocity.

4. **Internet commerce:** Companies that conduct Web-based commerce transactions, including airlines, manufacturers selling online, entertainment, and professional services. Examples are Amazon.com, Drugstore.com, and American Airlines.

Look in Appendix B for more information on the number of employees and dollar sales in each layer of the Internet economy.

## *Reason Three: It's Working—It Really Is*

We talked earlier about the great computer scare of 30 years ago. Once we got past that point and computer technology (particularly personal computers) started becoming mainstream, there was a "great computer hope" that computers would increase worker productivity over time. We have already seen that computerization has created exciting and very large opportunities. Now we are seeing definite signs that productivity is also coming along.

Here are two ways to look at the bottom line on this whole Internet phenomenon:

➤ People and companies alike are turning to the Internet for information, communication, and transactions. A lot of money is changing hands, and a lot of relationships are being built. What about you and your brand? Where are your opportunities in each of those areas?

➤ The Internet is turning to people and companies for innovation, productivity improvements, and transactional devices. Do you have something that you can sell to this enormous group of growing companies whose revenues are escalating and whose desire for great products and people is insatiable?

Will you be a user of the Internet or a supplier to it? Or both?

Here is some wonderful food for thought. In that same Internet Economy Indicators study that I just mentioned is a table that is just too good to ignore. The study posed a series of questions to companies positioned within the Internet economy and those in the general economy of the United States.

## Productivity and Competitive Advantage

| Percent of Respondents Who Said "Yes" | Internet Economy Companies | Sample from United States as a Whole |
|---|---|---|
| 1. Have any of your Internet-based products or services created any significant business or competitive advantages for your company? | 87 percent | 44 percent |
| 2. Have you seen any gains in employee or equipment productivity? | 73 percent | 29 percent |
| 3. Have you seen any increases in your market share that you would attribute to your Internet-based products or services? | 68 percent | 24 percent |
| 4. Have you been able to increase your penetration of a new market as a result of implementing your Internet-based products or services? | 72 percent | 25 percent |

*Source: The Internet Economy Indicators™ © 2000*

The third question has somewhat expected answers. If your business is serving the Internet, it makes sense that the Internet would create a higher level of market share gains for you. But look at the other three questions in depth. Both Internet economy companies and many of the others have good reason to have Internet-based products these days (for example, bookstores and department stores that have real buildings and a Web site). There are dramatic differences in the improvements in productivity and competitive position among the companies actively involved in the Internet.

This all makes sense because it is all so new. Of course, you expect to see something new have big jumps in numbers at first. But remember this, the extraordinary growth of the Internet economy did not *cannibalize* the general economy. Our national economy continues the longest expansion in history. There is something else going on here, and we want to make sure that you get your fair share of it.

**Big Brand Insight**

Take another look at the preceding table, and this time focus on the column on the right, the general economy. If you think small, you see how far behind these numbers are. If you think big, you see lots of opportunity to sell these companies your products and services.

# Will the Internet Encourage Brand-Building or Brand-Busting?

One of the biggest worries in the general economy is that this strange and mysterious Internet will somehow cast a spell over the good citizens and render them incapable of making intelligent decisions. Get a life.

A lot of companies with established brands are simultaneously worried and elated at the prospects of what the Internet can do for them. They have spent years and millions of dollars carefully constructing brands that have proven consumer appeal. Each of those CEOs has a group of people whispering in his ear that a new world of untold riches awaits with the click of a mouse, if he will just put $10 million into the Web development budget. And who knows, these people just might be right. After all, the business magazines and newspapers are loaded with stories of daring and visionary leaders who made their stockholders, and themselves, rich.

**Talk the Talk**

The word **cannibalize** is commonly used to describe what happens when one product or business gets its share by simply taking it away from another competitor. You would say that this happened if the total market size stayed about the same and these two businesses simply traded sales from one to the other, resulting in no net gain to the total market size.

**43**

**Talk the Talk**

The advent of selling things over the Internet created the need to distinguish between "real" stores and "virtual" stores. A store or office that you can walk into was referred to at first as "bricks and mortar" to distinguish it from an Internet store. That got shortened to **bricks and clicks.** Today, many product and service brands are sold in both kinds of stores.

Of course, that CEO has two ears, and another group is whispering dire admonitions and rebuttals to everything that the other guys say. For every glorified Internet czar mentioned, they have an unemployed has-been to name. For every established brand that is surviving with both *bricks and clicks,* they serve up the latest rumors of red ink ruining the carpet in some executive suite. No wonder people are taking early retirement.

What will happen to the power of brands in this new environment?

Let me take you through two different schools of thought on this issue. The first says, "Watch out," and for a very good and valid reason. The second says, "Watch" and then makes you pay attention to who does what with whom and when.

First the negative argument. There are many very good articles on this subject. One that I recommend for you is an article in the *Harvard Business Review,* March–April 2000, titled "Cost Transparency: The Net's Real Threat to Prices and Brands." The author, Indrajit Sinha, makes a very good argument that the vast amounts of information made available by the Internet allow the consumer to know so much about the pricing of any item that they can now "see through" the brand image and get right to the cost and relative value of the product.

The argument goes on to bring up a number of important points:

➤ People never really knew the direct cost of an item before; they knew only its market price relative to other choices. Now they can get a much better handle on what it may be with just a few keystrokes.

➤ Will brands be able to continue to generate good margins if consumers become trained to focus so much on cost? If cost overrides the specialness, or unique benefits of a brand, then all brands are threatened with being reduced to simple commodities; and commodities, like soybeans and crude oil, are not perceived as being different in any way. This would be the end of branding as we know it.

➤ When consumers can get a better handle on cost and pricing, will this result in reduced brand loyalty and possibly even bad feelings against the brand for perceived price gouging?

This article neatly sums up some of the biggest issues for brands in today's environment. And, interestingly, these issues apply whether those brands are actively marketing themselves in bricks or clicks or both kinds of stores. It doesn't take long to check four or five Web sites and compare prices. And, as we know, there are Web sites whose entire purpose is to do the comparison for you.

# Brand Name Recognition Closes the Virtual Void

Now, where is the good news for brands? Right in front of you, every day, everywhere you go.

How are Web sites letting us know they exist? Given the millions of Web pages out there, how do you know about Amazon.com, Yahoo!, Drugstore.com, WebMD, 1-800-flowers.com, Iwon.com, AOL, freeinternet.com … shall I go on? When you wanted to find a Web site and weren't sure of its address, did you ever just type in something, like "nameofmagazine.com"? It works a lot of the time.

The reason we know so much about Web sites is because they are driven by two things: a brand name that people can remember or a *link* that drags us to the site. In the case of the Internet, a memorable brand name means a whole lot. Are you familiar with the term *domain name?* As brand people, you need to know that one, too. And while we are at it, how about *cybersquatting?* Talk about new words for the dictionary writers to keep up with.

### Talk the Talk

A **link** is a software device that takes a person from one Web page to another by just clicking on the word(s). You can buy links to be placed in other Web sites. A **domain name** is the actual set of words or numbers in your Web address after the www. part, such as www.patricianicolino.com. **Cybersquatting** means getting ownership of domain names that you think someone will want and be willing to pay you good money for.

So, on the Internet, your domain name is very important. It is your brand identifier, just like the words on a soft drink can. As a matter of a fact, it is more important than the soft drink brand name. Why? When I go to buy a cold drink, I actually see the products on the shelf and can be reminded on sight just which is the one I liked so much last time. Try that when you are staring at your computer monitor at midnight.

Isn't it interesting that lots of big, successful, and want-to-be-successful Web sites are using traditional advertising methods to teach us about their brands? The brand name is so incredibly important that lots of old ideas about brand-name recognition and awareness are being talked about like they are hot off the press. We old brand managers have found another new incarnation for our talents.

Quickly, name the Web sites that ran the following ads:

➤ Men's singing group doing corny songs around the holidays

➤ Talking baby with or without big-name athletes

➤ Giving away $10,000 a day

When you put these two schools of thought together, what do you get? A confusing situation filled with hope and fear. Yes, that's right. Both positions are valid. The best guidance I think anyone can give you on this subject right now is to bet that, in fact, the Internet will make brands hotter and more important than ever. If you go back to the basic definition we are using of what a brand is and does, it makes specific promises of value, and that takes on an increased level of importance in the confusing world of the Internet. However, beware any illusions you may have about "making a killing" in the virtual world.

By the way, the answers to the little advertising quiz are Amazon.com, freeinternet. com, and Iwon.com.

# Be Clear: What Do You Want the Internet to Do for You?

Here is a good basic question for you: Are you creating a brand for the Internet or an Internet strategy for your brand? They are different things. Start right here: What do you want the Internet to do for you?

The best way to start answering that question is to get very simple and basic, before you get all jazzed up with big goals and ideas. Think about these things—and, for all you ultra-competitive types, there is no right or wrong answer. You can check off as many as make sense for your business:

I want the Internet to …

➤ Be a communications or access device:

\_\_\_\_\_ E-mail

\_\_\_\_\_ Research or analysis

\_\_\_\_\_ Customer service

\_\_\_\_\_ Newsletters

\_\_\_\_\_ Press releases

➤ Be a transaction device:

\_\_\_\_\_ Provide a service

\_\_\_\_\_ Sell something

\_\_\_\_\_ Order something

\_\_\_\_\_ Modify something

➤ Pick the words/phrases that best describe what you want the Internet to help you do:

_____ Smooth out communications throughout the company and with our customers

_____ Reach out to our customers to build their loyalty and value perception of us

_____ Sell something that we make or do

_____ Help somebody else sell something that helps us out, too

_____ Keep the competition from stealing our customers

_____ Bide time until we figure out if there is something meaningful for us to do on the Internet

_____ Save time on lots of little things, such as ordering office supplies

_____ Become the premier brand in the X business

_____ At least make us look like we are in the twentieth—oops—twenty-first, century

As you sort through all of this, the big point is to differentiate between the Internet as a tool and as your product. When in doubt, go immediately to one of my all-time favorite questions: How will you make money? Is your Internet idea supposed to bring in the cash by itself or help you do a better job of making money somewhere else?

A good question for established brands is this one: Can the Internet open up some area of access to the customer that was not previously available?

Here are a few ideas. Complete this sentence: With a good Internet strategy on our side, we could …

➤ Sell things on the Internet.

➤ Explain things in more depth.

➤ Educate our loyal users.

➤ Convince new users.

➤ Sell people on new or different things.

➤ Get a dialogue going to find out what consumers really want.

➤ Customize our promotions or advertising.

➤ Become a more important player in their lives by providing some kind of solution or service.

Let me leave you with a very exciting thought. The powerful communications ability that is inherent in the Internet means that you can generate a great number of very different messages. The click-choices that people make within a Web page means that they can direct themselves to what they want to see. In essence, they do the work of target marketing, finding the right person for the product all by themselves. This could mean very high productivity for every dollar that you spend building a good site.

---

### The Least You Need to Know

➤ The Internet is here to stay because of its widespread popularity and its impact on our national economy.

➤ Internet usage is rapidly expanding around the world, drawing in a diverse demographic mix of all ages.

➤ As companies work with the Internet, they are starting to see productivity gains—a very exciting benefit.

➤ The Internet relies on brand awareness and recognition and uses a lot of traditional media tools to get them.

➤ The Internet will make branding hotter than ever.

➤ You must be clear: Are you looking to create a brand for the Internet or an Internet strategy for your brand?

---

# Part 2
# Thinking Like a Brand Champion

*We will start your orientation to Part 2 the way everybody always wishes a new job would start: We will actually talk about the big picture, the subtleties that will make you stand out, and the kind of thinking that signals to top management that you really do understand what is important. We will make sure that you are exposed to this kind of strategic thinking so that when we work through a lot of the details of managing a brand in Parts 3, "You've Earned It: The Fun, Creative, Inspirational Part," and 4, "Building Your Brand Perspective," things will make more sense.*

*Why do you want to know about brand management? Do you want to understand how your own company goes about making decisions? Are you interested in starting your own business, and you want to understand how to develop and nurture a unique identity for it? Maybe your background is in engineering or customer service or accounting, and you want to get transferred into marketing. No matter what angle you are looking at this from, brand management comes to life when you work through a series of decisions from the brand perspective. So let's develop that right now.*

# Chapter 5

# Your Brand Manager Orientation Begins

## In This Chapter

➤ Brand names become a comfortable shortcut in life

➤ The Five P's—oldies but goodies

➤ Learning to analyze the marketing mix

➤ Now you need to add the Four T's

Congratulations and best wishes from all of us. You said you wanted to be a brand manager, so we have moved you into a brand group as a brand assistant. Now orientation is about to begin.

We want to be sure that you get a solid foundation, so in this chapter we will cover a few marketing basics to be sure you have the jargon. Then we'll add in some newer thinking that puts a real strategic twist on those classics. In total, we will cover nine concepts that, when combined, give you a strong foundation as a businessperson and as a manager of a brand. These are the things you learn and memorize and recite over and over.

## You Already Know a Lot About Branding

The very fact that you have lived this long says that you have made lots of brand decisions. We have already talked about the fact that you grew up in a world where branding is so commonplace that often you don't even think about which soft drink you will buy. You have a range of brand names on your "already approved" list for clothes, food, cars, and maybe even the pens you like to use. The brand names are quick identifiers, and they make it easier for you to move through life without having to turn each hour of the day into a major decision point.

You see advertisements every day and have opinions about the ads and the products, services, and people that they promote. Parents of young children often dread the day their children refuse to put on the clothes that someone else chose for them. They want to start picking out their own outfits, and this is a major step for them in the process of growing into an individual. If you are like me, you cringe at being told what to buy by someone else. I get a little crazy with the person who repeatedly pushes me or nags me with "Just try it" 5 or 10 times. I DON'T WANT TO. GET IT? We like thinking for ourselves.

We are accustomed to the idea of having choices, and the whole idea of having the freedom to change our minds and make other choices is one of life's great pleasures. If you stopped to analyze how many choices you make in a day, if you actually made a note every single time you chose one product, one road, or one radio station over another, you might wonder how you manage to make so many decisions and still get home to the right place at night. Brand names become a short cut for us. They help us move through life a lot more smoothly and effortlessly because, at least in certain areas of life, we have things that we already know we like.

**Talk the Talk**

**Marketing mix** is shorthand for the basic components of how an entity will be marketed. This is a reminder that it takes a mixture of activities and strategies to bring any entity to life in the marketplace. Memorizing the Five P's is an easy way to remember what that mix is.

When you stop to study the idea of managing a brand, as we are doing here, rather than purchasing a brand as you do in your life as a consumer, you start to look deeply into the very structure of a brand's life. Some fundamental things about every brand determine how it will be perceived and how it will get known. Brands exist to be communicated, to be understood, and to stand out. If they don't do all of those things, they are just a dream in someone's mind, not a viable business.

It is the very fact that brands need to be communicated that puts so much marketing emphasis into brand management. If brands just needed to get out into the marketplace to sell, then they would probably be managed out of the operations/logistics group inside a company. One of the basics of marketing any entity, and something that is always considered in brand marketing, is the Five P's, often called the *marketing mix*.

# The Five P's: Oldies but Goodies

Now this is a trip down memory lane. It seems as though the first day of Marketing 101 at every college starts with either four or five P's, depending on where you go to school. Most marketing books talk about the four P's, which are often attributed to Philip Kotler, who authored some excellent marketing textbooks. Don't get confused. The first four I list will match what you usually see, but I, and a number of other people, add one more that I think belongs on that list.

First things first: The Five P's are product, price, place, promotion, and person. Let's take each one and clarify what we mean and why it is part of the marketing mix. As a caution, and to help avoid confusion, remember that whoever made up this list originally wanted to make it easy to remember, so everything had to start with a P. You'll see what I mean in a minute.

➤ **Product** is really a catchall word that refers to whatever the entity is that we are talking about. Please don't get too literal with it, but think of it as a generic term for the product, service, philosophy, or individual that is at the center of what we are working on. We talked a lot in Part 1, "The Power of Brand Management," about what can be a brand, and all those things are covered here by the word *product*.

➤ **Price** is just what it sounds like—but, of course, as brand management people, you can expect that we will focus on finding the *right* price. We will spend a whole chapter (Chapter 18, "'What's the Price?' Has No Easy Answer") in Part 4, "Building Your Brand Perspective," talking about how you calculate pricing.

➤ **Place** used to be so simple to define: It was the store or office or movie theater or ice-cream shop where the product was bought. With the advent of personal computers and then the Internet, there is a much wider definition for where and how a product can be bought. This one element of the mix just may be the most dynamic of them all these days. We will spend a whole chapter (Chapter 16, "Channels of Distribution: Getting from Here to There") on place in Part 4.

➤ **Promotion** is a little bit of a catchall phrase, too, because it refers to the activities that encourage people to purchase the product. In this context, therefore, both advertising and what is commonly called promotion incentives, such as coupons and rebates, are bundled together under the one word: *promotion*. Part 4 and Part 5, "Taking Ownership: The General Management Part of Brand Management," will talk more about this.

➤ **Person** is the fifth one, and it means just what it sounds like: Who is going to buy this product? In marketing jargon, we would call this the target market. I think it is a pretty important part of the marketing mix because we need to be clear with ourselves just who we think wants or needs what we have to offer. The advent of new technologies and things such as frequent shopper programs makes this a fascinating and almost brand-new part of the business to work with, much more challenging and exciting than ever before. You guessed it—we will spend a whole chapter on this, too (Chapter 22, "Promotion Is Changing Fast, and So Should You").

**Mentoring Memo**

The Four/Five P's is an idea as old as dirt, but it has stood the test of time. It is a great fallback checklist when you are tired. It is a great memory jogger when you are writing something really fast and need to cover the bases. It is pretty easy to memorize. When you give the original author a little leeway for making everything start with a P, it also makes sense.

If you can identify the Five P's of a product, you are on your way to learning how to make the decisions about what each of those elements should be on your own brand.

# Warm-Up Exercise: You're the Consumer and the Analyst

Let's take a few minutes and have you work with the Five P's so that you see how to bring them to life and see that each is really the result of a specific decision.

Let's start with what you already know as a consumer. I want to make this exercise easy for everyone to do, so I want you to choose a specific brand of a soft drink, which can be either carbonated soda, bottled water, iced tea, lemonade, or whatever you like best. Using the chart that follows (which you may want to just copy onto a piece of paper so that you can do this over and over), start with the left column and work your way across the page.

In the left column, put a specific <u>product</u>—in this case, the brand name and maybe even the size that you like best. Moving across, list what you know, as a consumer, about its <u>price,</u> a <u>place</u> where you can buy it, a <u>promotion</u> you have seen for it (if a commercial, just write in TV or radio, and so on; if a coupon, write that in), and who you think is probably the <u>person</u> the brand is targeting, even if this doesn't describe you. The person column might include teens, or mature women, or kids, or males 25 to 40—whatever word or two says what you think.

| Product | Price | Place | Promotion | Person |
|---------|-------|-------|-----------|--------|
|         |       |       |           |        |
|         |       |       |           |        |
|         |       |       |           |        |
|         |       |       |           |        |

*The Five P's of Marketing.*

So, as a consumer you can actually analyze a little bit of the brand strategy by simply looking at the individual pieces of the marketing mix. You can do this for any product, and it is a great way to get yourself into thinking like a brand marketer.

## Bringing the Five P's to Life

Now, let's get one step closer to the real brand strategy. Go back to the chart you just filled in, and see if you can fill in at least two other lines for the same brand by doing this:

➤ Using the exact same product and size, can you name two other *types of places* that it is sold (not two other store names) and what its price is there? Specifically, if you first listed the name of a grocery store as the place, what other kind of store sells this product?

➤ Can you name two other promotion activities that you have seen or heard?

➤ Under the person category, can you name two other possible target groups that you think this product tries to attract?

Are you starting to see how many possibilities there are for this one product? Want to have some more fun?

➤ Now add a second item under the product category that is from the same brand but that is a different size or is packaged differently. Stretch your mind and purposely try to think of where you have seen something different. An easy one with a lot of beverages is a 12-ounce can versus a 2-liter bottle. In many cases, they are both sold in probably 90 percent of all outlets. Can you think of a situation in which they are not both sold?

➤ Next to that product, put down the place and price; if you think that this product has a different target, write that in. If you want to jump to the head of the class, you can start to refine what you write about the person by thinking about who would buy this product in this form, and maybe for what occasion. (Hint: If this is a 2-liter bottle versus one 12-ounce can, maybe you start to think families, parties, heavy drinkers of this cola, and so on.) There are many possible combinations of the Five P's for just one brand of soft drink.

**55**

## The Five P's Are All Conscious Decisions

When you look at the Five P's this way, you see them as critical components of a total brand strategy. There is nothing old-fashioned or out-of-date about them. The place may be as old as a country store or as new as a Web site. The promotion may be as tried-and-true as a television commercial or as leading/bleeding edge as an artificial intelligence program tracking click-through on the Internet (don't worry, we will talk about all of these in Part 4).

The big message for you as a brand manager in training is that each and every element of your brand needs to be thought through and decided upon. You don't leave out pieces of the brand's identity or strategy and assume that the world will figure it out. Every single piece of the puzzle is your responsibility.

Want to add a new product or a new size to your line? Want to start selling to some new outlet? Want to get rid of some discontinued product in some out-of-the-way place? Want to start attracting young, working, single people to your brand? A simple way for you to start thinking about the ramifications of any of these changes is to draw up that chart that we just used and then do three things:

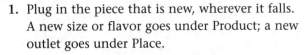

**Big Brand Insight**

Working through the Five P's may not sound too enthralling to some of you right now, but brand management is a long, complex, and highly disciplined set of decisions that never ends. These five basics explode out into a hundred or sometimes a thousand little issues a year, and you own every one of them.

1. Plug in the piece that is new, wherever it falls. A new size or flavor goes under Product; a new outlet goes under Place.

2. Fill in all the other spaces on that line so that you have at least one thing that makes sense all the way across.

3. Now go down as many of the columns as you can, adding more possibilities as you go. For instance, if what you started with under Product is a one-gallon plastic bottle of ready-to-drink iced tea, you might have lots of different things under Place. What about supermarkets, warehouse club stores, mass merchandisers, large drugstores, convenience stores in resort areas, and maybe even sandwich shops?

Now you are thinking like a brand manager. You may not choose to target all of those places in the end, but you are looking at the possibilities and seeing what makes sense. This little chart idea is a very simple way to look at your facts arranged in front of you, and we will use it again when we talk about promotion and place in Part 4.

# Now Add the Four T's: Newer Thinking and So Very Timely

The Five P's have been identified as key to marketing thinking for a long time. Many of the changes of the last decade have led me to look at four other key issues that are critical to good business thinking, and I want to introduce them here. They should be understood, memorized, and integrated into your thinking right along with the P's. I call them the Four T's. I have never heard anyone talk about the Four T's, so I don't think you will find them in another book as the Three T's or some other confusing number of T's.

The Four T's are technology, timeliness, teamwork, and truthfulness. Each of these will be discussed in the sections that follow.

## *Technology Is a Critical Factor*

Technology is now a basic component of every business to some extent. Technology may be what the business is about, or it may be something that supports the business function. Whether you are looking at an existing business or playing around with ideas for a new one, you want to ask questions about where technology fits or can fit.

When you are analyzing an existing business ask questions such as …

➤ What impact does technology have on this business?

➤ What technologies could help grow this business?

When you are working with an idea for a new business, ask this question:

➤ How can technology make this work "better," which, by the way, needs to be expressed more specifically as faster, smoother, cheaper, more responsive, and so on.

Technology can play a lot of different roles in your business, so let's spend a few minutes and go through five of them.

**Big Brand Insight**

Technology is often referred to as an enabler. This means that when a company has certain goals and strategies, it sees that it can use the power of technology *to enable it* to reach those goals. The technology becomes a strategic tool when used to send e-mail newsletters or special discounts to encourage purchases.

➤ **Technology as a product:** Many products and services are involved in supplying users of various technologies. Is your business a component (hardware, software), a solution (a package of pieces that together provide certain value), or a service (storage)? If technology is what your core business is, and if it is what you sell, then you are heavily involved in the uses of technology in business. However, be sure to read the other roles of technology here to be sure that you don't overlook an opportunity that may be right in front of you.

➤ **Technology as a promotion device:** When you think about the person in your marketing mix, be sure that you look at how you will reach this person. Is there an opportunity to sign up consumers for e-mail notices? When they go through the cash register at a store, can you give them a receipt that becomes a discount on their next purchase? Can you get them to sign up for a frequent shopper membership so that you can send them incentives?

➤ **Technology as a customer service strategy:** How can you use technology to better serve your customers? Can you shorten turnaround time, answer questions quickly, provide online support or ordering, or give them access to information that helps them in some way? How can the technology that you own be adapted to make life better for your customers?

➤ **Technology as a relationship builder:** Why do you suppose that Kraft, Inc., has put so much money into www.kraftfoods.com, its consumer-oriented Web site? It is full of recipes and meal ideas. It doesn't take orders from supermarkets or restaurants, things that you could tie into a profitable sale. It exists only to serve consumers like you and me—millions and millions of us. Think back to what we discussed when we talked about what a brand is. By building and actively maintaining its Web site along with everything else that the company does, Kraft, Inc., reinforces the value of its brands to the consumer.

➤ **Technology as an efficiency tool/advantage:** This one may be pretty straightforward for you or a really big idea. The basic fact is that most businesses use computer technology to some degree. All you may need to do is stay reasonably on top of things by using e-mail, spreadsheets, and the basic software programs well.

**Mentoring Memo**

Someday you will find the makings of a big idea for your business buried in a news report about some new whiz-bang technology. So always look at new things with this question in mind: Could we do something with that idea to make our product better?

If your business is providing people to build displays in department stores, for instance, is there value in knowing exactly how many displays they build each day, in which stores, using which products? If you had this information on a daily basis, instead of waiting to read their reports mailed in at the end of the week, could you turn that into a competitive advantage for clients? How will you get that information daily? Probably by computer.

Please don't ignore the questions of where technology fits or how it can help you reach your goals. Your business may be consulting to the widget industry, and what does technology have to do with that? If you ignore these questions, I can guarantee you only one thing: Some morning you will wake up and find a big, hairy competitor on your doorstep who is using technology to his advantage.

## Time Waits for Absolutely No One

*Timeliness* has gone from an element of having good manners to a basic function of life, kind of like breathing. I don't imagine that I need to say much about the speed of change these days. It seems like every businessperson I know is feeling more and more like a gerbil on a treadmill, running as fast as he can to just keep up.

If you take a minute and really think about time and making timeliness a part of your work culture, some interesting things start to happen. For our purposes here, the focus is on two issues:

➤ As a brand manager, you need to be on top of all the brand's priorities, and you need to shift emphasis from one project to another if time becomes a factor.

➤ As a business manager, you need to watch carefully for the impact of time on your ability to serve your customers. Time may present itself as an opportunity or a threat. One day it shows up as "If we could only have the Chicago market ready in two weeks instead of three, we could …," and just a week later it barrels through your door as "If we don't have the product shipped by October 1, the customer says don't bother shipping at all."

When you look at time this way, timeliness just may need to be as much a part of your total brand strategy today as promotion and advertising.

## Teamwork: Plays Well with Others

*Teamwork* is a plus in kindergarten, it is the winning ingredient for a football team, and it is both essential and mandatory in business. I really don't think it has ever been as important in business as it is today.

Generally speaking, when people who work together actually work together (I know, that was a little corny), things go more smoothly. Little problems don't always become big problems, and you have some nice relationships at work. Today, teamwork is a lot more than a nicer working environment, though. Today, teamwork is a do-or-die element.

What is so different today? It is probably just these two things:

➤ Technology makes information readily available and communication much faster and more efficient. It is pretty hard to say that you don't know something or didn't get the memo when an e-mail was sent to 10 of you. Most businesses today have lots of ways for people to find the information they need, so the idea of one person controlling the mother lode of knowledge is gone. You now hold responsibility for finding out what you need to know.

➤ Everything we just said has created a business environment with an interesting combination of *understanding and expectation*. Everybody *understands* that, in fact, there is too much for one person to know, even if it is all at your fingertips. No one can possibly know everything going on. At the same time, this creates an *expectation* that you can and will find out what you need to know. So you need—and your business needs—to rely on a group of people who care about the same goals as you but who have different sets of knowledge. And, frankly, nobody wants to hear, "That's not my job."

## Truth or Dare? I Don't Think So

*Truthfulness* is another one of those old words with all kinds of new meanings. There has been a significant and growing emphasis on personal accountability in the last decade. Let me give you some food for thought as it pertains to you as a businessperson and you as the manager of a brand. Frankly, I am going to do a mentoring thing here—cut right through all the fluff and get to the heart of the matter:

➤ Don't lie—you will probably get caught. Remember everything we just said about technology making information widespread and highly accessible? Guess what? That means people can find out if you know what you are talking about or are lying—in a matter of minutes.

➤ Don't stretch the truth about your brand. Your competitors have 10 eyes in their heads and ears the size of California. Do not imperil the brand for the sake of a quick moment of glory or an easy way out.

➤ We live in litigious times. (Now there's a quote.) *Litigious* is related to *litigation*, which is related to *lawsuits*, which is related to *expense and agony*. Not only will you get caught, but you also may be sued.

➤ It ain't worth it. The stress is going to get you, whether it means that you can't sleep at night or can't stop pacing around the office. It just isn't worth jeopardizing your own integrity or that of your brand and your company.

Those are the Four T's, and that is a lot to think about. Did you ever think you would hear that telling the truth and doing things on time are business requirements? When you hold the integrity of a brand name in your hands, business becomes very personal indeed.

## The Least You Need to Know

➤ Brands exist to give us choices and to make it easier to get things that we like without too much hassle.

➤ The Five P's are the basics of product, price, place, promotion, and person, sometimes called the marketing mix.

➤ The Four T's are a mix of old and new, and they are technology (the new one), timeliness, teamwork, and truthfulness.

# Chapter 6

# Brand Champion— Your Toughest and Most Important Role

> ## In This Chapter
>
> ➤ What is a brand champion?
>
> ➤ How brand champions talk and act
>
> ➤ Defending and building your brand
>
> ➤ Extending the life of a brand

Brand champion—now there's an important-sounding phrase. It evokes images of a superhero—caped and masked, for sure—whose heart is pure and who dedicates his life to taking care of those he serves. Well, the job I am about to describe is kind of like that, but you will have to supply your own outfit. We don't allow clothing on your expense account.

We have been talking about brands as identifiable entities that make specific promises of value. Whether your brand is built around 15-minute oil changes, a mutual fund, or an amusement park, those promises and that value are the bulk of what you have to work with.

This chapter is all about attitude, discipline, and change. If you think of the brand's promises as the tools you have to work with, then the brand champion role becomes the technique that you work with. You can be a painter or an artist. The choice is yours.

# Brand Champion? That Means You

This chapter is more about you and how you approach the job of managing a brand, the skill that you use in assessing opportunities, and the passion that you bring to the job than it is about the brand itself.

In the end, every brand is subject to the whims and faults and brilliance of its managers. In some ways, that is a scary thought. The business press is full of stories of long-established businesses foundering and failing after a change or two in management. It is also an encouraging and motivating thought. How many businesses can you think of that have been kept fresh and relevant for many years? What about the ones that have been created in just the last 5 or 10 years, that are vibrant and alive because of the energy and intelligence of the people who run them? That could be you.

I came up with the phrase "brand champion" a few years ago as a way to express both the fun of working with something as lively as a brand and the inherent responsibility of taking care of an asset so valuable and so needy. *Needy* may seem like a strange word to use here, but brands are inherently needy; they will pull in every ounce of creativity and commitment that you make available to them. You will hear me say repeatedly that a brand is alive, but understand that it gets its life force from the people who manage it.

The concept of brand champion has a lot of appeal to it. It challenges our intellect, fuels our drive, and encourages us to reach higher. It pays us back over the curve of our entire careers with a reputation for smarts, dedication, and strategic ability—in other words, for being good businesspeople. That's why I so strongly encourage you to embrace it.

So what exactly is a brand champion? It is someone who makes the brand come to life for everyone in the organization. It is someone who embraces the idea that a brand is a living, dynamic entity that needs leadership, direction, and challenge—and, yes, even someone who will defend its honor, when necessary. A brand champion always asks, "What is in the best interests of the brand?" A brand champion makes the rest of us care about doing right by the brand.

That is a pretty tall order, isn't it? Let me reduce all of that down to a single statement. A brand champion is a leader within the organization, no matter what his or her title may be, because he grasps the fundamental truth: The brand *is* the business.

# A Company's Greatest and Most Overlooked Opportunity

The role of a brand champion, like so many other things we have talked about so far, has two levels: the spirit of brand management and the practice of it. Most of this chapter talks at length about the practical role of being the central brand champion or the brand manager, but first let's look at the bigger picture. The spirit of being a brand champion is so underappreciated and so often overlooked, and yet so powerful in its being, that I would say this is the single biggest problem in most businesses today: Most of the people in the organization have no sense or appreciation for how important it is to build and defend the company's brands.

That is a big statement. I can hear some of you right now thinking that it is a crazy statement. What about rampant competition, cost pressures, problems hiring enough good people, and a hundred other good, tough business issues? Yes, indeed, every one of them is big, and many of them are downright threatening. But, if you and your organization do not grasp or truly embrace what the business is really all about, these other issues cannot be resolved well, no matter how much time and money you put into them.

Your business does not exist separate from the brand; it exists to serve the brand. Think of it this way: If a company simply acts as though it owns the brand, then it may make decisions for the corporate good without carefully considering the impact on the brands. The brand champion philosophy recognizes that the brand owns the company. If your brands all die, the company does, too. And if your brands die, all you have left to sell is empty buildings or office equipment. If the company dies because of some financial management issues, you can still sell off a good brand name and see your work continue out into the future.

So, the big opportunity for all of us working to manage brands is to engage the minds and hearts of the whole organization around this idea: A brand is a living thing, and a good brand is a very valuable asset. This mind-set should come from the very top of the organization and should be reflected constantly in communications between employees, and then to the outside world when employees deal with suppliers, customers, and the media.

Let's get practical and bring this idea down to everyday life. What does it sound like to hear people across the company who "get" the brand champion philosophy? The following table lists the kinds of things they would say.

## Listening to Brand Champions Talk

| Speaker | Talking With | Saying What |
| --- | --- | --- |
| President | Brand manager | "I hear your argument for a price increase to provide more money for marketing programs, but I worry that it will push the brand out of reach for some loyal users." |
| Purchasing manager | Supplier | "We feel strongly that Brand X must remain the best cavity-fighting toothpaste on the market. What new developments are you working on that can help us with that?" |

*continues*

## Listening to Brand Champions Talk   (continued)

| Speaker | Talking With | Saying What |
|---------|--------------|-------------|
| Secretary | Outside printer | "I am sorry, but these signs are not acceptable. We feel strongly that the copyright symbol should always be used with the brand name and that every piece of selling materials must be clean and clear. That is why we asked for it the way we did." |

What are you hearing? What messages are you taking away from these little conversational clips? Here is what I think you can hear loud and clear:

➤ Everyone in the organization understands that the brand is a living thing and should be treated with respect.

➤ Everyone in the organization understands that there is a set of standards for how the brand should be handled, and some of them are nonnegotiable.

➤ The long-term health of the brand is directly tied to the care that we take with it today.

➤ Brands are built over time and by lots of people. A whole village of brand champions can do a lot that one single brand manager never can.

Will you be a brand champion? Can you see yourself, no matter where you are in the organization today, talking differently and spreading the philosophy of the care and feeding of the brand wherever you go? If your senior management does not have this mind-set today, does that mean it is a waste of time for you to adopt it? No way. Start your own revolution by asking questions in meetings and by phrasing things in a way that encourages other people to focus on the brand. Try things like this:

➤ **Subject: Proposed price increase to up the profitability of company.** Have we looked at how this higher price will position us versus our competitors? Do we think that our loyal consumers will find any reason to turn away? Do we have enough of a quality differential to feel comfortable that we can continue to bring in new purchasers? Should we consider taking this price hike in two smaller stages? It will take longer to get the profitability that we want, but it could be much less disruptive to the brand.

➤ **Subject: Cutting the brand's marketing budget.** How much do we know about whether advertising or promotion has the greatest impact on the brand's sales? If we cut back on our promotions, will we have problems getting our vendors to support the brand during key buying seasons? One opportunity for a cut is the brand equity study that we planned to do. We can save that money now, but how will we feel this time next year when we are still stumbling around in the dark over decisions like we are trying to make right now? Will we still be guessing at what our purchasers really think about the brand?

There's an old saying that an opportunity is just a problem turned upside down. As corny as that may sound, it is a truism for sure. If the lack of a brand champion philosophy is a big problem in your business today, is this an enormous opportunity for you? Where does this fit in our goal of building Brand You/brand champion?

Now let's turn to the functional, hands-on role of being the brand manager with the brand champion blood in his veins. There are four specific skills and strategies that you need to develop: being a proactive defender of the brand, making others care about it, building a long and productive life for it, and finding smart ways to keep it fresh and relevant.

# Take Ownership: Be a Proactive Protector

If somebody was threatening your kid brother, you would jump to his defense. If somebody insulted your mother, that person would be met with a barrage of emotional responses, and maybe more, from you. What would you do if your father was poisoned by a pill that was supposed to cure his headache? What would you do if I went on television and told the whole world that you were an underhanded, manipulative snake? I keep saying that brands are alive and are personal—oh, boy, do they get personal.

Is there anyone reading this book who doesn't know about the United States government's proposed breakup of Microsoft Corp.? The concerns that Microsoft has become monopolistic as a result of its extraordinary success led to the most public airing of business emotions in our country's history during 1999 and 2000. Hundreds of interviews have been done in the media, and articulate, educated people have lined up on both sides of the argument.

What I want you to focus on from this case is the kind of things that have been charged and said and how the company responded. Your own opinions and mine about Microsoft have nothing to do with this exercise. I want you to take away from it how a brand champion responds to challenge.

What makes this such an interesting case to study is the combination of professional and personal attacks. It is very rare that a government investigation, usually the driest and most tedious of business stories, becomes exceedingly personal. Why did Bill Gates, one of the co-founders of the company and now its chairman, become a human punching bag?

Because Bill Gates *is* Microsoft in many people's minds (although I would guess that Mr. Gates himself might say that it is more the opposite, that Microsoft is Bill Gates, the expression of his ideas and drive). From our perspective as observers eager to learn, I encourage you to study the Microsoft case for both the personal and the business learning that it provides.

### Mentoring Memo

The case against Microsoft is the kind of thing that will be talked about in every industry for years to come. You have got to have an opinion and must be knowledgeable about it to carry on intelligent conversation in the business world. Even if you don't own a PC—which is hard to believe, but possible—this case still pertains to your business career.

As I write this, a judge has ordered the breakup of the entity into two separate companies. The basic idea is to open up more opportunities for competition to flourish, which in turn feeds our free market national philosophy.

Enough of the background—what have you seen the management of Microsoft do in response to all this very public and, I would have to think, personally painful publicity? If you built a company from an idea to an icon of successful innovation, how would you respond to this intense confrontation? Think about this as brand Microsoft and brand Bill Gates:

➤ Whenever it is you are reading this, go back over what happened already and see how the judge's decisions of 2000 are unfolding.

➤ Watch carefully how Microsoft communicates with the average citizen. Do you remember the newspaper ads and the television commercials throughout 2000 with Gates and Steve Ballmer, the president of Microsoft, talking with us one on one about the company's commitment to excellence? What are they doing in 2001 and 2002?

➤ Make it a personal mission to stay on top of what happens between 2001 and 2005, repeatedly asking yourself five questions:

1. What does this mean for the Microsoft brands?

2. Is this what I would have guessed?

3. What are the implications for the entire technology industry of products and services?

4. What do I think of the way Microsoft is handling itself publicly?

5. What would I do differently if I were Bill Gates?

I know one thing for sure. Gates and Ballmer are passionately committed to their company and are very much proactive in defending it. They have no intention of letting their company's reputation be sullied. You can see in their communications with the public that, no matter what the structural outcome of all this legal wrangling may be (and we may not really see any of that for some time yet), brand Microsoft' must be defended.

Another high-profile case, although one that happened a long time ago now, of a brand needing fast, smart, and passionate commitment is the Tylenol® tampering case. It was discovered that a few bottles of the popular pain reliever had been tampered with, and poisoned capsules had been placed inside. This caused an enormous level of fear throughout the country and, indeed, around the world. The Tylenol® brand, owned and managed by Johnson & Johnson, immediately became identified with grassroots terrorism. Imagine being the brand manager, just trying to get rid of headaches all over the country, and finding yourself inundated with media people and a public terrified of your product.

A lot has been written about Johnson & Johnson's response to this crisis, and every bit of it that I have ever seen is positive and full of respect. Why? The company chose quickly and decisively to do the right thing for the brand: Come forward, communicate openly, spend whatever it took, and commit whatever manpower it took to reiterate that Tylenol® did not create the problem, but that Tylenol® would absolutely be part of the solution.

**Big Brand Insight**

The Tylenol® tampering case and the way in which it was handled has become legend in the brand management world. I encourage you to do some research on it by working through the archives of the major newspapers and business magazine Web sites. Having a working knowledge of the basics just might start a great conversation in an interview someday.

I remember the public hysteria surrounding this episode well, with a number of media and business analysts saying that this would be the end of the brand, that it could never regain the trust of the public and the medical profession that it once enjoyed. That trust factor carries an extreme burden for a product that we ingest. It is analogous to me having your whole family over to dinner and then finding out that your father was poisoned somehow. That kind of confusion, anger, and accusation is what Tylenol® was subjected to on a national level. Just look at the brand today. The credit for its overwhelming rise from the ashes of "certain" defeat is a testament to the brand champion skill and dedication to proactively defending the brand.

These are two larger-than-life examples of living the brand champion philosophy and carrying that philosophy into everyday action. You want to be a proactive defender of your brand.

## Teach Us to Care About Your Brand

I have had the good fortune to work with more than 100 companies in the United States who make and sell branded products. I have seen the smaller ones struggle to gain a toehold in the market and the biggest of them struggle to hang on to what they have. I learned one of my greatest lessons about caring for a brand from one of the smaller companies, The King Arthur Flour® people in Norwich, Vermont. Since then, I have become a keen observer of how companies do or don't draw us in to caring about their brands. There is another company, bigger and more famous for sure, that also does an outstanding job: the Saturn® car company.

What is it that the people at King Arthur did so well? You should have seen them give a sales presentation! They exuded energy, enthusiasm, passion, and product knowledge like no one I have ever seen. Maybe you are having a little trouble seeing yourself getting wild about flour. Not these people. They made their product (and, basically, we are talking about a bag of flour) as vital and important as the brand, and they made their brand as important as the biggest of national competitors. In fact, they positioned the King Arthur brand as better than the competition, a premium product that had better promises of value and that sold for a higher price, and they never missed one single opportunity to make sure that everyone in town knew it. But you see, they didn't just position the product as better—they lived and breathed that positioning into life.

**Heads Up**

Notice that the people from King Arthur worked through their customer, the supermarket, to reach the consumer. This kind of promotion is cooperative by nature and is the kind of partnership thinking that you want to develop. We will talk much more about this in Parts 4, "Building Your Brand Perspective," and 5, "Taking Ownership: The General Management Part of Brand Management."

The energy and enthusiasm of the people in the company went a long way. Two fundamental things that they communicated in those presentations made all the difference:

➤ They clearly and very simply honed in on what made their flour different and better, and they found simple ways for salespeople and consumers alike to "measure" the difference.

➤ They reasoned, quite successfully, that they couldn't really sample the dry flour and have people say, "This tastes better." So instead, they put their marketing monies into teaching baking classes all over the place, and they had the classes "sponsored" by the local supermarket. That way, the customer (supermarket) got great PR for providing a valuable free class to the consumers, and King Arthur reps got to teach people to use their flour in simple recipes with glorious results. The customer learned that they could count on King Arthur to make them look good, while the consumer learned that working with a great product really does make a difference.

What about the Saturn® car people? "A different kind of car. A different kind of company." Does that sound familiar? That slogan has been repeated on television, in magazines, and on the Saturn Web site over and over again. This was a radical idea:

that a car company, just about the biggest of the big industries, could get people like us to care about what it did and what it made by letting us in on what the company thought and felt. Huh? What about cold corporate America? What about commercials that all said their car was the sexiest or fastest or safest? Now we are hearing that nice people—in Tennessee, no less—have decided to band together to be the anticorporation, to make the kind of car that real people want and value.

It worked. Can you remember some of the Saturn® commercials? Do you remember things like the woman on crutches getting her specially equipped Saturn®? Remember one of the times the local dealer went out of his way to help a customer? Do you remember hearing anything about Saturn's community-level events? Everything they communicate, and the programs they sponsor and support, all tie perfectly into that very personal, caring message. Saturn is involved in Habitat for Humanity, sponsors a cycling team, and even rebates up to $1,000 to purchasers of its cars who need to add special equipment for people with physical disabilities. Do these people love their purchasers or what? It makes you want to go to your local dealer and give the guy a hug and a handshake, doesn't it?

What can you do to make us jaded, advertising-saturated consumers care about your brand?

# Not Just a Lifecycle, but a Life

What makes brand management so exciting, and so risky, is that a brand really is a live entity. It doesn't matter if the product is as unglamorous as trash cans, because that is just the physical product. If the brand of trash cans is Rubbermaid®, for instance, it has an equity and a reputation of quality and dependability, and that is worth a lot.

The idea that every brand has a lifecycle makes sense. It is introduced, hopefully gets established, and has a long, successful run. Then perhaps at some point, it fades as its relevance to the modern world is lost. Button hooks and buggy whips are the weary examples always dragged out for this.

Just because it makes sense doesn't mean that it is inevitable, nor is there a known time frame in which all of this may happen. Do all products and all brands warrant decades and centuries of existence? No. But before you give in to the old lifecycle concept, look hard at what options your older brand may have. After all, many prophets of doom have been wrong before.

Look at these issues for clues as to how you might extend your brand's life:

➤ Why does the brand look "old"? Be specific: Is it package design, lack of pizzazz in its image, poorer quality than new competitors, or less convenience? Or has it fallen off everyone's radar screen because it hasn't been advertised since Moses was a baby?

➤ If the problem is the product itself—its claims, promises, and real value to the purchaser—can you change that with some type of reformulation? If so, what will that cost?

➤ If the problem is image, what kind of pizzazz do you think it needs? Will it be better served by a fresh new package design or by keeping the old design and doing some nostalgia advertising that it is still the same great thing? Can the brand support newer, fresher claims as it is, without reformulating it?

➤ If the problem is awareness, and if people have simply forgotten about it because it hasn't been promoted or advertised very much, is the brand worth that level of investment? Advertising can be very expensive, so make sure that the brand's promises and value can actually deliver what they claim before you invest.

The bottom line is this: Do not fall into the old-think school that the death of a brand is inevitable and that you should just move on. The hard part of doing the analysis is the emotions and attitudes of the people in the company. As brand manager, you need to give the brand a more-than-fair assessment before casting your vote one way or the other. Try very hard not to be swayed until you have a good, solid list of pros and cons for investing in the revitalization of the brand. It is alive until you hold its funeral.

# Make More of a Good Thing: New Products and New Uses

One of the most famous rescues of an old brand name has got to be the revitalization of the Arm & Hammer® brand. One of the newest and jazziest expansions of a brand is the Chrysler PT Cruiser®. And, not to be outdone by jazzy cars, what about taking a clear liquid that smells bad and creates problems if it is spilled but that has a reputation for sanitizing and cleaning like nothing else. What could you do with something so mundane?

There are wonderful examples of keeping brands fresh and relevant all around us. The Arm & Hammer® example is used all the time, but you have got to like the creativity and gutsy personality that it took for those brand people to step out of the old mold. Baking soda was becoming a ho-hum product, probably more than anything else because of the trend away from baking at home. As more baked goods were purchased in stores, home cooks found less reason to keep the little yellow box around.

The brand people took a good look at what the product can do and what claims and promises it can make (even though they hadn't made those claims before), and they found another story to tell—a whole different story. The product that our grandmothers used to make their blueberry muffins rise was also good for keeping disgusting food odors from running amok in our refrigerators. It also does a nice job of polishing our pearly white teeth. Who would have thought? Oh, by the way, it cleans our clothes, too.

All of these new items under the Arm & Hammer® brand are new products, and really new brands, in themselves all working under the master brand name. Any advertising or package claims build on the inherent good reputation of the master brand, but the products have branched out into completely new categories. This is a new product strategy that leverages the strengths of the original master brand. It keeps the same brand name overall but moves it into a new area.

What about Chrysler Corporation's introduction of the PT Cruiser in 2000? That is a whole different story. In this case, the product is completely new, not being repositioned and reformulated for different uses. This is a great example of using a new product to expand and refresh the master brand's image.

Notice that when you see an ad for this car, it is called Chrysler PT Cruiser®. When you talk with your friends about it, you probably just say PT Cruiser, eliminating the corporate brand name. But, were you aware before you read this book that Chrysler owns and manufactures this new brand? Probably so. The positive halo from creating a fun car that is generating lots of interest spills over onto the parent or master brand in a flattering way. Chrysler's investment in widespread redesign of its line over the last few years will probably pay out handsomely, and this one model is helping to spread the message that Chrysler builds cars that people really want.

What about that smelly stuff I mentioned earlier? Got a bottle of Clorox® bleach handy? Probably so. Millions of households do. Have you seen what these people have been up to lately? Would you guess that people think the Clorox® brand stands for things like a powerful stain remover, germ-killing ability, and other good words that imply clean? So would I. That's probably why Clorox created new products such as a spray disinfectant and antibacterial cleaning wipes. The company also created *line extensions* to the basic bottled bleach business with Lemon Scent and Fresh Scent. Notice that in the first case, these are completely new products, still within the cleaning category; in the second case, it is the same product with more pleasing scents.

All three of these companies are good examples of people dedicated to creating more of a good thing. What else could be done with your brand?

**Talk the Talk**

A **line extension** is a product that is added onto an existing brand in a slightly different form. The difference might be flavor, size (a 10-ream case of printer paper vs. a single package), packaging (squeezable mustard vs. jar mustard), color, or type (C batteries vs. D batteries). The important thing is that it makes sense within the same brand.

# More Good Things: A License to Grow

Not enough people are aware of a very powerful way to grow a brand name. Licensing is a legal arrangement in which you give another company the rights to use your brand name to produce items that you cannot produce on your own but that make sense under your brand. It requires very careful structuring of the deal and is well worth investing in expert legal guidance.

For our purposes here, let's look at licensing as an opportunity for you to either expand your own brand name or seize the opportunity to work with someone else's brand name. Let's look at a few examples of licensing deals that are right in front of you but that you may not even think about:

➤ When you see a designer's name such as Ralph Lauren on sheets and towels, do you think there is a Ralph Lauren factory somewhere making them?

➤ When you walk through a toy store, maybe you know that the Barbie® doll is a famous brand manufactured by Mattel and that there is a Hasbro Co. as well as a Hasbro® brand. But, when you walk through The Disney Store, do you ever think about who makes all those *The Lion King*® cassettes and books and stuffed animals?

➤ Got a hunger for an ice-cream bar—maybe one of those super-premium, drenched-in-dark-chocolate fantasies? Do you really think that this famous candy maker has an ice-cream factory out back?

Where are the business opportunities here? Before we go any further, think back to our discussion in Chapter 1, "Living in a Branded World," on private label brands. To make things easy for all the readers, we focused there primarily on things that we would all commonly see in mass-market outlets such as supermarkets and drug stores. In those venues, the private label would typically take the form of the store's own name on the label or a special brand created just for this purpose.

In other venues, the same basic concept applies: The person or company named in the brand does not actually make the product itself, but it has it made under guidance. Licensed deals work like this. So, for instance, if your company makes and markets a brand of sheets and towels, you may also enter into a license deal with several big name designers to make similar items for them. The department stores who order the product would know that you make the designer brands, too, and would order them all directly from you.

The logic is terrific, really. The cost of setting up your own linen factory would be outrageous. The cost of building an ice-cream factory and then having to ship such a fragile product all over the country at −20° would bankrupt you in weeks. Instead, you find someone who can do those things (who does them well already), and you give them more volume to help cover their overhead costs and generate incremental profit. It often makes the whole idea feasible instead of impossible.

From a brand champion standpoint, the single most important thing is to be excruciatingly clear and relentlessly dogged about ensuring that anything produced under your brand name must meet specific guidelines for quality. You must maintain control over any communication, whether it is advertising or package design. You cannot simply hand over your precious brand name to someone who may mean well but who doesn't have brand champion blood coursing through his veins. Sound overly dramatic? Not dramatic enough, maybe.

---

### The Least You Need to Know

➤ Brand champions play a vital, energizing role within a company.

➤ One of the best things you can do is to get people throughout the organization to appreciate the value of the brand.

➤ You may be called on to defend your brand. Stay cool and always act in the best interests of the brand, not your ego.

➤ There are many opportunities to extend and refresh your brand through new products, new uses, and even licensing deals.

---

# Brand Equity: Like Money in the Bank

*Brand equity* is a phrase that is quickly moving into the mainstream after spending its whole life in the confines of the marketing department. The equity is the sum total of all the different values that people attach to the brand name, which can be an eclectic mix of practical and emotional factors.

A brand's equity is the ultimate intangible, existing only in people's minds, and yet it has bankable power. In this chapter, we will study three brands and their equities in detail. Each is quite different from the others. In total, they represent a vivid cross-section of industries and images.

We will talk about their brand equities here; then, in Chapters 11, "Branding Inspiration: Information and Education Go Branded," 12, "Branding Inspiration: Product, Service, and Science Brands," and 13, "Branding Inspiration: People and Entertainment as Brands," we'll spend some more focused time looking at how they think about and manage their businesses. These companies represent new (Media Metrix™), established (KISS 108-FM™ radio), and old (Welch's®) brands, and they couldn't be more dissimilar in product line if they tried. All of them are highly conscious of the value in the brands that they serve.

# What Is Brand Equity?

I recently heard a story from someone who used to be a brand manager at one of the biggest consumer products companies in the United States. He told me that one day the president was meeting with a group of people. When he talked about how important a good brand name is, he explained it pretty much this way: If all the offices and manufacturing plants burned down that night, within one day they could have hundreds of millions of dollars of investment capital to rebuild. In the midst of the rubble, the brand would retain almost unimaginable value, and not even a fire or explosion could destroy it.

That is the simplest explanation I know for how valuable a good *brand equity* is. And just what is it about a brand that is referred to as its equity? Let's look at a working definition: Brand equity is the sum total of all the different values that people attach to the brand name.

## Talk the Talk

Are **brand equity,** brand personality, brand image, and brand identity all the same thing? They are often used interchangeably. However, be aware that brand identity is the term often used when discussing things like development of the logo, what color scheme the brand's stores should use, or how the package design will look. Consistently using "brand equity" when discussing the values associated with the brand name is the best idea.

What kinds of "values" do we mean? Perhaps the most interesting and most approachable aspect of studying brand equity is that it is so much like talking about a human being. What kinds of things go into your opinion of another person?

➤ Both positive and negative images

➤ Whether you know this person a little or very well

➤ Things that you learned about this person firsthand

➤ Things that you heard about this person from someone else (reputation)

➤ Things that make this person seem more familiar (ethnicity, attitude) or more distant (too formal, too different from you)

➤ Is this person important or special somehow?

➤ Do you like being associated with this person?

These are the same kinds of thoughts and feelings that go into brand equity. And when you look at it this way, you can see how those thoughts and feelings translate into decisions:

➤ We like this person, so we will probably like their friends and family, too (or vice versa).

➤ Do we feel any sense of loyalty?

➤ If you could choose between joining Friend A or Friend B for dinner Friday night, which would you choose and why?

Translate these two lists into business talk and know what you get?

1. Brand awareness. (You know this brand a little or a lot.)

2. A sense of brand loyalty. (How strong is your relationship?)

3. Reasons why you like the brand. (This is also known as the attributes of the brand.)

4. Brand benefits. (These are what the brand gives you in return.)

A terrific and somewhat unusual example of how seriously people are taking their brand equity is what is happening in Vermont. The land of the Green Mountains, maple syrup and all that fall foliage has realized that the state has a distinct set of values.

The state shows some real insight in the naming of one of its groups: Department of Tourism and Marketing. I like the addition of "Marketing" in there. This is a state that derives a large percentage of its revenues from tourism, so it has taken steps to understand and defend the equity of the brand called Vermont. When you think of Vermont, what comes to mind? If you saw the name Vermont on a product, what would you think? What if you then realized, by reading the fine print only, that the product was made in Arkansas and was just named Vermont?

Would you ever have thought that you might find a brand management position in government? This is another example of the thousands of opportunities waiting for brand champions.

# How Brand Equity Is Built over Time

Another very important aspect of understanding equity is the notion of equity that is "vested" as opposed to just potential. This is particularly important for newer brands.

You may find this easiest to understand by looking at a home that someone has purchased using a combination of a down payment and a mortgage to close the sale. The amount of "vested equity" the homeowner has changes over time. As the house goes up in value and the mortgage goes down in size, the equity (what the homeowner actually owns) increases. This homeowner could feel that his $100,000 home will someday be worth $1,000,000 and that a $90,000 mortgage will look like peanuts then. But that is looking at potential equity, not the real (vested) equity today. Brands are like this, too.

When a brand is getting established, it has unlimited potential for equity building. As people get to know it, the positive and negative attributes come through. More people and more opinions add up. The brand has five years of consistent quality and attention to customer service, and the equity keeps building. Then the company has a product recall. If the problem is small and the recall is handled well, the equity suffers, but hopefully not too much. If someone dies or the recall is bungled somehow, one week's problems can do what a devastating fire could not: destroy the brand.

The younger or weaker the brand equity, the more vulnerable it is to problems. A new brand can have all the signs of great potential, but it isn't a strong, powerful brand until it earns that status. It is what it is today, not what it should grow up to be tomorrow. A brand cannot trade on the future. It is so important for the people in the company to understand this; it is the heart of what being a brand champion is all about. The brand really is an asset of the company, and its value can move up or down.

When things are going well, when the brand is growing and its reputation is strong, this is a good time for the management team to sit down and envision what the full potential of the brand equity could be. This is a wonderful exercise for a management meeting because it gets everyone focused on what *could* be and *should* be. It can contribute to the creation of a vision statement or the understanding of the one that exists.

## How Is Brand Equity Measured?

In the three examples that follow, you will see three different approaches to measuring brand equity. Each company goes about the assessment differently; the important thing is that they all consciously do some type of process. Even the youngest of them, at only four years old, is sensitive to what people see and feel about its developing brand.

Brand equity research requires a fine attention to detail and a commitment to getting a breadth of opinions. This is an area that is particularly difficult to measure without strict discipline.

The discipline that is needed involves basically three things: 1) the number of inputs that you generate; 2) the frequency with which you test; and 3) the quality and consistency of the questions.

All of these are hallmarks of good market research; in equity studies, they are mandatory. Within these, there can be all kinds of different ways to do your study. For instance, contrast how Welch's and KISS 108-FM get their input.

Brand equity research focuses on things such as perceptions of quality, levels of awareness and familiarity, and how the brand ranks relative to its competitors. It probes satisfaction levels and tries to get responses that get to the emotional images tied up in the brand name.

If you would like to have a brand equity that is the envy of many marketers because it broadcasts uniqueness and expertise, and evokes the warmth of good memories, I think I have one for you to study.

# Welch's®: The Billion-Dollar Brand Name

How much would you give for a brand equity that consumers can easily articulate, that is consistent across your product line, and that practically glows with warm, emotional, positive connections? Many, many companies would envy the extraordinary equity of the Welch's® brand name. Just look at some of the dimensions of that image.

Here are 10 descriptors that Welch Foods, Inc., (the company refers to itself simply as Welch's most often) found in its research: 1) high quality; 2) time tested; 3) use of fine-quality ingredients; 4) Welch's special pride; 5) rich in roots and heritage; 6) old/well-established, dependable, reliable, traditional, old-fashioned; 7) special/unique connection to consumers; 8) emotional ties to childhood, growing up, and the good old days; 9) Welch's for the whole family; and 10) for everyday usage and occasions.

These kinds of attributes are truly million-dollar words; they are also the key to having this 130-year-old company break the billion-dollar mark in sales very soon.

Welch's® is a terrific example of how a clear equity takes on very human qualities—and the more humanlike it is, the easier it is for people to verbalize what they feel.

The Welch's® brand equity is studied in three different ways. The company hires outside professional research firms for the first two that we will review and then internally applies an equity research perspective to other studies. The sum total is a very rich bank of knowledge.

Welch's feels that the richest, most evocative insights come from talking directly with consumers, one on one or in small groups. The interviewer uses guided questions to draw out the feelings and thought of the participants. One of the managers at Welch's told me about having people weep as they recalled the good childhood memories evoked by their brand recollections.

Large, highly controlled studies in which hundreds of people are interviewed using the exact same questionnaire are much better at quantifying differences or changes. This is an area in which the discipline we talked about earlier becomes very important. By using the same questions and carefully probing for detail, you amass a

### Mentoring Memo

When a brand is this well established, every piece of research can feed the understanding of equity. This is one of the great benefits of having a long heritage, even in our current era of "new is better." There is a depth and breadth of experience with this brand that no dotcom/Internet pure-play on earth can possibly have.

statistically significant body of data that is reliable across time. The people at Welch's see this research as most valuable in helping them understand how their brand ranks relative to their competitors in key areas such as quality and value.

The third piece really speaks to the discipline of experience. When Welch's evaluates the results of testing on new advertising ideas or new products, they are looking for guidance on whether to invest in these specific projects. A secondary benefit arises when they take the longer view of brand equity, studying each and every piece of research for what they can learn about the brand's role in the outcome. Was the new product idea interesting, but people just couldn't see it with the Welch's® brand on it? Was the advertising funny and memorable, but people scored it low on its appropriateness for Welch's?

Welch's does a formal equity study every 7 to 10 years, and obviously does the ongoing assessment all the time. The company has committed to this process and believes that it is an integral part of its success. One of the major changes that came out of this research was the redesign of the company logo and all the packaging back in the 1980s. When you think back to all the things that you read about this equity, you can see how the new logo captures so much of the emotional quality.

*The old Welch Foods logo.*

*The new Welch Foods logo.*

One of the questions that I like to ask a company is whether it can give me examples of decisions made that were *clearly and knowingly influenced* by what the brand equity was understood to be. This is pretty much saying: Show me. I have some good ones for you.

➤ Welch's has created a director of marketing communications position with an interesting twist to it. This person has veto power over *any communication* that she feels is inconsistent with brand equity. That's right—she gets to say "forget it," not just to the things that her own department creates, but to what every department does. They put some muscle in the job.

➤ "A consistent message in a consistent manner" is one piece of learning to come out of the equity work. This has directly influenced—and, in some cases, torpedoed—new advertising campaign and package design ideas. Managers admit that this can cause some tension as they argue their own positions to push for new glory versus staying true-blue. The challenge is always to have the learning inspire wonderful marketing moves without stifling creativity. This is a difficult task.

Here is another good question for you: Who "owns" the brand? This simple question can generate all kinds of answers, and I purposely let people self-define what I mean. At Welch's, the number-one brand guardian is the CEO, with the VP of marketing and the director of marketing communications as his lieutenants. It is made clear that all corporate officers are held responsible for brand building.

I can almost hear the more cynical among you thinking, "How would you see something like that in action?" When two departments have different opinions about something (timing of a new product or acceptable costs for a project), the most senior people are expected to resolve it in the best interests of the brand, not themselves, their own egos, or their department budgets. And that is part of how they are evaluated.

Studying the Welch's® brand equity is a great way to build a sense of the importance and extraordinary value of finding a clear, positive message and sending it every day, year after year. Welch's has had 130 years to perfect its story—so what if the company was just a new kid on the block?

# Media Metrix™: New Company, New Industry, Big Idea

I talked briefly about Media Metrix, Inc., in Chapter 4, "E-Commerce Makes Branding Hotter Than Ever." I had originally contacted the company to get some Internet usage data for that chapter. Two weeks later, I attended one of its Users Group client meetings to see what the company was all about. I walked out of there convinced that this company had not just extraordinary business potential, but also a brand equity potential that was out of sight. I also walked out with the company's commitment to provide the exclusive bonus section on Internet movers and shakers for you; you can find it in Appendix B, "Resources and Revelations Guide."

We will take a closer look at Media Metrix's business in the case study section of Chapter 11, "Branding Inspiration: Information and Education Go Branded." Before we talk about this brand equity, though, I want to make sure that you understand enough about what the company does to put this discussion in perspective.

Media Metrix, Inc., was born in 1996. In those four short years, it made two acquisitions and is about to finalize a very important merger. These people are the pioneers and leaders in Internet and digital media measurement. They track the usage and popularity of Web sites and the effectiveness of advertising in this environment. The Media Metrix merger with Jupiter Communications will now incorporate the leading provider of research on global Internet commerce into this mix.

For those of you who look to build a career in the burgeoning Internet-related world, this company is a model of success and is likely to be a part of your own business future as well. Let's take a look at what its brand equity is all about.

Media Metrix is synonymous with high-quality, independent, reliable Internet measurement throughout the world. Some of the descriptors of its equity include …

➤ Cutting-edge technology.

➤ Innovative.

➤ Global vision.

➤ Forward-thinking.

➤ Entrepreneurial.

➤ High standards.

This is a particularly interesting mix of words and phrases to me, combining the best of what many people might call Old Economy and New Economy images. It is a testament to the hope that many of us share: that technology is enabling both new business formation and older business revitalization, and that the two *together* create unprecedented innovation.

An existing, successful market research company, NPD Group, created Media Metrix. That kind of stability right from the start is certainly an important component of the company's rapid success. It is similar to but still different from a number of Internet-related businesses with strong venture capital involvement. I would guess that some of the equity descriptors such as "global vision" and "high standards" are a product of being able to have a solid, deeply experienced management team right from the beginning.

*The Media Metrix logo.*

Take a good look at the Media Metrix logo. It is one that I particularly like, although the catchy graphic isn't the big reason why. It is the circle of words that makes this logo really sing for me: "The Power of Relevant Knowledge." In the age of information overload, the company puts its primary promise right up front. Media Metrix will help its clients get to what is good, strong, and actionable. Nice.

What are these people doing to understand their equity? There are some great lessons here for those of you at the early stages of brand development. Until you have enough awareness and customer contact, you cannot get a good read on brand perceptions.

Want some good advice from some big brands? Get in a regular program of talking with your customers and gathering clean, unbiased reactions to "What does our business/brand mean to you?" and "How are we doing?" Make a short but very focused list of questions—10 is plenty—and figure out whether anyone inside the company is objective enough to get the answers. Otherwise, hire an outsider.

Media Metrix fielded the first significant audit of clients' perceptions of the brand at the beginning of 2000. Before that, the company used an ongoing audit of smaller scale and collected lots of informal input. The company foresees an even more important need for ongoing research as it continues to evolve after the Jupiter/Media Metrix merger.

Media Metrix's understanding of brand equity has been slowly emerging over the four years. In early 2000, managers created a firm baseline to measure future studies against. When I asked for concrete examples of how brand equity has influenced some important decisions, I got more answers than I have room for here, but let's look at a few.

The Internet is obviously a global phenomenon, and that requires companies that service this environment to make some decisions early on about how they will handle the challenge of needing foreign operations. While so many of us think of the Internet as dissolving international borders, as we e-mail cousins and friends all over the globe, that isn't an accurate picture for some companies.

Media Metrix needs to *access* information in foreign lands, not just broadcast it. That requires local interaction that cannot be done from New York headquarters. Media Metrix has made the strategic decision to maintain majority control of all its international businesses, rather than creating a series of alliances. This makes international expansion a more rigorous process, but the company believes that the payout will be ensuring that its standards are carefully protected.

### Mentoring Memo

There is a good lesson in this Media Metrix example for all of us brand champions: *The equity that these people wanted to have is the equity that they managed the company to.* That sounds obvious enough, yet it is a big statement when it is true and not a corporate platitude. When a company's management is *absolutely clear* on what it wants the brand to stand for, that knowledge becomes a *strategic tool.* The company can use it to guide decision-making, knowing that today's actions create tomorrow's equity. Brand equity is an asset to be managed, and sometimes mission and vision statements can miss that point. Ever seen one long on profitability dreams and short on brand dreams?

Data integrity is another area that Media Metrix cites as directly reflective of its commitment to brand equity. The company believes that it has the most rigorous research methodology in the industry and that it delivers the highest quality data as a result. This, coupled with its longevity (all of you laughing at that word describing a company younger than your own kids, just remember that longevity is a relative term), gives clients the ability to trend data right from the beginning of the Internet revolution.

So, in the 24/7, fast-paced Internet world that Media Metrix lives in, who "owns" the brand? The company feels very strongly that while the CEO and the president are the two "captains," an unusually deep sense of brand association runs throughout the company. This is attributed to an intense commitment to training, an enthusiasm for being part of creating something new and exciting, and making sure that the associates get to see how *their company* is respected in the press.

As an outsider looking in, I can tell you this much: Once I got to know this company, I asked to profile it here and in Chapter 11 for you. Between doing that, generating a mountain of data for various chapters, and building Appendix B, I know that I created a good-sized challenge for Media Metrix. My contacts were refreshingly open and honest, and they have a monster commitment to quality. My money is on these guys to win the race. And speaking of winning the race over and over again ….

# KISS 108-FM™ Radio: A Sharp and Fresh Identity

You know right from the start that you are going to like these people. Anybody who comes up with the nickname KISS for a radio station has got a sense of humor and a marketer's soul, for sure. And just to add a little wrinkle to that name, it is officially called KISS 108-FM™, but that isn't exactly where you'll find the station on the dial. It's really close, and apparently close enough, because KISS 108 gets thousands of listeners to turn to 107.9 without any confusion at all. And the call letters are really WXKS-FM, but I don't know if any listeners would know that off the top of their heads.

*The KISS 108-FM logo.*

This Boston radio station is a legend and, at 21 years old, is a proven performer; but somehow it doesn't seem to age. The lead celebrity on-air personality has aged along with the rest of us, but he still sounds fresh and full of energy.

KISS 108-FM™ is a chart-topper of long standing. The station has repeatedly led the market for the key demographic of women 25 to 44 and has made itself into somewhat of a cultural icon, not just an entertainment medium. As you will see in the case study, the station has very high listener involvement, completely overruling many people's belief that radio is a passive medium.

The brand equity is all about three things: 1) the music; 2) the fun; and 3) "Matty in the Morning."

It was interesting to me that when I was doing interviews to create this write-up and the case study on the station that you will find in Chapter 13, I asked several people what the brand equity was. I was delighted because they all gave me the exact same answer. That pretty much doesn't happen. Usually I get answers that are anything from close to forget it.

This raises two interesting questions: How can you be so sure that this is the equity, and how come you guys can all play it back to me so clearly? I got some good answers for you on both counts.

KISS 108-FM™ does a different type of equity research than both Welch's® and Media Metrix™. The station has constructed a rolling research program that it believes suits its type of business best. This style of radio is so highly interactive that the station wants constant feedback to make sure that it delivers on strategy.

➤ Weekly phone surveys focus on the music (the biggest part of the "product") to make sure that the station lives up to the target audience's expectations of the brand.

➤ Quarterly, people are brought into an auditorium to get feedback on the music, the on-air personalities, and the promotions.

➤ Twice a year, focus groups are conducted to do in-depth probes of how the brand image grows or changes.

This is a surprisingly rigorous research schedule, which reflects a business sophistication that might surprise some of you. You might look at a radio station—particularly one that plays the top hits and has a constant stream of promotions—and think, "This has got to be the greatest job on earth." And, when I tell you about its annual concert in Chapter 13, you will want to send your resumé, for sure. But, in fact, this is a tough business and is living testament to the old adage that it takes a lot of work to make something look so easy.

Let me circle back to the second part of my question: How come the people who work at the station can play back the brand equity instantly and without hesitation? The answer to that question, coupled with the research commitment that you just saw, is the key to the station's success in building a powerful brand equity.

An amazing number of people at the station get involved with the business of building business; it would be pretty hard to hide out and just collect a paycheck in this place. They have weekly promotion meetings. They have brainstorming meetings. They invite people such as secretaries and computer specialists to join in. They have a town meeting once a month in which every associate attends and every department talks about what is happening.

KISS 108-FM™ does an audit of employee happiness and satisfaction every year. The station uses an outside firm so that there is no bias. The station firmly believes that if people *want* to come to work, have friends at work, and are doing what they want to be doing, they will get more involved. Is this just because they are in a "fun, people business"? I don't think so.

KISS 108-FM™ takes its brand equity very seriously. These people are in a business where they need to make it fun for their customers, even when it may be stressful at headquarters. They are very conscious of protecting their equity. For all the laughs and the good times they create, they exist only because they can generate advertising revenues to stay on air. They cannot charge you one penny for the music, the fun, or the charm of "Matty in the Morning." It is all of us freeloaders, spinning the dial at our leisure, who decide which stations live or die. Now there's an interesting thought, isn't it?

### The Least You Need to Know

➤ Brand equity is the sum total of all the different values that people associate with the name. It can be a mixture of all kinds of pragmatic and emotional elements.

➤ Brand equity is built over time, which makes it harder for new businesses to know how they are doing. A good, clear vision of the brand equity you want is one of the best guiding lights that you can have when tough decisions must be made.

➤ Welch's® has an equity steeped in tradition and warmth. Recollections of childhood and wonderful flavors mingle with trust and respect.

➤ Media Metrix™ is only four years old, yet it is already picking up clear signals of how its equity is developing. The company has used the equity that it wants to guide it through very fast growth and a lot of change.

➤ KISS 108-FM™ promises and delivers on a simple combination of music, fun, and "Matty in the Morning"—and it is working beautifully. The station stays focused on keeping the target audience happy and loyal.

# Chapter 8

# Your Brand's Mission, Vision, and Core Values

## In This Chapter

➤ Mission statements are meant to clarify

➤ Vision statements are meant to inspire

➤ Analyzing mission and vision statements

➤ Understanding a brand's core values

Many companies developed mission statements of some type during the 1990s. You may see them labeled as mission statements, goal statements, statements of purpose, and probably other names as well.

My own take on the situation is that a lot—and probably most—of them went up in corporate offices and were promptly ignored; a much smaller percentage was worked into the company's culture. I see some interesting changes happening in people's attitudes toward these statements: They are being taken much more seriously now.

The newer trend is to give voice to a vision of what the company sees happening in its future. The idea of giving life to a vision for the future is becoming a new element in the definition of a strong CEO. As the vision statement idea grows, we will see more emphasis on another idea: The company and the brands will need to understand and express their core values, too.

## Mission Statements Are Most Prevalent—for Now

Over the last two or three years, *mission statements* have started to become living documents for a lot more people. The days of framing or laminating these documents and putting them up all over the building as proof that the company actually has a mission are over, thankfully. Something different is happening now. People can actually tell me what their company or brand is all about without having to read it off a chart on the wall. That signals to me that mission statements have come of age. I attribute this to two different factors:

➤ Developing a mission statement in the early 1990s took on the air of a "we need one of those, and I want it on my desk by Monday morning" kind of phenomenon. The herdlike mentality of so many companies rushing to produce one made it pretty easy to dismiss it as another here today, gone tomorrow activity. It took time for us to adjust to a mission statement as a living document that really did reflect a deep insight into what the company wanted to be.

➤ The birth of so many new companies, propelled into business by technology innovations, led to a new emphasis on defining what makes one company different from another. Could the entrepreneurs clearly define what they wanted to be and who they would be better than? Could they attract vital employees by clearly defining what the cultural goals of the company were all about? This put a lot of emphasis back on the written word.

**Talk the Talk**

A **mission statement** is a declaration of the goals of the organization. It should clarify for the reader what the organization is focused on *doing*. When you look at it this way, you can see how other terms grew out of this, such as "statement of goals" or "statement of purpose."

So, why did I write "for now" in the heading for this section? Because mission statements, which are very prevalent, will soon be joined and probably overshadowed by vision statements. My vote says, let's add a vision statement, not make it replace the mission statement. I think they do different things.

I have worked with a number of mission statements in my career, and I helped to write a few of them as well. Whenever I approach one, I always look for the "so what," the proof that there is more than fluff in the statements. To me, the true acid test of any mission statement comes when you ask someone in the company to prove that the ideals in the statement can be seen in the real world.

In this chapter, we will look at four different mission statements to see what they are telling us. You will find two more mission statements in the case studies in Chapters 11, "Branding Inspiration: Information and Education Go Branded," and 12, "Branding Inspiration: Product, Service, and Science Brands." Altogether, these six give you a view into very different businesses, ranging in size from a dental office to a manufacturer with hundreds of millions of dollars in sales. They cover both product and service businesses.

I am purposely leading off with a mission statement from the smallest of the five organizations to be sure you see that the size of the company has nothing to do with the value of the statement. Let's look at the mission statement for the Center for Esthetic Dentistry (the bold and italics are just as shown on this company's Web site):

## Our Mission

To guide our patients along a path of **optimal health and wellness,** for life. To *nonjudgmentally* deliver the highest possible level of care, with empathy and understanding.

To continually **pursue excellence** through continuing education, personal and team growth, and mastery of leading-edge technology. To treat our patients as individuals.

To deliver this care with **first-class, five-star service.** To respect our patients' time. To accept our patients **as partners** in their wellness. To assume a leadership role as a resource—a window of information with concern for our patients' overall well-being.

To consistently **deliver more than would reasonably be expected.**

© *2000, Center for Esthetic Dentistry. Permission granted.*

When I came across this mission statement, it was the first time I had seen one from a dentist. I found it at www.starsmile.com, the Web site name that I had memorized (quite easily because it is a catchy name) from some advertising. I went to the Web site to see how good a communications device it was; I left it very impressed with how much I knew about the dental practice after just five minutes. And that is how I ended up choosing this statement to use in the book, calling for legal permission to reprint it and meeting a brand champion in the process.

### Mentoring Memo

As brand managers, you are expected to have an intimate knowledge of the brand's personality and equity. As brand champions, you have a keen understanding of the emotional aspects of the brand's promises and values. And, at the same time, you are expected to have a businessperson's professional ability to be objective. Look at your current mission statement. If you subjected it to the scrutiny that we are doing here, how well would it stack up? How good is the fit between what the statement says is important and the way in which the brand is managed?

# Dissecting a Mission Statement

There are a number of ways to analyze a mission statement, and each is simple and straightforward. All you are really trying to do is see how easy it is to understand what this organization says it is all about. If that becomes a difficult task, then you already know something very important about this group.

Here is one way to analyze a mission statement. With just one reading of the statement, ask yourself these questions:

1. What do I think are this company's real priorities?

2. What kind of feeling/image/impression do I get about this company?

3. Without reading the mission statement a second time, write down five things (words, phrases) you remember. Look at your list and rank order them from most to least important.

4. If I owned this company, what would I want my customers to think about us after reading a mission statement; and then, what would the statement need to say to help the associates focus on what we need to deliver?

5. Read the statement again. What do you see/hear this time that you missed before? Did the mission statement communicate what you thought were the priorities? If you made another list of five things you remember after this reading, how different would that list be?

By doing this quick exercise, you are simply getting at the real messages being communicated. How many people read a mission statement more than once? Not many. That's why it needs to be clear.

Now, what about how representative it is of reality? There are two different ways to get at this. If you can talk with someone who has worked in the company for a while, that is ideal. These days, you may be able to get a lot of information off the company's Web site. This is detective work: What you want are concrete examples of how the mission statement reflects what the company actually does.

Let me use The Center for Esthetic Dentistry's mission statement and Web site as examples. The practice is owned by Dr. Tom Orent, and it specializes in dental work to make the teeth much more esthetically pleasing. In other words, Dr. Orent's focus is giving you a better smile. The mission statement puts five areas in boldface type, so I assumed that those are key issues. Using only those five, and only information that I could find in the Web site, here is what I know about how Dr. Orent's practice delivers against those promises.

➤ Offers a "last-time guarantee" on its work.

➤ Uses state-of-the-art computer imaging technology so that you can see how you will look after a procedure you are contemplating.

➤ If you are traveling from out of town, his office will arrange hotel reservations for you and make sure that you are picked up at the airport and brought to the office.

➤ The chairs in the treatment rooms have back massage pads and heated neck rests. (Just as a side note, this is sounding pretty good to me so far.)

➤ While the dental procedure is being done, you can choose from cable TV, movies, music, or silence, whichever makes you more comfortable.

➤ Dr. Orent has been a leader in the field of esthetic dentistry, has held positions within the industry association, and has taught seminars and college programs.

➤ If you suffer from jaw pain, you can order Dr Orent's book *Freedom from Chronic Pain* online, or you can download the file.

That list is a lot of support to pull together just off a Web site. I called and spoke with Dr. Orent, whom I had never met, to get permission to reprint his mission statement here for you. Fifteen minutes later, I was convinced that this man is a brand champion in dentist's clothing. He was enthusiastic about the practice that he and his staff were building. He talked easily and willingly about their commitment to satisfying the customer—and, if I didn't know better, I would have thought that he was a marketing director for a big consumer packaged goods firm. I hung up a happy person: Dr. Orent was further support for my contention that brand champions can be found in any type and size of organization.

## Are Mission Statements Impacted by the Size of the Company?

The size of the company has nothing to do with the quality of the mission or the mission statement. You can read many mission statements online by visiting the Web sites of major corporations. Quite a few of them have their statements right there, which is exactly why I am not using them in the book. I want to expose you to some mission statements that you might never see and yet are for organizations that you can relate to. Dr. Orent is probably not your dentist, but you are familiar with local dental offices in your area. The next time you visit your own dentist, look around and see if the office has something like a mission statement. Now, let's switch gears to look at large national associations you know and that have some influence over your life but that you probably never interact with.

Because our first example was for a dentist, let's take a look at the mission statement for the American Dental Association. You can find this on the organization's Web site at www.ada.org.

Before you start to analyze a statement, be sure you are focused on the fundamental question: What is the job, the primary function, of this organization? We are not talking about an individual dental practice now. The ADA is a professional organization, a service business. Who is *its* customer? The customer here is the individual dentists across the country who pay dues to support the organization's activities; in turn, those activities are supposed to support the individual dentists.

## ADA Mission Statement

The ADA is the professional association of dentists dedicated to serving both the public and the profession of dentistry. The ADA promotes the profession of dentistry by enhancing the integrity and ethics of the profession, strengthening the patient/dentist relationship, and making membership a foundation of successful practice. The ADA fulfills its public and professional mission by providing services and through its initiatives in education, research, advocacy, and the development of standards.

*© 2000 American Dental Association. Permission granted.*

Let's use a second method for analyzing what a mission statement really says. In this case, the challenge is to see how easy or difficult it is to turn the statement into an outline:

This is a professional association serving …

➤ The public.

➤ The profession of dentistry.

The ADA promotes the profession of dentistry by …

➤ Enhancing integrity and ethics.

➤ Strengthening the patient/dentist relationship.

➤ Making membership the foundation of a successful practice.

The ADA fulfills its public and professional mission …

➤ By providing services.

➤ Through initiatives.

➤ Through education.

➤ Through research.

➤ Through advocacy.

➤ Through development of standards.

This is a very easy statement to look at structurally. It is a relatively short statement, and yet it does answer who the association sees as its constituency, what it promotes about its members, and how it does this. When you outline a statement this way, it is very easy to then "check" how well an organization or company lives up to this ideal by asking what kind of education, what kind of advocacy, how you strengthen the relationship, and so on.

Our third example is one that I found while doing some research for a later chapter. I wanted to see what kind of information I could find online on the bowling industry. I was quickly led to www.bpaa.com, the Web site for the Bowling Proprietors' Association of America. I was struck by its mission and vision statements, and I want to share them here with you.

## BPAA's Vision Statement

It is the Vision of BPAA to Drive a Growing, Prosperous and United Bowling Industry.

## BPAA's Mission Statement

It is the mission of BPAA to enhance the profitability of its members.

*Source: www.bpaa.com, © 2000, Bowling Proprietors Association of America. Permission granted.*

These two statements are terrific examples of clarity. They are also good to study as you are trying to clearly discern the difference between a mission and a vision statement. Look what these do:

➤ The vision statement paints a picture of the future that the association wants to see.

➤ The mission statement tells us plain and clear what the association is focused on doing day to day.

When I called the BPAA office in Texas to get permission to use these statements, I think I surprised a few people. They probably haven't been mentioned in too many business books, but I congratulate them on the thought that they put into developing this work. And, this is another example of brand champions at work in every kind of business we have.

The fourth example is different yet again, and I chose this one for three reasons:

1. It is the mission statement developed specifically for the *Web site* of a well-known organization.

2. The structure is a short, one-sentence statement followed by nine critical objectives. This may give some of you a different model to follow as you develop your own statements.

3. This group also has a vision statement, and that will lead us into the next section of our discussion.

**97**

The American Medical Association, or AMA, as it is commonly called, is a well-known professional organization. It is regularly talked about in news broadcasts, and its publications are quoted in the press all the time. The Association has created a Web site at www.ama-assn.org. When I first visited it, I was struck by the fact that the Web site is seen as a serious and distinct component of the Association's communications strategy. How did I know this? Here is what the introductory paragraph on the mission statement Web page says:

> The AMA Web site launched in August of 1995. The Mission and Objectives of this site reflect the organization's continued commitment to the Internet's importance in meeting the AMA's goals.

Think about this in the context of our discussion in Chapter 4, "E-Commerce Makes Branding Hotter Than Ever," about the need to be clear on what role the Internet should play in your overall business strategy. The AMA has a specific mission and objectives statement *for the Web site*. That is a nice sign that the Association takes the Internet very seriously. So, what about the mission statement? Here it is:

## Mission

To promote the art and science of medicine and the betterment of public health.

## Critical Objectives

1. Disseminate up-to-date information on health and medical practice to physicians.
2. Disseminate up-to-date information on health and medical practice to the public.
3. Use innovations in Internet technology to provide information on medical ethics, practice, and education to physicians.
4. Enable physicians to remain informed in multiple areas of medicine, including developments in fields other than their own.
5. Provide members with information on the Association and membership activities.
6. Provide members with a forum to communicate with other members using Internet technology.
7. Provide physicians with information on the Association's advocacy activities for physicians and their patients.
8. Provide the public with information on the Association's advocacy activities for physicians and their patients.
9. Provide information on AMA policy.

© 2000, American Medical Association Web site, www.ama-assn.org. Permission granted.

As you look this over, remember to identify what the focus is here and who the customer is. The AMA, just like the ADA, serves its own professional base of members but has a very public persona as well. The two organizations have very different styles of mission statement; both are clear, and both would be very easy to "check" by asking specific questions.

# Vision Statements Are the Newer Direction

In the mid-1990s to late 1990s, a new discipline started: identifying a master vision for what the organization could be, and would be, if everybody got the passion for the picture. I would source a lot of this thinking back to a fine book called *Built to Last—Successful Habits of Visionary Companies,* by James Collins and Jerry Porras. The book first came out in 1994, was updated in 1997, and is still a good read.

I was excited when I came across this *vision statement*. I went looking for a mission statement example to show you and found this, too, at www.ama-assn.org, the American Medical Association Web site. I was particularly excited to find this because it was one of the few examples I have seen in a public forum that specifically addresses the idea of core values. It also has a nice, short statement of what the AMA wants its future to look like.

After I decided to use this, I went back to the *Built to Last* book to check something: Sure enough, the format in this statement was clearly inspired by examples shown in that book. Here is the AMA vision:

**Talk the Talk**

A mission statement talks about what a company is *doing*. A **vision statement** is a declaration of what the company is focused on *being*. The ideal vision statement is a short, easily memorized sentence that conveys spirit, drive, and enthusiasm for the business.

> The vision reflects a shared desire by the Board of Trustees and Senior Management that the AMA approach the new millennium with renewed vigor based on a solid understanding of purpose, values, and envisioned future.

### Core Purpose

To promote the science and art of medicine and the betterment of public health.

### Core Values

**Leadership:** the stewards of medicine, caring advocates for patients and the profession.

**Excellence in all we do:** the highest quality service, products, and information.

**Integrity and ethical behavior:** the basis for trust in all our relationships and actions.

## Envisioned Future

The AMA will be an essential part of the professional life of every physician and an essential force for progress in improving the nations' health.

## Objectives

AMA will pursue being:

➤ The world's leader in obtaining, synthesizing, integrating, and disseminating information on health and medical practice;

➤ The acknowledged leader in setting standards for medical ethics, practice, and education;

➤ The most authoritative voice and influential advocate for patients and physicians; and

➤ A sound organization that provides value to members, federation organizations, and employees.

*© 1995–2000 American Medical Association. Permission granted.*

I encourage you to analyze this statement as we have earlier mission statements before you read on.

## Heads Up

Take the time to analyze a company's mission statement and anything else like it that you can get your hands on before you go in for an interview. Don't get carried away by the poetry in it or turned off by the brevity. Do a quick structural analysis and turn it into an outline, which takes only a minute. This way you have a better sense of how valuable it is, and you are armed with great questions to use.

Let me point out my favorite phrases and see what you think:

➤ Shared desire

➤ Renewed vigor

➤ Science and art

➤ Stewards of medicine

➤ Caring advocates

➤ Excellence in all we do

➤ Integrity and ethical behavior—the basis for trust

➤ Envisioned future

➤ Essential force for progress

➤ Setting standards

What do these have in common; why do you suppose I like them so much? They use emotional words, words that take our attention to a plane high above getting from Monday to Friday. These are the words that inspire and that paint a picture, or a vision, of what a group of people can do, if they choose to. This is the language of vision.

# What About Core Values?

Core values are the "shoulds" of the business, the things so basic and so important that you won't let yourself walk away from them. The simplest analogy that I can give you is that a brand or company's core values are to it what your own guiding beliefs are to you. If a cashier gives you too much change back after your purchase, and you say, "Thank you, but you gave me too much," you have a core value around the subject of honesty. Somewhere inside, you are programmed to stay that course.

When you think about core values, it personalizes the world of business pretty dramatically. It takes away a lot of the slick veneer—and, frankly, the sarcasm and disbelief—that a lot of people feel about business. Core values bring us back to the understanding that any business and every business is about human beings making choices. And that is true even when you work for the biggest companies in the country.

Let's look at the AMA's core values and see what messages they send. This discussion should help you think hard about what your own brand/company core values are all about. Remember to look at these in the context of being "should/must be" declarations:

1. **Leadership:** the stewards of medicine, caring advocates for patients and the profession.

   A steward is someone who cares for and/or guides in a caring way. Being an advocate means taking on an active role. These are highly descriptive words that combine activity with intent.

**101**

2. **Excellence in all we do:** the highest quality service, products, and information.

    *Excellence* is a big word and a very big promise. The biggest problem with using it in a vision statement is that you are left open to the individual definitions of success that your readers will attach to it. That is also the best reason for using it: You intend to live up to their expectations.

3. **Integrity and ethical behavior:** the basis for trust in all our relationships and actions.

    When I read this my mind immediately went to the famous phrase "First do no harm." In a time when medicine is accused of being a heartless business and our newspapers run stories of doctors indicted and sued, this statement is gutsy. It is also necessary. It is also just the kind of visionary reminder that a sometimes beleaguered membership needs.

Can you see, hear, and feel the differences between mission and vision statements? What about your own? Your company may have a worn out, dog-eared mission statement somewhere that no one but the president can quote or explain. If so, it is useless. No matter where your title may place you in the hierarchy, I encourage you to write two vision statements in the next month: one for Brand You and one for the brand that you work on. You may never share either one, but both are invaluable in making you the kind of businessperson you want to be.

---

### The Least You Need to Know

➤ Mission statements are designed to provide a clear sense of purpose for what the company does. When you look at the investments that a company makes, for instance, they should make sense in light of the mission statement.

➤ Vision statements capture what the company wants to be, what it wants to stand for, and why it deserves to be looked up to. A personal vision statement for Brand You is a terrific way to better understand your own values.

➤ Core values are the "shoulds" or the "we must be" kinds of things that guide the company's decision-making. You cannot claim purity of product as a core value and pollute the environment at the same time if you live up to your core values.

# Part 3

# You've Earned It: The Fun, Creative, Inspirational Part

*Brand management is hard work, but it does have a lot of creative times, too. Most people are fascinated, although that could be in a positive or negative way, with how strange words are made up to create a name for a new car or a headache medicine. The average consumer would probably be shocked to realize how many brand slogans they know by heart and how quickly they can identify the music they hear in commercials.*

*All of these things are part of the brand naming and positioning process, and all require both creativity and discipline.*

*Part 3 explores both the naming and the positioning of a brand. Then we will have three chapters that let you sit back and look for inspiration from some new areas in brand management. We will look at things happening in science, education, and celebrity branding. Things and people as diverse as the Human Genome Project, charter schools, and chef Emeril Lagasse are all up for discussion. The whole idea is to build up your brand radar system, your ability to find the branding nuggets of wisdom all around you.*

# Brand Names Are Just Words, Right?

If I asked you to name 10 brands right off the top of your head, you could do it easily. If I changed that to 100 brands, it would still be a snap and take only a little more time. Move it up to 500 brands and give you a day, and my money says that you could do that, too. One week and a request for 1,000 brand names? Not all that tough.

When you can come up with that many brand names so quickly, there are two things happening: You have a high level of brand awareness for many brands, and, there is something inherently memorable about those brands. I have heard a statistic used several times in recent months that we get about 8,000 messages a day as we go about our lives. How can we possibly find room in our brains to remember anything given that barrage?

When you are choosing a brand name or making decisions about how to work with the name you've got, the issues that you are dealing with are far more human than strategic. The brand name—and how you talk about it and make it come to life—is the ultimate marketing communications challenge.

# What's So Hard About Choosing a Brand Name Anyhow?

The United States Patent and Trademark Office (USPTO) put out a press release on June 15, 2000, announcing that 15 brands were celebrating their centennial that year (more on trademarks in the section "Use It or Lose It: Copyright and Trademark Issues," later in this chapter). Among the group are such fixtures as General Electric's "GE medallion," Nabisco's CREAM OF WHEAT® picture of a chef holding a bowl of cereal, and Carnation® Brand condensed milk. Looking at these three brand names, what role did the name itself play in helping the brands to endure?

Did these brand names help the brand to endure, or did the brand help the brand names to endure? I don't know for sure, but my money says that the brand kept the name alive. Not one of these brand names would be a likely candidate today. They would be deemed too common, not very memorable, and not particularly descriptive, although CREAM OF WHEAT® pretty much describes what it is and what it looks like. So let's talk about what you see in that bowl of cereal for a minute.

CREAM OF WHEAT® is pretty much nondescript stuff; a mass of off-white, smooth, slightly thick cereal derived from wheat. No offense meant, I assure you, because it is a very good product. It just doesn't look like much by our current standards. The brand name is descriptive of what the product *is*. If this was a new product to be named today, there would be long conversations about whether to describe what it *is* or what it *does:* the choice between product attributes and product benefits.

### Talk the Talk

**Brand awareness** is vitally important for all brands. It is measured through market research that probes for both top-of-mind and aided awareness. Top-of-mind is the ideal: When asked to name brands in a category, some brands pop up right away. Aided awareness occurs when identifying familiar brands when shown or read a list of brands.

A lot of older brands have very simple names like this; the brand name might be the founder's family name, hometown, or something that describes the products. So, names such as Welch's®, Pabst Milwaukee® Blue Ribbon Beer, and General Electric® made plenty of sense. Also, there wasn't much competition out there to muck up the competitive scenery, so naming was pretty easy.

The big idea was to build *brand awareness,* to keep the brand name in front of people so that they would recognize it.

Choosing a brand name today is much more difficult. More than 2.3 million of them are already registered in the United States, more than 1 million are in active use, and more keep pouring in. In 1999 alone, the government registered another 104,000 trademarks. How many more combinations of letters, numbers, lines, and words can we dream up?

A very important thing you need to know is that it isn't just the brand name that can be trademarked. The USPTO's press release says that "words, phrases, symbols, designs, shapes, and colors have established the identities of countless sources of goods and services." Did you notice, by the way, that when I first mentioned the USPTO's press release, I actually said that it was the GE medallion, not the name General Electric? Was it the chef holding the bowl of cereal or the name of the brand that was celebrating its anniversary? In both cases, it was the graphic, the symbol itself, that was registered 100 years ago, not the brand names.

# The Many Roles of a Brand Name Today

Talk with someone involved with new product development today, and you will hear that person lament how difficult it is to find a new brand name. Even easier, just look at the names of cars you walk by the next time you park at the shopping mall. Where did those words come from?

What is it that a brand name needs to do for the business? What roles can the name itself fill in the overall business strategy? Let's look at five possible roles:

➤ **Motivate involvement/purchase:** The brand name is often the primary hook in getting the customer's attention. It telegraphs, "This is the one you want."

➤ **Create memorability:** The brand name itself needs to stick in people's minds. It can do this in a lot of ways, such as by being quirky and different, or by evoking an image that is calming and reassuring. The key is that it is memorable. The marketer's worst nightmare is the customer who says, "I saw what I want in an ad, but I don't know what the brand is."

➤ **Create a focal point:** The brand name should provide a center of gravity that holds everything else together. The brand name has to be relevant to what the product is about and ideally should provide some type of inspiration or guidance to all the facets of brand communication.

➤ **Describe what the product is or does:** This rule doesn't always hold up, that is for sure. All you need to do is think about the names of laundry detergents or cars and wonder which is which. But, for some brands, the name says it all. Look at the household cleaners aisle in a grocery store for some very straightforward names.

➤ **Create positive feelings/identifications:** A brand name that can make customers feel good about purchasing is one that is a big contributor to loyalty. Think about very expensive jewelry and watches. Just owning certain brands seems to make people feel great.

**Mentoring Memo**

In the following chapters of this part, we will talk about creating a brand profile as a living document that embodies the personality, promises, and values of the brand. When you work through that section, you may want to refer back to this chapter and review the roles that you think your brand name plays for you. The idea of the brand name as the center of gravity around which the rest of the elements circulate is an important one.

# Brand Names Convey Images and Promises

If you were to ask a dozen companies involved with creating brand names and images "What makes for a good brand name?" I don't know how many different answers you would get, but here are some of the ones you would hear for sure: Memorable; Evokes a positive image; Not offensive to an ethnic, racial, or religious group; Pronounceable; Projects a personality; Different; Sounds nice when spoken; Describes a key product benefit; Describes a feeling; Distinctive, stands out; and Trademark-able.

Is there a straight-line relationship between the brand name and the brand equity? Well, yes and no, is the only realistic answer.

Back in Chapter 7, "Brand Equity: Like Money in the Bank," we saw that the equity research on the Welch's® name ties to strong emotions, feelings, and childhood memories. That equity practically shouts "dependable, high quality." Does the word w-e-l-c-h-s in itself mean anything? No, it doesn't, but the products and the value that have been delivered for the last 130 years have imbued the name with all kinds of very meaningful characteristics. If you applied that same brand name to tires, it would be meaningless. In the context of fruit-based foods, it is magic.

What about KISS 108 and Media Metrix? KISS as your brand name implies a lot of personality and a fun, upbeat sensibility. That actually works very well as a descriptor of the product and the promise (music and fun). Media Metrix is a descriptor of the product (measurements, also known as metrics, of the online medium) and a quick, jazzy tie to the world of media in general, which has the image of being cutting edge. These two names have a more linear relationship between the name and the equity than the oldest brand in the group.

There are so many brand names to choose from to show examples of how a name develops over time. Let me give you some food for thought by presenting 20 names from many different sectors:

➤ **Best Buy.** This certainly tells you the basic promise of this chain of general merchandise stores: Buy from them, and you will get the best deal.

➤ **Toys "R" Us.** The name tells you what this company is about in no uncertain terms. The company declares itself *the* source for toys; a pre-emptive positioning that implies that it is somehow better without ever having to say how or why.

➤ **Kids "R" Us®.** If ever there was a name for a store that handles the things kids need, this is it. Again, a wonderful play of words positions this company as the ultimate source.

➤ **SmarterKids.com.** I like the name of this Web site a lot because it provides such a clear benefit statement and practically announces the target audience.

➤ *Complete Idiot's Guide®.* This is a great example of a brand name that plays with the way we commonly talk. Of course, as *you* already know, since you are reading this book under that brand name, the readers of this series are a very sharp group of individuals.

➤ *Chicken Soup for the Soul®.* A completely different title for a book series that once again plays off common language. It creates a quick association with comfort.

➤ **IWon.com.** You've got to like the simplicity and clarity of this name. It has a lot of quick appeal and is great for promotional purposes. If you want to cut through the clutter out there, this name is a winner. I do have one big concern, however, and that is a lack of clarity about what the Web site is all about. Do you know?

➤ **Grandmother's® Pie Fillings.** All right, all you domestic goddess wannabes, doesn't this brand name just make you want to rush out and buy a couple of jars to put into the ready-made pie shell that you picked up in the freezer case? The brand name conjures up an image, and the image is what leads you to the promise.

➤ **Dell® Computers.** Fifteen years ago, Dell was the family name for a young guy with a dream. Today, when you put the name *Dell* next to the word *computer*, magic happens.

➤ **6FigureJobs.com.** This may get my award for the best Web site name that I have ever seen. I laughed out loud—in delight, I assure you—when I saw this advertised in *The Wall Street Journal*.

➤ **Business Week®.** So, do you think you know what kind of magazine this is just by the name? It's clear and right to the point, and you even know how fresh the news inside it will be.

### Big Brand Insight

Big companies in the consumer packaged goods business spend a lot of time and money researching brand names. Usually they will involve ad agencies, the brand group, and a number of outside resources. Conducting focus groups followed by in-depth market research testing is commonplace to be sure that the name picked is clear and communicates the message and the image that is perfect for the new brand.

➤ **Colgate Total®.** This is a fairly new brand name, which is obviously an extension of a very well-known name. It is so simple and works so well to convey a multibenefit toothpaste that it must have surprised everyone at Colgate when it was actually chosen.

➤ **FreeInternet.com.** Here is another one that says it all really quickly. I think you know the number-one promise.

➤ **Streamline.com.** How do you describe the benefit of something as new as an online grocery shopping/errand service that delivers to your home? You tell them that it will streamline their hectic lives. The name works.

➤ **MasterCard.** When is the last time you even thought about the name of that plastic card in your wallet? The use of "Master" is brilliant to describe a card that can be used for all kinds of purchases. Here again, it's just a play on common language.

➤ **Tiffany®.** There really was a famous person named Tiffany, though very few of us know much about him. But we certainly have an image associated with his name after years of extremely careful branding work by the managers of the company that bears his name.

➤ **Fast Company®.** This is a nice double entendre that is clean enough to discuss in this book. "Traveling in fast company" is one common expression that sounds very much like something our grandmothers warned us against. Then again, we live in a time in which companies themselves need to be fast at the change-switch or perish while they rest. Nice name. Do you think the target audience thinks of themselves as "fast"? I do, too.

➤ **KFC®.** Didn't these restaurants used to be Kentucky Fried Chicken? Yes they did, and they still sell all that chicken. But now, they have more than the old fried chicken buckets. They have a new image, new advertising, and new signage to go along with it. An old brand has been refreshed more so than changed.

➤ ***The Wall Street Journal®.*** This is another terrific name, this time for a newspaper that specializes in financial news. The content and look of the paper keep evolving, but the publication has certainly broadened out what constitutes financial news into the latest in business news. As "the Street" has changed, so has this paper.

➤ **Hewlett-Packard®**. Two men you know nothing about gave their names to a company that now has a charismatic woman CEO who stars in the television ads to tell you that the original two men were brilliant and that the modern-day company is living up to their standards. Nice way to make an old company name something to talk about.

# A Promise to Protect and Defend

When blue jeans are being sold at off-price outlets, a designer gets mad and then gets going. When diamonds are getting a bad image because of politics in Africa, a leading brand name disappears. And, as Internet businesses get the message that "dotcom" on your name signals "new and not profitable," even that hottest of monikers gets changed. There is a whole lot of shakin' going on.

These are three very different examples of things that are happening with brand names these days. Calvin Klein's issue was with the company that licenses the rights to use his name on a line of blue jeans. He found out that the manufacturer was selling the product to warehouse clubs and other off-price retailers, which he believes hurts his brand equity. He has brought a lawsuit to stop this action.

DeBeers, the diamond company, has taken its name off of its own advertising, leaving behind the tagline "Diamonds are forever." Why? The ongoing political situation in parts of Africa has led to charges that diamonds from local mines are being used to arm rebel soldiers. The DeBeers name has come up a number of times in news reports because it is such a prominent brand in the diamond trade.

Dotcom no more? This one is fascinating. I worked with a company two years ago that had just *added* the ".com" to its name to make sure that is was seen as part of the new economy excitement. Then *USA Today* reported on July 3, 2000, that some companies are dropping the extension so that they appear more stable than risky.

What happens with company names when there is a merger, or, conversely, when some elements are sprung out as separate companies? There are some basic options:

1. Slide the names together somehow, as in AOL Time Warner.

2. Find a whole new name, such as Verizon, the merger of Bell Atlantic and GTE.

3. The "little" guy's name goes away, even when it is worth billions, as in Warner-Lambert becoming Pfizer.

4. One guy's name wins out, and the other's disappears, as in when Pharmacia & Upjohn, which was already the outcome of a merger of the two named companies, merged with Monsanto, resulting in what is now Pharmacia.

5. Spin off two divisions to become a new company, as when AT&T spun off Western Electric and the world-famous Bell Labs into Lucent Technologies.

6. Now, this may be my favorite: Hoechst Marion Roussel merges with Rhone-Poulenc Rorer to become Aventis. How's that for getting rid of lots of name baggage?

Some of you will be very envious of this next problem, but a problem it is. What happens when your brand name is so well known that it *is* the category?

➤ Would you hand me a kleenex, honey?

➤ You know, that toilet is the cadillac of plumbing fixtures.

➤ Well, we will just put a band-aid on that budget and hope that no one notices the boo-boos.

### Talk the Talk

When a brand name is used to mean a type of product rather than a specific brand, it is referred to as being **genericized.** The biggest problem for the owner of the trademark is that allowing this to go on weakens your own case for exclusive ownership. If someone else wants to use your brand name, you may not be able to defend yourself.

When your brand becomes so well known that people use it without thinking, it has become *genericized*. That may seem flattering at first, but, in fact, it creates a world of problems.

Look at the three bullets you just read. Did you notice that I didn't even capitalize the names, never mind use the ® symbol? I wrote them in the context that they would be used in common conversation. And that is exactly the problem: They don't get any respect. This is why you see advertisements that say things like "Band-Aid® brand adhesive strips." The addition of the three words "brand adhesive strips" may seem redundant to you, but it is critically important to Johnson & Johnson that people understand that the generic descriptor for products like this is adhesive strip, not the brand name. If they didn't defend the brand name, they may leave themselves open to challenge if someone else wanted to use the Band-Aid® name for another product.

## Use It or Lose It: Copyright and Trademark Issues

What is a trademark? The USPTO has an excellent four-page document, "Basic Facts About Registering a Trademark," that you can download from their Web site www.uspto.gov to get a lot of information. The definition of a trademark given in this document is this: a word, phrase, symbol, or design, or combination of words, phrases, symbols, or designs, which identifies and distinguishes the source of the goods or services of one party from those of others. A service mark is the same as a trademark, except that it identifies and distinguishes the source of a service rather than a product.

That Web site also has a search feature that you should know about called TESS, for Trademark Electronic Search System. It lets you do a quick search of the government database of trademarks to find out who owns a mark, whether it is still active, and a number of other pieces of information. I have used this database extensively for this book, so let me offer a little bit of advice to first-time users.

➤ I had much better results, and a lot less frustration, using the Free Form Search (Advanced Search) function rather than the Structured Search.

➤ The first time you use it, I would suggest you get acquainted by trying four or five different tests. Simply type in a brand name that you know exists, and see how many results you get.

➤ Try a one-word brand name, and then try a two- or three-word name. Scroll down through the results, and look at what it is giving you. You will see a list that could run to thousands of entries, of all trademarks that contain the word you typed in.

➤ Try a two- or three-word name again, and this time enter it with some basic search discriminators, like the words *and*. For instance, when you type in the three words "King Arthur Flour," you get 41,241 records to look through, with everything that contains any of those three words. When you type it in as King and Arthur and Flour, like magic, you get what you want, with only three entries to look at.

If you want to register a mark, you can get the forms from the USPTO online. By the end of 2000, the government expects to have an online registration service by which you could handle the whole application via Internet.

I want to be sure you are aware of a few basic facts about registering and protecting a trademark, because too few people are familiar with these regulations. If you work in a big corporation with your own legal department, you probably will never run into any of these issues. However, if you work for a smaller company, or even a startup, these can be thorny problems to find out about at the last minute.

1. The rights to a trademark are established in one of two ways: by using the mark regularly, or by officially registering it with the government.

**Heads Up**

The USPTO system allows you to do a quick search of all trademarks similar to yours, or to one that you are considering. Do pay attention to the warning note posted on the Web site: You should not assume that a trademark you are interested in is free and clear just because you can't find it yourself in the database.

2. Holding on to a trademark, however, if someone else wants to use the same name or symbol, can be very tricky if you never registered it. If two parties both used a name and neither registered it, the ownership would have to be resolved in court.

3. Official ownership of a trademark (certified by the USPTO) is for a period of 10 years. It needs to be renewed every 10 years after that.

4. A trademark owner who doesn't use the mark leaves himself open to challenge.

5. You can file an "intent to use" application for a mark that you want to use and fully intend to use but that you have not yet gotten out into the marketplace.

6. Once a trademark is registered and a 10-year term of ownership begins, you must file an affidavit between the fifth and sixth years that you intend to continue using it.

These six items give you an important overview and should get you asking a few questions about the status of your brand names and logos. If your company used a brand name at one time and you are considering bringing out a new product under that name, check right now for whether you still own it.

I strongly encourage you to use this government Web site for patents and trademarks, and to link to the copyright Web site to learn more about copyright regulations. These are terrific sources of information and are pretty easy to use. You will absolutely want to get good legal advice before investing time and money, but these Web sites can give you a good grounding in the issues and questions that you need to ask. That alone could save you thousands of dollars in legal fees.

---

### The Least You Need to Know

➤ Brand names conjure up images and feelings that are attractive to customers. Some names are highly descriptive of the product itself, others are descriptive of the benefits.

➤ Brand names provide a center of gravity around which everything else revolves. Over time, the brand name really develops a personality that infuses the rest of the communication.

➤ Brand names should never be allowed to become genericized; this weakens the trademark owner's claim that the name signifies something unique.

➤ Trademarks provide legal protection for your brand names and logos. A trademark needs to be actively used to be kept alive, and brand managers should know the legal status of their own brands.

# Chapter 10

# The Powerful Duo: Brand Name + Positioning Statement

---

## In This Chapter

➤ Positioning statements clarify brand promises

➤ Promotional hooks add immediate appeal

➤ Qualitative research requires good listening

➤ Quantitative research takes away some of the risk

---

Okay, you have three seconds: What product has used the line "Good to the last drop" for years? How about this venerable gem: "Takes a licking and keeps on ticking."

These are classic positioning statements, or you may see them called taglines, and you hear them all the time. When a brand finds one that really works, the brand team often, quite wisely, hangs on to it and uses it over and over again. And that is the whole idea of a positioning statement: to position the brand name firmly in the mind of the audience.

Finding the right statement is hard work and is an area in which doing some very well-thought-out market research is critically important. It is also one of the most fun and creative parts of brand management. In this chapter, we will look at a number of different brands and see what they choose to say about themselves. Then you can decide: Do you think these positioning statements are working hard enough for the brand?

# Positioning Statements Make Brands Come Alive

"Good to the last drop" is a phrase that must be burned into the conscious minds of millions of Americans. Just hearing it immediately brings up the brand Maxwell House® coffee. And I am old enough to remember Timex® watches as a major advertiser on television. The Timex® ads were always focused on the watch surviving some kind of torturous experience that would surely destroy an ordinary watch.

**Talk the Talk**

A **positioning statement,** also called a tagline or a hook, is a set of words that capture the essential, the most dynamic, and the most important message of the brand. It is like the subtitle of the book: It explains what the catchy title is all about.

These two statements, just a few words each, have accompanied the brand name so many times that many of us link them together as one unit. Now that is a powerful duo. When you cannot think of the brand without thinking about what it stands for, you've got an image and a clear value that is priceless.

Just to make sure you don't think that *positioning statements* can never change, let me tell you about one that has changed ever so subtly over the years. The next time you see an ad for Maxwell House® coffee, you may very well see "Make every day good to the last drop." Do you hear the subtle shift from the coffee itself being "good to the last drop" to the coffee helping to make all of your days "good to the last drop"? The latter has a little more of a lifestyle feel to it, but it carefully weaves in all the equity of the original.

# The Mix-and-Match Game: Who Says What?

Anyone who hears, sees, or reads any type of advertising is familiar with lots of brand-plus-statement combinations. Here is a list of brand names and a list of statements used. See if you can match them up. The answers are at the end of the chapter (refer to the section "Mix-and-Match Game Answers").

## The Mix-and-Match Game

| Brand/Company Name | Statement |
| --- | --- |
| Salesforce.com | We're the dot in .com™ |
| Sprint PCS® | The clear alternative to cellular. |
| Honda® | All day strong. All day long. |
| State of New York | Coach has more class.™ |
| Lipitor® | How the world shares ideas. |
| Sun® Microsystems | The lower numbers you're looking for. |

| Brand/Company Name | Statement |
| --- | --- |
| Nortel Networks™ | Thinking.™ |
| Office Depot | Point. Click. Close. |
| United States Postal Service® | New Attitudes. New Opportunities. |
| Aleve® | Taking care of business. |
| American Airlines® | Fly like an eagle™. |

# Is It a Positioning Statement or a Promotional Hook?

Did you notice anything different about some of the statements in the right column? Did you notice that when I was introducing the game, I simply referred to them as statements, not positioning statements? That is because some of them are most likely being used as temporary hooks or taglines for a specific advertising or promotional campaign, rather than more permanent positionings.

Look at "Coach has more class," for instance. I hope I am not ruining the surprise, but that line should be paired up with American Airlines. The airline has put a lot of emphasis on the fact that it has created more room in the coach cabin of its planes by removing some seats. The particular line I am showing came out of a magazine ad, and to me this is much more of a temporary statement. It works well to reinforce a very important message, but it may not still be around two years from now.

Car dealers are probably the most well known for running advertising that uses promotional hooks. Quite often, you will not see the car brand's own positioning line anywhere in the ad because all the emphasis is put on the President's Day Blowout or Summer Sale Celebration. They are putting the focus right where they want it: Come in now before all the good deals are gone.

One of the better promotional lines I have seen was used in a television ad during the summer of 2000 for Mitsubishi® vehicles. The line was "The Car Envy Event." Now that does a nice job of communicating that there is a special sale event going on, but it keeps the focus on the idea that Mitsubishi® is something worth coveting. Contrast that with another car ad at the same time that talked about the Olympic Countdown event. You get the idea of the promotion and a sense for the timing, but it doesn't rise to the level of the other example. We brand champions are a tough crowd, aren't we?

Let's try just four more statements and see if you can recognize them without any prompting (you will find the answers in just a minute):

➤ The relentless pursuit of perfection.
➤ The point of contact.

➤ We love to see you smile.

➤ Think different.

Once you start looking and listening for these types of statements, you will very quickly learn to analyze them for effectiveness and memorability. You will find it fascinating to watch some brands as they weave promotional hooks in and out of their advertising. All of these marketers are trying to get the attention and interest of their target audience, and that is difficult on a good day. The amount of advertising message clutter makes it hard to break through.

By the way, the brands that use those four statements are listed here:

**Lexus®:** The relentless pursuit of perfection.

**Sprint®:** The point of contact.

**McDonald's®:** We love to see you smile.

**Apple® Computer:** Think different.

# Let's Talk About Market Research

This is a good place to talk about some market research studies that you may have heard about but probably have not worked with firsthand. We will talk about some types of qualitative and quantitative research, and each has its place in your arsenal.

You should know the difference between qualitative and quantitative research. Qualitative research is a study done among smaller groups and in a setting that is not too highly controlled. For these two reasons, what you are getting is not projectable; it is not reliable enough to reasonably predict what the general public would think. It can offer a lot of *quality,* however, because you hear people talk in their own words. Quantitative research uses larger numbers of people and makes sure that they are all asked the same questions, in the same way, without anyone else's opinions interfering. The higher level of control, plus the increase in people, makes the data much more *quantifiable* and projectable.

Generally speaking, companies do qualitative research first to help refine their ideas. When you understand that the costs for doing large-scale, statistically sound, quantitative studies can easily run from $50,000 to several hundred thousand dollars, it makes sense to do some smaller work first. Each element that you want to test in a quantitative study adds cost to the total, so taking a list of 10 alternatives down to the best 3 or 4 saves tens of thousand of dollars.

# Qualitative Research: Rich in Texture and Direction

Let's focus on the development of positioning or promotional statements as our project to be researched. The process that I will describe is representative of what many companies would do to be sure that they were developing the strongest possible messages. If you work for a very small company with little or no research budget, you still want to understand the ideas here and then see what elements you can replicate to some degree. The more good research input you have, the more confident you will be that the marketing money you are spending will pay you back in profitable sales.

When you are trying to identify strong messages for your brand, you are usually looking for a number of different kinds of feedback. You want to know people's reaction on things such as these: Easy to understand; Clear, communicates what you intended; Believable; and Pulling power, whether it draws people in to listen/read.

For the rest of this chapter, let's assume that you have developed a list of 10 possible statements and want to find the very best one. All the people who developed the list will each have their own favorites and probably some firm opinions, but— let's face it—all of you are a little biased. And some of you may not even be anywhere near the target audience description. You can see that it would be great to get some reaction from people who are likely targets.

The most common form of qualitative research is a focus group. The idea is to bring together a group of people who fit the target audience description and then get their opinions and ideas on subjects of interest to you. There should be a moderator or group leader who guides the questioning and tries to elicit input from all the participants. You need to clearly define what type of people you want to talk with, based on what you want to learn. This definition is called the "screening specs."

**Heads Up**

The characteristics usually considered in the screening specs are things like these: Do you want current users or people who don't use this type of product? What about age, income, and whether they have children? What about housing? Do you want only apartment-dwellers or only single-family homes? The key question is this: What perspective do you want them to have, to give you the most valuable input?

When you organize a focus group, usually a research company near the community where you want to meet is hired to find 10 to 12 people who fit the specs that you provide. Depending on how much time, money, and patience you have, you may choose to specify several different groups, each one representing a different spec so that you get varied input. One example would be to have one group of current users of competitive products, one group who uses your brand,

119

**Talk the Talk**

Let's do a quick rundown of the who's who in a focus group. The **participants** are the target audience individuals invited to offer their opinions. The **client** is the person(s) representing the brand and paying for the session. The **moderator** is the person meeting with the participants and guiding the discussion. Generally the client does not ever go into the room or meet the participants.

and another group who is thinking about buying something like this but that hasn't done it yet.

Before the focus group starts, you will need to develop the statements that you want to test and decide how those statements will be shown to the *participants*. Will you print up signs, write up a paragraph, and read it to them? Will you put your brand name on the statement, or just probe what they think of the statement and then ask them about the fit with the brand name? These are decisions that have to be made in advance.

Also, before the group starts, the *moderator* needs to be given what is called a discussion guide, which is simply an outline of the steps and questions that you want addressed. The guide needs to specify what your priorities are so that if there isn't enough time to do everything, the moderator knows which things to cut or speed through.

At their best, focus groups are a wonderful way to hear real, unscripted comments. Once the group gets talking, there is a dynamic that takes over, which can yield some insightful, funny, unexpected, or pretty hairy results, depending on who is in the room and what the moderator's instructions are from the *client*. The biggest downside of this dynamic is that one or two of the more outspoken personalities can dominate the conversation. They can end up overinfluencing the more reticent people, or leaving the client and moderator with an impression that many people agreed with just these few.

## Focus Groups: Watching and Listening

You are now part of "the client," and that usually is a whole team of marketing and ad agency people. This is your first focus group. What do you need to know about what is going to happen?

First of all, yes, it's true: You will be sitting in a separate room looking into the meeting room through a mirror. This is just like in the detective shows on television. There will be a microphone in the meeting room so that you can hear what is going on. Your room will be quite dark. Your room will have whatever snacks and goodies your budget allowed.

Having been the client or the moderator in perhaps 200 or more focus groups, here are five golden rules for smart client behavior during the session: 1) listen; 2) don't talk; 3) don't take every comment too personally; 4) don't take every comment too literally; and 5) don't start rewriting the statements or discussion guide after one group.

Here is what happens all too often: The clients are so keyed up and eager to hear what "real people" have to say about their fantastic ideas that they keep talking and revising those ideas until show time. The client people who have been to a hundred other groups get bored in the opening 10 minutes and start whispering to each other. Within five minutes, at least three other client types will say that they can't hear the people talking. At that point, the moderator will already be able to hear a low-level buzz coming from your room, which is supposed to be silent. You can see where this description is headed, can't you? Enough said; now back to our five golden rules.

1. **Listen** to what these people are saying. Listen and take brief notes when they introduce themselves up-front so that you will know who has five children and who has only one, who is a struggling single parent, who just took up the computer six months ago, and who has been working with one for 10 years. You put the specs together, so find out what kind of group you actually got. The input that these people are about to give you in the next two hours will be colored by their life experience. If you don't understand a little about who they are, how will you know how to interpret their comments?

2. **Don't talk**, out of courtesy to everyone involved, and because if you are talking, you are not listening.

3. **Don't take every comment too personally.** You put a lot of thought and effort into these statements, and now some rude, crude, and obviously unsophisticated human being is saying that it is the dumbest thing he ever heard. You *asked* for his opinions, remember? Listen carefully for *why* he thinks it is dumb. It might just be a word or a phrase that is throwing him off; he may hear a condescending tone that you didn't pick up, or it just may be a dumb statement. You invited him, so listen and learn. On the flip side, don't get wildly excited when a few people say nice things about your favorite statement. The next group will probably hate it.

4. **Don't take every comment too literally.** Let's keep this process in perspective. There are two basic facts of life colliding in front of your eyes: Some people don't want to say negative things because that's not nice, and some people don't have the interest, education, or personality to give full expression to their ideas. This is why you want to do more than one or two focus groups.

5. **Don't start rewriting the statements or discussion guide after one group.** This is a cumulative process. If you are listening to just 10 people at a time, and you do three groups in one day (which is almost beyond human capacity to sit through), you have heard from a grand total of 30 people. This is not projectable to the other 285 million people in the United States, never mind in other countries. If you feel that there is something worth changing, I strongly encourage you to leave the statements as they are so that you get another clear set of starting opinions, and then have the moderator say something like, "If I were to change that statement to bippity-boppity-boo instead, does that change anything for you?"

## Balancing Structure and Risk-Taking

One of the hardest things to do with focus groups is to get a consensus among the client group on where the line is between staying with the planned structure and breaking out to try to generate more passionate, involved responses. I have become a proponent of the latter tack more and more over the years as a result of seeing far too much money and time wasted on boring focus groups.

If there is enough experience within the client team, it is great to make a conscious decision to break out of the mold and go for the learning. Some groups simply never take off, while others are terrific and very vocal. If you have a dull group, you are wasting a lot of time and money anyhow, so why not try some different tactics?

How different? Let the moderator throw away the discussion guide and come out of her shell. Have her pose much bolder questions, purposely trying to elicit some emotion. This helps get the true feelings out on the table. What kinds of things? Nothing all that radical, just more assertive: "You know what? I think you are bored with this subject. Look, I need to write a report to this client about what you folks think of these ideas, so just tell me this: Which one stinks the worst?"

Within 30 seconds, you will have a conversation on your hands. The onus is on the moderator to sense how much assertiveness to keep pouring on to get the responses flowing. She will need to jump around a little more to get at which idea is the best, or stinks the least, depending on how she has to phrase it. And what about the client? If you are a good, really good client, and you are there to listen and learn, you will love this approach instead of being scared by it. One comment on behalf of all the moderators in the world: Don't take it personally when we say things like "which stinks the worst," okay? It's a technique, not a report card.

# Quantitative Research: When It All Adds Up

We have now done 8 focus groups and seen that our 10 beginning statements have really come down to only 3 different messages. We have changed some of the language and tone based on what we heard and what our collective best judgment tells us is right.

*Judgment*—now there's an interesting word. How do you know whether to rely on personal judgment or the conclusions out of the research? The biggest and most sophisticated of brand marketers struggle with this just like you do. When you are deciding what messages to test, there is a lot of judgment needed. In our example, we have 80 people (8 groups of 10) who gave us their thoughts on a set of messages. In a big brand company, there are more than 80 people who have a stake, and a strong opinion, on what is best for the brand. Can you afford to test an alternative that pushes beyond what you think the brand equity can or should handle? Can you do this even once a year? Over time, it is a great way to learn how the target audience really feels and what your equity may be able to expand to. On the other hand, you may learn that what sounded fascinating in an energetic conversation among 20 people sounds ridiculous when people sit quietly and listen to it themselves. Either way, it is good learning for the future.

Quantitative research uses a lot of techniques to control the environment in which people are exposed to your statements. Depending on how your message would usually be conveyed (on a package, on the radio, on television, on a Web site, or by direct mail) the researchers may want to control things like these:

➤ How much time people get to look at or hear each message.

➤ Top-of-mind opinions before the statement is shown, immediately after exposure, and perhaps a day or a week or a month later. Capturing the starting opinions and the ones immediately after exposure are pretty much universal; the variable is usually whether to do a third check and, if so, at what point in time.

**Big Brand Insight**

What about the role of judgment relative to research? The best guiding light is a clear picture of the brand equity you already have, or the one you want to build. That way, if focus groups liked an edgier, sexier message, your own judgment may say that it isn't where you want to take the brand. So, you discard the statement before final testing.

➤ The order in which the statements are shown. The idea is to eliminate or at least control for *order bias*.

➤ Which questions are asked when. Generally, the sequence moves from the more general to the more specific, but within that, there may be an issue of wearing out the participant's attention span. In this case, you want to control the *question sequence*.

**Talk the Talk**

Two of the many important elements in controlled-environment research are often not appreciated. **Order bias** and **question sequence** are two pieces of the same concern: Beware of unintentionally creating bias in the responses. Order bias is the order in which the things being tested are shown; what you just saw can influence what you see next. Question sequence is the order in which the probing questions are asked; the first 10 questions are fine, but the last 10 may be tiresome.

The best outcome of quantitative research is the increased reliability of the conclusions that you can draw from it. As I look back over the many pieces of research that I have been involved with, I see three things that I want to make sure you know are critical success factors:

➤ *Sample sizes* must be adequate to give a statistically sound set of conclusions. You must get someone with a knowledge of statistics involved in determining how many people you need to recruit to have the answers be meaningful. A lot of factors are involved in making this calculation, and, yes, all those old terms from your one statistics course will come back to haunt or delight you. Remember things such as standard deviation, areas of confidence, and the mean and the mode? You probably don't remember them well enough to do the calculations yourself, so get someone else involved. FYI: When you hire a market research firm to run the test for you, their experts can calculate these.

### Talk the Talk

**Sample sizes** are critically important and should not be skimped on or ignored without the recognition, all the way to the top of your company, that the conclusions you will draw from the research are not too reliable. If you cannot afford to test among enough people to make the results statistically sound, rethink whether to do the test at all, or agree that the test is only an aid to judgment. By the way, if the test is not sound, you cannot use the conclusions to make claims in television advertising—and, these days, other media groups may ask for proof of your claims as well.

➤ Skillful questioning is critical to a meaningful outcome. Again, the research people you hire to do the testing can bring tremendous experience and guidance in this area. Listen carefully to what they are saying. Ask what their concerns are about things such as order bias. You can get an education just by talking with these people.

There are a wide array of market research techniques and many variations on how they are conducted. With the advent of the Internet as a communications device, older techniques are being adapted to be useful and meaningful in this environment. Market research is a terrific field in which to build a career these days and is attracting creative thinkers who can conceptualize well and then translate those concepts into testable programs. This is a whole new area for brand champions, not just math majors, to consider.

# Mix-and-Match Game Answers

How aware are you of which brands use which lines in their advertising? How many did you know for sure and how many could you guess at? Be forewarned: once you start focusing on this you won't be able to watch television or read a magazine without having certain ads jump out at you.

**Salesforce.com™**: Point. Click. Close.

**Sprint PCS®**: The clear alternative to cellular.

**Honda®**: Thinking.™

**State of New York:** New Attitudes. New Opportunities.

**Lipitor®**: The lower numbers you're looking for.

**Sun® Microsystems:** We're the dot in .com.

**Nortel Networks™**: How the world shares ideas.

**Office Depot:** Taking care of business.

**U.S. Postal Service:** Fly like an eagle.™

**Aleve®**: All day strong. All day long.

**American Airlines®**: Coach has more class.™

---

### The Least You Need to Know

➤ Positioning statements help define what is most important and appealing about the brand. They are like subtitles on a book, explaining what the short title really promises.

➤ Statements that are used temporarily to convey a special promotion are usually called promotional statements, hooks, or taglines. They usually bring attention to the details of a specific offer more than they reinforce the long-term message of the brand.

➤ Qualitative research, such as focus groups, is very helpful for learning how people react to different ideas or even product samples. The small group format allows the participants to get more specific and verbal about their feelings.

➤ Quantitative research uses a highly controlled environment to predict the true market reaction to an idea or a product. Professionals who can look at each aspect of the test design must handle these tests.

---

# Chapter 11

# Branding Inspiration: Information and Education Go Branded

---

## In This Chapter

➤ Information is being packaged and marketed

➤ Technology innovation changes information access

➤ Education is a new branding opportunity

➤ Internet information creates enormous opportunity

---

It wasn't so long ago that "information" was what you called to get an out-of-town phone number, and "education" was what happened in school for 12 to 16 years. When did this become the stuff of marketers' dreams? Information and education have largely blended, which to me is one of the most exciting concepts around. I firmly believe these two areas are true marriages of product and service, where any lines separating the two are blurred forever.

So much is going on with information and education right now that it really is mind-boggling. It has pretty much all gone branded. Even going to the local public school is slowly being turned into a branded experience. And, should we talk about the number of people who put an infant's name onto a waiting list for preschool and kindergarten programs to start three or four years from now?

Grade-school children are wearing pagers, teenagers have their own cell phones, and adults are battling information addictions. For every 100 people who complain about technology invading our lives, another 100 are essentially training their own offspring to be even more info-saturated than they are. This could be your dream come true if you have some great ideas for merging information and education. The world is definitely waiting. But you'll have to hold on a minute; call waiting is beeping.

# News and Information Are Friendly, Fun Businesses

Not even in the wildest days of the Excessive Eighties (1980s that is, pre-market crash, of course) did we have a newsperson called "the money honey" or a television show called *Hardball*. And no, these are not Hollywood sitcoms; this is your financial news that we're talking about. I don't remember *People* magazine doing features on stock market types or CEOs back then, either. That was the province of the sedate business magazines.

### Talk the Talk

**Infotainment** describes the move toward making information exchanges more entertaining, easier to grasp, and, therefore, more palatable to a wider audience. You see its impact every night in the way network and local news programs are delivered. Have you noticed the increased use of color, graphics, jazzy stage sets, and lots of personal impact stories? Look at the warm interaction between the on-air personalities.

Now, "business" is news, and what used to be "news" is often considered too boring and tedious, so we move increasingly toward narrowly defining what information we want to get through to us, and being fed a lot of *infotainment* broadcasts in the mass media.

Information reigns supreme, it seems, and our need to know is changing our everyday lives. Take a look at your own life:

➤ How do you get the news and the information you want? Where do you get it? How often? Do you use a mix of media, or is one medium your favorite?

➤ How differently do you interact with news/ information today relative to 10 years ago?

➤ If there is a major news event, whether it is the Gulf War or a massive hurricane, where do you turn for updates? Is that different than 10 years ago?

➤ Do you have a favorite evening news station on the television, or do you just watch whatever station is already on? Do you watch television news at all?

➤ How have your magazine subscriptions changed in the last five years? What is new? What got dropped?

➤ Did you hear the one about how newspapers and radio were going to be obliterated by the Internet? Did you believe it when you heard it three years ago? What about now?

If a sociologist spent a week in your home, he would learn a lot about you by watching what you watch, observing how you gather information, and questioning you about why you will spend 30 minutes with one magazine and barely skim another.

Each element of your information world has developed a brand equity with you, and as your list of choices gets wider and easier to access, you will form all sorts of new equity images as you try out new ways of satisfying your need to know. You have probably already started trading out one source for another. Don't think so?

➤ Do you read any of the newer business magazines, such as *Fast Company, Wired, Red Herring,* or *Business 2.0?* Did you drop another subscription to make time for this one?

➤ Do you get most of your daily news input from the Internet instead of the newspaper, radio, or television?

➤ Have you ever searched the online archives of a newspaper or magazine Web site?

➤ Do you have a favorite search engine on the Internet?

➤ Are you intrigued with the commercials for wireless Web services that bring the news to your portable phone? Do you have one yet?

## We Want to Control and Personalize Information

Many of us have changed both *how we gather information* and our definitions of *what we need to know.* These two factors are at once the cause and the effect of sweeping changes, and there will be many more innovative businesses growing to serve them.

How we gather information and what we need to know are both fed by the choices we have, and those choices are defined by the access we have. It is access that has exploded in the last decade: access to new ways to get and send communications. Branded businesses are rushing to fill the new void, and access has expanded even faster than we can create *content* to fill it.

The general public has what appears to be an insatiable desire for information. Interestingly, what keeps fueling this desire is our assumptions and expectations about how much we *can* know and how customized it can be.

**Talk the Talk**

**Content** is an old word that is being used every day in the Internet era, so let's be sure that you are comfortable with how Web site people use it. Content is the matter contained within a Web site, whether that is reports, things to buy, a database of statistics, or your horoscope. Think of it just as you do the matter contained in a magazine or newspaper. "Content developer" is a job description that you may see advertised.

Are you looking for hot areas to build a brand management career? That last sentence gives you two places to start looking: "how much we *can* know" and "how customized it can be."

Follow this thought process: The first one addresses the dual issues of *access and ability*; there can be new businesses that open access in new ways or to new audiences. There can be other new businesses that address the ability to extract and use the information, since getting at it is only part of the challenge. The second issue combines ability and person-ability. Once you find the information and extract it, the wizardry of modern technology falls prey to the oldest of problems: Human beings are not all wired the same way. We learn differently, at different speeds, and we bring different cultural experiences, expectations, and intellectual abilities to the process. To make the information valuable, not just usable, it must be matched with the person's own ability. All kinds of new businesses will scale this mountain of challenge. In fact, in just a minute, we will talk about some of the things that are already happening in education.

Before we do that, let's talk about one more factor in this puzzle. And, let me plant a question in your mind right now: We use technology to *get at* information for sure, but does technology *create* information, too?

**Big Brand Insight**

Brand marketers who have been around for a while learn to watch and listen for clues on when a category is about to have a growth spurt. Technology adoption has been a wild ride; it appears to be lightening fast, and yet millions of people still haven't even bought a cell phone, never mind digital phones, pagers, personal digital assistants (PDAs), and wireless Web devices.

## Technology Feeds Our Expectations

Technology has created new ways to access information, and each technology innovation feeds our expectation level. An exciting new communications medium or device is introduced; it is quickly adopted by some percent of the population. The mass media pays so much attention to it that the impression is built that *everyone* has one of these gadgets. And soon, that gadget and its abilities become the expected norm and we look to the next innovation.

The reality is that enough people are adopting the new technologies to make them economically feasible, and a much wider group is being educated into accepting this new lifestyle. The bulk of the population will always be mid-to-late adopters, but they enter the category in such huge numbers that the sales revenues that they generate fuel continued innovation.

For brand management thinkers, the magic in this formula is that the advertising and general media attention around these innovations is priming the pump for even more expansion. This raises some interesting questions and challenges to a lot of the marketing thinking around the Internet-centered economy.

What is the real advantage to being first to market? Most of the business theory of the last five years has pushed very hard that companies need to be first or forget it, that there is only room for a few players in any market. I don't argue that Amazon. com has built a fortress by being first, and that company deserves a tremendous round of applause for what it has accomplished. I do think the jury is still out on the "first or forget it" idea. The recent collapses and consolidations in Internet companies point to a retrenching, and we need more time to analyze whether the "losers" were the late-comers or those with weaker business models. Given the short life cycles of many products, it may be hard to be first in innovation *and* first in ongoing sales.

# Information as a Lifestyle and a Business

We consumers are being educated by a blitz of advertising that is selling a new lifestyle more than anything else; the devices promoted in the ads are the means to the end. In this way, information has moved to the very center of our lives. What an opportunity for brand marketers.

What do the advertisements for wireless Web devices imply will happen to your life if you buy one? Do you remember when cell phones were first introduced? How do you feel about people who carry beepers/pagers: Is it okay for some people, like doctors, but annoying for others? Did you ever think you would be so incredibly opinionated about something so small?

Now, confession time: Have you read some of the articles in the New Economy–type business magazines and found yourself thinking, "Oh, yeah, I am definitely a 24/7 kind of guy"? Isn't there a little bit of romance and an air of Huckleberry Finn in the stories of dotcom fortunes built on a stack of empty pizza boxes in some guy's garage? If you see the appeal in these stories, and you want the gadgets and mind-set that you read about, then you understand the lifestyle impact of information.

What kinds of information businesses need brand champions? Here are five ideas for you to consider: 1) content providers; 2) research services; 3) education developers for both childhood and adult education; 4) media companies; 5) manufacturers of consumer-driven software.

As information becomes more and more a routine part of our lifestyle, new career opportunities will be created. There is a lot of evidence that technology is creating a craving for more goodies and gadgets to make us feel smarter and more in touch. Let me close this lifestyle argument with an example of tech-envy from way back in the mid-1990s.

One of my favorite stories about the lifestyle impact of technology goes back to around 1994. To put that ancient time into perspective, laptops were pretty widespread, but cell phones and telephones on planes were still not big things.

This true story is about the president of a company who somewhat hesitantly had agreed to move his business into the computer age during the prior few years. He never really understood what all those expensive computers were going to do, but after a while, it did seem like just about every company had them.

After a series of business trips, he arrived back at the office with an announcement: He wanted one of those laptops, too. Many people, thinking that he had finally been converted, greeted this with great enthusiasm. A laptop was purchased and brought to his office, and he was offered private tutoring so that he could learn how to operate it. He didn't really want any tutoring, he announced. He just wanted it to do one thing: When he sat down on a plane, he wanted to open it up and have those nifty-looking reports that all the other guys on the plane had. Stop laughing. This is a true story, and it gets worse.

When told that something like that could be arranged and that he would need to hit just a few keys to make it happen, he then specified what those reports should be: up-to-the-minute sales showing orders received in what you and I would call real time. The need for a modem connection was explained and met with growling anger. He was *positive* that these other guys had *real* sales reports because *they moved on the screen*. The explanation of a scrollbar and a mouse did nothing to calm his anger, and that pretty much brought the meeting to a jarring conclusion. As far as I know, the laptop never made a business trip. Right now, at least 500 of you are wondering when I met the president of your company.

# Education Gets More Branded Every Day

One of my favorite topics is education. I have a passion for the subject and am a huge proponent of adult education, in particular. The term "adult ed" sounds as antiquated as my grandmother's aprons because it has been reborn as lifelong learning for inquisitive minds. That works for me, too.

Education is a rich and complex mixture of access, information, ability, and individual learning style. Technology has already enabled a type of mass education whose value is totally under-recognized: the teaching that happens on television and radio. And I am not talking about teaching youngsters their colors and their ABCs.

Let me name a few of the things I mean (by the way, to me, each of these is a branded entity):

➤ Discovery Channel

➤ The Learning Channel (TLC)

➤ Biography

➤ History Channel

➤ Home & Garden Television (HGTV)

➤ Food Network

➤ National Public Radio (NPR)

➤ Public Broadcasting Service (PBS)

➤ PBS University

What are they doing that I get so excited about? They use what is essentially a mass entertainment medium to encourage people to keep learning new things. They inform, encourage, inspire, cajole, and explain. On television they use the power of visual images to show *exactly* how to construct a spreadsheet, bicycle rack, bookshelf, or fruit tart. Radio programs that use in-depth, lengthy interviews with scholars and writers and musicians and philosophers create magical moments of introspection and delight. Is this going to affect world peace? Probably not. But I am convinced that it is starting to affect family life.

As more adults awaken to the idea of lifelong learning, they set an example. They also reset our cultural expectations. So now we look at the Internet's awesome communications ability and ask: Why not an online university? Can I learn astronomy in a virtual classroom? If I never had the opportunity to go to college in my teens, can I capture some of that now?

And a very important business-to-business product is creating interactive learning programs so that companies can train more associates, letting them learn at their own pace, with as little or as much repetition as they want. For many subjects, this is a far better way to learn than in a classroom.

So now, what about my earlier question: Does technology give us access to information, or can it *create* information?

# Case Study: Media Metrix™ Pioneers Internet Information

In boardroom meetings, you may hear "What's your Media Metrix™ number?" Open up *The Wall Street Journal* and see a feature article that says "Source: Media Metrix." Study one of *USA Today*'s great charts, and it may well announce the same thing, "Source: Media Metrix."

This company is in the spotlight all the time, and there are two basic reasons why:

➤ Media Metrix is the leader in Internet and digital media measurement.

➤ The Internet and digital media are the hottest topics in town.

Media Metrix, Inc. (www.mediametrix.com), was created as a spin-off of NPD Group, a well-known market research firm. The initial work on the idea of measuring Internet traffic was done within NPD Group in 1994 and 1995. It was recognized as having the potential for a separate business and was spun out in 1996. Its heritage and service orientation are very much market research-based, but this is definitely a new breed of market research house.

### Big Brand Insight

There are actually several brand names under the Media Metrix, Inc., corporate structure, including Media Metrix™ and AdRelevance™. After the company's merger with Jupiter Communications, Inc., is finalized in late 2000, the new corporate entity will be Jupiter Media Metrix, and the brand lineup will add Jupiter Research™ and Jupiter Event™ as well.

Media Metrix clients include advertisers, ad agencies, Web publishers, technology companies, financial analysts, venture capitalists, and consultants, to name a few. Anyone with a business impacted by the Internet or some type of digital media, or someone who wants into that world, has a high interest in this company's product line.

The primary goal of the organization is to help its clients understand and profit from the Internet, which has changed business and also our personal lives forever. Those two things combined, business and personal life, create the "matter" that needs measurement, definition, and analysis. Millions of us log on to check e-mail, do some research, buy a few things, and maybe sell a few things every day, and that is the heart of the revolution. There is a world of activity related to the Internet that is not understood without the kind of work that Media Metrix does.

Media Metrix uses an expression that I particularly like: "to chronicle and help shape the most important new medium of our time." I like it because of the words *chronicle* and *help shape*. The Internet is so vast, and yet so new, that it is like a story waiting to be told. We see it, we are the ones creating it, and yet we don't know what it means to us as a people until someone captures it and shows us what we collectively are doing with it. It takes a series of those "captures" to bring the story to life, just as the scenes in a play or movie show us what is happening. One month at a time, we see the changes happening.

How does this "help shape" the medium itself? We get to watch the evolution, see what is changing and what is working, and, with that knowledge, write the next scene. Do you have a Web site today? Are you looking for a business opportunity to start up? All kinds of clues are waiting for you in the data that these people produce.

As a consumer, the only glimpses that you get of this story are what is reported in the media. Luckily, this is such a high-interest area that you can find stories every week in the major newspapers and magazines. Here is where you put your entrepreneur's hat on.

Study every piece of information in this area, and see what is happening. As a consumer with a television, radio, newspaper, and Internet connection, you are on the receiving end of thousands of messages from Internet companies. You form your own opinions of those companies. With Media Metrix data, you can go one step further and learn from them: See the effects of advertising, promotion, zany messages, and straightforward sales pitches. Go visit the top five Web sites in a category that you are interested in, and see what they are doing that is so right. That study will help you visualize where the opportunities are. A thoughtful analysis of the reports and data tables in the section on Internet movers and shakers, in Appendix B, "Resources and Revelations Guide," is an education all by itself.

## All People, All Places, All Platforms

What is it that the company does, exactly? Media Metrix created the first Internet audience measurement service and has continued to refine that product with methodology and technology improvements. Today the company captures a picture of how people are using all types of digital media, including online services (such as AOL), using streaming media (such as audio files), browsing the World Wide Web, and using wireless devices.

**Heads Up**

It is important for you to know that Media Metrix clients access the data via a site license, which is a contractual arrangement in which the client receives the data electronically for use within its own company. The Internet movers and shakers data in this book is an exclusive bonus for our readers. This data is not publicly available.

➤ Media Metrix captures usage both at home and at work, which is unique in the industry. Workplace usage has become vitally important to get a clear picture of how we use digital media.

➤ Media Metrix measures usage starting at the age of two. Yes, you read that right.

➤ The company measures things like the number of unique visitors that each Web site receives (one person counts only once, even if he visits the Web site twice in the same month) and what percent of the total available audience each site reaches.

➤ The data is used to gauge the advertising value of one site over another, the effectiveness of promotions, competitive analysis, and certainly some investment decisions.

➤ Media Metrix tracks where, when, how, and how much Web marketers advertise.

➤ Media Metrix tracks e-commerce to better understand the shopping transactional element of the Web.

➤ The company operates in the United States, Australia, France, Germany, Sweden, the United Kingdom, and, most recently, Japan. These countries represent 80 percent of online usage.

### Mentoring Memo

Media Metrix's acquisition/merger strategy has been strongly influenced by the vision of what the company wanted the Media Metrix™ brand to stand for. It merged with a start-up competitor, Relevant Knowledge, in 1998. In 1999, the company recognized that although it had created its own ad-tracking capability, it was not able to live up to the standards that it set for the brand, and so AdRelevance was acquired. In 2000, Media Metrix will complete the next merger. Along the way, the company also created a strategic alliance with McKinsey & Company, one of the most highly regarded consulting firms. This partnership, formed in 1999, is already paying out in a deeper understanding of consumer behavior in the online environment.

## Can a Business-to-Business Player Have Consumer Awareness?

The new Jupiter Media Metrix is going to be fascinating to watch, for many reasons. Everything that we know about its marketplace would predict explosive growth opportunities and the potential for all kinds of confusion as the players sort themselves out. I have another reason for you brand champions to keep an eye on this one in the future: My personal prediction is that this company will evolve into having consumer-level brand awareness, and that adds a whole other twist to the story.

Let me give you two analogies of the kinds of things that could happen here:

➤ The ACNielsen Company is a worldwide powerhouse in market research. There is no particular reason for the average citizen to know anything about them. But, the company has this television ratings system that is quoted on the news and in magazines all the time. Its name shows up in newspaper articles every time a new TV season starts up, and its data is the source for declaring a show a hit. The consumer is aware of the Nielsen name, to some extent. There is a precedent here.

➤ Isn't it interesting that the average person, out to buy a new PC, knows enough to check whether it has "Intel Inside®"? Now, if most of us were to take a screwdriver and open up the case, we wouldn't know just where inside this thing is or even what it looks like. Just knowing that it is in there makes the whole box more attractive and makes us feel more secure. This is outstanding marketing, for sure, but I want to focus on just that last sentence. If Intel Inside® is critical to making all those gadgets and wires inside the box work together like a great PC, could "Source: Media Metrix" be what makes all those gadgets and Web sites make sense?

The opportunity for this to become a consumer-aware brand name, even if the consumer never buys a thing directly from this company, is one of the marvelous new delights waiting for us in the wild world of Internet-driven business. This is a very interesting idea to contemplate, and if it can happen here, it can happen to other businesses as well.

When this book is in your hands, the Jupiter Media Metrix merger will be complete, so let's look at the mission statement for the new company:

> To be the global leader at the center of the digital economy, combining data and analysis, and creating the ultimate information platform to drive the digital economy.
>
> © *Jupiter Media Metrix, 2000. Permission granted.*

Global leadership built on the ultimate information platform—now there's a simple picture to guide all their associates.

---

### The Least You Need to Know

➤ Information and education are blending into a very dynamic product mix.

➤ Information is an integral part of our lifestyle. The current pace of innovation promises to deliver easier and less expensive means of accessing and using information—and the pace will only get quicker.

➤ Media Metrix™ is a company to watch closely as Internet activity becomes a global interest. Study this type of data for leads and ideas on where to build your own Internet success.

# Chapter 12

---

# Branding Inspiration: Product, Service, and Science Brands

## In This Chapter

➤ Branded products are everywhere

➤ Branded services are growing fast

➤ Science has become consumer-friendly

➤ Old product brands can stay fresh and relevant

This is a fun chapter. I want to mix up all kinds of ideas for you. Some of them will show how consistency and clarity pay out over the long haul. Others are here to surprise you, to open your mind to new thinking. I am combining products and services, the two most basic types of brands, with science, which we don't think of as branded at all. I want to mix them up and have you see that they are full of exciting, inspiring examples of people using creativity and brain power to build new business. There are a lot of challenges here: You can use them for brainstorming new ideas for your brand or for identifying new career opportunities for yourself.

Let's take a tour of some of the new things happening with brand development. You are probably aware of all the examples I will use, but maybe you haven't thought of them as branded entities. It is fun to take a look around and identify surprising trends. It is also interesting to see "branding" in action when the people running the show might not be thinking of their business as a brand at all.

One of the most interesting new branding activities has been making science into a consumer product. It is happening in many ways. Some of these companies are consciously trying to learn how to become brand management types, and they are making great strides very fast. Interesting stuff, indeed.

# Wild and Exciting New Products for Branding

You don't need me to give you a laundry list of 100 different products that have proven to be good brands. Products are the easiest things to imagine taking on a branded identity.

So, let's think about some things that aren't so obvious and have some fun looking at what is happening with them. Frankly, sometimes the biggest challenge is deciding whether the subject at hand is a product or a service or something else. But here is an example that I think is a product at heart, although I would be the first to say that it blends product and service.

Here is a wild one from left field for sure: the Human Genome Project. In the rare event that you were sequestered underground and missed all the news during the summer of 2000, I will give you a one-sentence description of what this is: A group of scientists has identified the 3.1 billion pieces, or "letters," that make up human DNA. This work is expected to open up an exciting new world of opportunities to eradicate disease and find new treatments or cures that can help millions of people around the world. This is genuinely exciting news. In fact, it is so big, so abstract for most of us, and so far beyond the common man's understanding of science that most of us can only guess at its true power.

So what has this got to do with powerful brands? The Human Genome Project is leading-edge—maybe bleeding-edge is a better term—brand development. It certainly meets our criteria for a brand: an identifiable entity making specific promises of value. And, even more fun, there were actually two competing teams who each wanted to "own" the project (does that sound like warring competitors to you?). In a much-heralded act of chivalry, the two teams agreed to merge into one unified front to present the announcement and findings to the world.

Okay, so this meets the basic criteria for a brand. But so far there is no real product per se, just what seems to most of us like ethereal pieces of information and squiggle designs on paper. I think this is going to be a fascinating project for you to study over the next five years. Here is your opportunity to study how an idea becomes a master product, which creates or enables a whole series of other products.

What kinds of products and services will spring out of this beginning? We will probably see test kits for hospitals to diagnose disease at earlier and more treatable stages. Those will create testing services and counseling services. The new technology will undoubtedly raise ethical and legal issues. That will create books, associations, and other new services. In five years, I will be amazed if there are anything fewer than 100 new products and services related to this first announcement. It is the birthplace of a new business community.

# Services Are Big Business, and Now Big Brands

Once again, you know about lots of services that are branded, such as insurance, drain cleaning, and package delivery. There are tremendous opportunities there for differentiation, and every chapter in this book has things to help you build a strong service brand.

So, let's stretch our thinking with one of my new favorite examples of a service business: hospitals. This will be one of the great marketing challenge arenas of this decade.

Perhaps I should forewarn you: I recognize that this example is riddled with politics and high emotion for a lot of people. My only mission here is to have us look at the opportunity for hospitals to adopt more brand management thinking as they reposition themselves within the community. By studying something we are all familiar with, and something caught in a crisis state, we can identify some tough challenges for service businesses.

I am not going to comment on the competency of the staff or how tangled up the paperwork is. That is for someone else's book to discuss. I am just looking at the whole operation (no pun intended) from a brand marketer's eye and challenging *you* to consider what brand management approaches you would bring to this business.

Hospitals are in a double bind. They are caught in the crossfire between high emotion and pragmatic decisions. We are in the midst of explosive changes in healthcare, and I don't know if there is any social policy area, even education, that can top the emotionalism of this one. Hospitals are something we don't think about unless we are in crisis; the rest of the time we drive right by and don't even glance over at the building.

Many politicians are echoing the general public in the concern that today medicine is a business, and no longer the noble profession to which we always assigned such esteem. A hospital is the ultimate service business, and yet sometimes we don't even spend as much time choosing which hospital to visit as which hairdresser to cut our hair.

There is an interesting aspect to this kind of service business. With the exact same customer (you or me), Hospital A, by virtue of location, may have no competition one day, and then two weeks later have four different competitors for you to consider. When we have an emergency, time overrules everything else, and that makes location the critical factor. The nearest hospital is where we go. (Note: The exception here is that some residents of big cities have three hospitals

**Heads Up**

What is it that can totally change our choice of hospital? Our perception of expertise and the reputation that we have heard about the facility will often win out over the convenience of location. In plain brand management talk, the brand equity rules the day.

within 10 minutes.) However, when we have time to choose, because we need a planned surgery or some special treatment, location falls far down on our list of priorities.

What if *your* customers made different buying decisions at different points in time—how would you handle that? And furthermore, what if the only time you saw your customers is when they were stressed out and scared? Now compound that with the fact that your cost of service *is* very high, your industry is under attack as uncaring, and you have a severe labor shortage with constant, high turnover in critical areas. I know, I know—you don't want this job.

But I know this much: There will be great opportunities for brand champions who want a real challenge to work alongside the medical professionals and bring brand discipline to this industry. It is an extraordinary challenge for hospitals to learn how to position themselves, how to construct mission statements that their workforces can relate to, and, most importantly, how to translate those words into promises that they can keep. Didn't you tell me you were looking for exciting opportunities?

# The Newest Frontier: Science Gets Cozy with Consumers

I distinctly remember my mother and grandmother telling me to just take the medicine that the doctor gave me and not to ask questions. A simple "What is it?" was always met with the exact same answer: penicillin. That stuff apparently cured everything because they assured me that it was the wonder drug. Enough said.

**Talk the Talk**

**Direct-to-consumer,** or **DTC** for short, occurs when pharmaceutical companies and others take their message right to the end user: us. This does not mean that they abandon all communication to the service provider, by any means, but it clearly alters their own communications plans and programs.

Today, I cannot spend one hour at a cocktail party or a family gathering without a lengthy conversation erupting over which brand of cholesterol-lowering, diabetes-regulating, or arthritis-relieving drug is being used by most people in the neighborhood. And, by the way, there is almost never a doctor or a nurse in one of these conversations, just all the everyday pharmaceutical experts that we all seem to know. What happened to all these people? How did they slip in a few years of medical school while I wasn't looking?

You and I both know that they don't need medical school. They have television—that's much faster.

So how did all these medical "experts" we are related to come by their education? They are stunning examples of the success of the *direct-to-consumer* (DTC) strategy of the last few years.

The eruptions in the healthcare field in the 1990s contributed to a consumer movement to take charge of our own health and wellness education. As managed-care programs replaced traditional healthcare systems, many people realized that they couldn't be passive consumers any longer. This created the perfect environment for the pharmaceutical companies and many other kinds of care providers to talk directly with us. Now they don't have to hope that the doctors and nurses are explaining all the differences in medications and treatment options. They differentiate themselves from the competition by talking one-on-one with the end consumer.

There is a terrific article in the June 2000 issue of *MedAdNews*, which is one of the big trade magazines in the pharmaceutical industry, on how DTC has evolved and is maturing. These companies are learning to be consumer product marketers, and that means more new career avenues for people like you. As brand managers, there is a lot for us to learn from this evolving new field of marketing.

This is another good topic for you to follow and study over the next few years. It is also a good example of innovative change, which we will talk about in Part 5, "Taking Ownership: The General Management Part of Brand Management." An industry that has always made consumer products, although we didn't think of medicines that way until recently, has been brought much closer to its real customer. Until this point, its sales and marketing efforts were focused on doctors. Now healthcare needs to satisfy *us*, and that changes the game substantially.

The article provides a nice overview of how this new field is developing:

> The change in the philosophy of advertising of prescription products to consumers has been evolving over the past several years. As recently as five years ago, the consumer was an enigma to pharmaceutical marketers. As marketers have increased their expenditure in the direct-to-consumer area, they have had to educate themselves about an audience outside the physician-based community. Marketers have learned that they need to connect better with consumers.

The article goes on to quote Terry Gallo, president and creative director of Becker Consumer Health, a healthcare advertising agency in New York, as she talks about how the industry has learned about the power of consumer branding.

> We have to make sure there are strong advertising ideas and strong branding ideas connected, because a lot of what has been done in the industry up until now has felt rather generic.
>
> *Source for both quotes:* MedAdNews, *June 2000; © 2000, Engel Publishing Partners. Permission granted.*

Here is a quick way to see just how much this new trend has impacted you and your family. Take a look at the brand names in the first column, just to see how many you recognize. Now, do you know what illness they are used for? See how many you got right. Then read off the list to five people in your family who are of different ages, and see how many of the names they recognize and how many they can link to an illness. Then take a look at the last column; you will see that these are becoming big consumer brands.

## Direct-to-Consumer Spending by Brand

| Brand Name | Indicated For | 1999 Promotional Expenditures ($ in Thousands) |
|---|---|---|
| Claritin | Allergic rhinitis | 123,744.8 |
| Prilosec | Ulcers | 79,435.8 |
| Xenical | Obesity | 76,152.9 |
| Propecia | Male pattern baldness | 71,116.4 |
| Zyrtex | Allergic rhinitis | 57,068.4 |
| Lipitor | Hypercholesterolemia | 55,456.7 |
| Zyban | Smoking cessation | 53,904.9 |
| Flonase | Allergic rhinitis | 53,457.4 |
| Viagra | Erectile dysfunction | 53,034.5 |
| Nasonex | Allergic rhinitis | 52,333.6 |
| Ortho Tri-Cyclen | Prevention of pregnancy and acne vulgaris | 50,133.9 |
| Meridia | Obesity | 43,513.9 |
| Glucophage | Type II diabetes | 43,098.0 |
| Allegra | Allergic rhinitis | 42,788.0 |
| Valtrex | Herpes zoster | 40,899.5 |

*Source: © 2000 Competitive Media Reporting. Permission granted.*

Between the Human Genome Project and the new strategies in the pharmaceutical, field you can see a lot of news in the area of science. There are many more examples that we can't fit into this book, but take a look at how the news magazines educate us about new technology, how we learn about the latest in computer hardware, and how medical devices and science museums and television documentaries are being marketed. Science has indeed become a consumer product, and there are wonderful opportunities waiting for brand champions who want to get involved in building those businesses.

# Case Study: Welch's®: An Agricultural Co-Op in the Twenty-First Century

In choosing the case studies for this book, I spent a lot of time making lists of possible companies to approach. I wanted to be sure that you got to examine a mix of products and services, and I wanted three very different kinds of companies. I also wanted you to study companies of three very different ages because the age factor is often a subtle, unspoken element when brand managers assess where they want to work. Does age really matter?

For our product-driven brand, I chose Welch's®, a brand name that I am sure you all recognize, whose products you have probably enjoyed at different times in your life. In Chapter 7, "Brand Equity: Like Money in the Bank," we saw how rich this brand equity is and how the company carefully manages that asset.

### Mentoring Memo

Using Welch's® as our brand gives us the chance to study one of the oldest brand names in the United States, and one that has a business structure distinctly different than anything that most of you have seen. Brand decisions are made a little differently in this company, and those differences are a rich area for you to explore. Every company has some bit of uniqueness. Learning to spot it, and then to make that work *for* rather than *against* the brand, is how successful senior managers are built.

The Welch's® brand is owned by one of the small number of agricultural cooperatives in the United States. It operates a very large consumer products food business, and yet is not publicly owned, which is unusual. The company, Welch Foods, Inc., and the brand are owned by the members of the National Grape Cooperative Association, Inc., a group of more than 1,000 growers who supply their grapes directly to the company.

One of the most interesting things for you to know about an agricultural co-op like this is the impact of the rather unique ownership arrangement. The owners are the ones supplying a very large percentage of the raw material, so they have a clear incentive to grow superior-quality grapes. In addition, because the coop owns the company, it sets the rules: All incoming grapes are tested, and only the ones meeting very high standards are accepted. Yes, even if one of the co-op's own growers is bringing in the product, if it doesn't meet standards, it is turned away. The grower has to sell the shipment to someone else.

So, the ownership arrangement impacts product quality. It also impacts how the company is run. Take a look at the corporate mission statement:

> The mission of our company, as a cooperative, is to maximize long-term grower value, and to provide a reliable market for their grapes through excellence in product quality, customer service, market responsiveness, and consumer satisfaction.
>
> *© 2000 Welch Foods, Inc. Permission granted.*

Let's dissect that statement and see what it tells the employees of the company about their jobs day-to-day.

> … maximize long-term grower value …

Remember that you have a group of growers as your owners. Obviously, they are relying on the proceeds from the sale of the finished product to help them earn a living each year. And yet, if ever there was a group of owners who would be inclined to pay attention as you pitch the value of long-term versus short-term strategies, these people should be more likely to listen. This is very different than trying to round up thousands of stockholders who know very little about the company and then convince them to accept a lower dividend this year.

On the other hand, you have a group of owners who are far more likely to want to get involved. In some ways, this is like a family business, and this one has more than a thousand branches on the family tree. A number of times now, we have talked about how very personal the brand marketing business can be. I bet these owners take the brand name and equity very seriously and very personally. The managers of the business are likely to feel a little tighter rein on their activities.

> … provide a reliable market for their grapes …

"A reliable market" is a very interesting expression to contemplate, particularly if you have worked only for large, publicly traded companies. For the people who work in the company, the promise is that they will look at their decisions in all the usual ways (market size, competition, profitability, and so on) and that they will consider crop usage as a factor in the final decision. Crop usage? What MBA programs ever teach that concept?

The owners belong to the co-op to create a good home for their product. If you know anything about farming, the crop size of any product is not guaranteed from one year to the next. But these owners want to be assured that their crop will have a home each year and that the managers of the company will use that crop to best advantage.

> … excellence in product quality, customer service, market responsiveness, and consumer satisfaction.

These are four key strategies for the management of the company. Product quality and consumer satisfaction are key elements of the Welch's® brand equity and thus can never be ignored. Customer service includes the consumer and the supermarkets, convenience stores, restaurants, and other customers who buy the products to supply the consumer. Look at the mission statement again, and notice where this line comes in. It is tied to the phrase "provide a reliable market."

## Carefully Making the Old New, Again and Again

There is one more strategy in that last phrase that we haven't talked about yet: "market responsiveness." This is an interesting way to talk about a cluster of attitudes and activities, all of which relate back to providing that "reliable market."

Welch's® is certainly best known as a fruit-based product brand, and grapes are the fruit most often associated with the name. As we saw in Chapter 7, the equity is rich in emotional memories of childhood and good tastes that linger in the mind. But selling grape juice and grape jelly is not enough to sustain a modern food company, and those two products don't utilize a lot of the richness in the consumer's image of what the brand *can* be.

**Big Brand Insight**

Welch Foods gives customer service a lot of prominence in the mission statement, and it does so a little differently than many companies. The way it is phrased and positioned here clearly states the belief that satisfied customers contribute to a stable, reliable market for the products. Excellent customer service is a necessity, not a nicety. The message to the employees is crystal clear.

When the people at Welch Foods look at market responsiveness, they are again in somewhat of a unique position. The marketplace does shift in its tastes, particularly where beverages are concerned. That is probably one of the most volatile food categories. When deciding if and how to respond to a change, this management team considers the size of the opportunity and the fit with brand equity, just as you would; but then it has to stop and review its response in light of the "reliable market" element that we discussed earlier.

Choosing how to expand the product line, to keep the brand fresh and relevant to the consumer, is a much more complicated undertaking for these brand managers. They have developed the motto "new uses and new users" to guide the process.

Have you taken a look at the Welch's® product line recently? It is an interesting study of how a brand that is 130 years old has an image of old-fashioned dependability and how a simple rather than catchy brand name has grown in importance to its target audience. How did Welch's do it? The company focused on the combination of brand equity and mission. It utilized some good news from the scientific community, and it figured out how to get people into the franchise earlier and to stay there longer.

### Mentoring Memo

Committing to a new product that uses a lot of the growers' grapes may look great one year and be a disaster the next year if the crop comes in short. Conversely, using only a little of the growers' product generates more profit per ton utilized, but it may not be very helpful if there is a record crop next year and no place to put all those grapes. These are issues that most of us don't even have to know about, never mind grapple with.

Spend a few minutes in a supermarket near your home. Look through the bottled juice aisle, the frozen juice products, and the ice cream novelty area. Look in the dairy case at the refrigerated juice blends. The product line of 50 years ago was pretty basic: the finest grape juice and jelly. Today it expresses a much broader expertise, with lots of fruits in lots of forms.

Another interesting thing to observe is how the company has chosen to utilize some recent preliminary scientific findings that grape juice may be good for maintaining a healthy heart. This is obviously terrific news for the brand that is synonymous with grape juice. And yet, after studying their options, Welch's has chosen to incorporate this news, but not make it a major selling point.

Why? Welch's products don't have a negative health connotation to overcome, people already see fruit products as inherently better for you than many others, and the brand champions have more important things to say.

What other new elements is the company working with? We have talked about the need for a brand to be clear in choosing an appropriate Internet strategy, and this brand is a good one to think about. There isn't a need to sell Welch's® products over the Internet, so clearly the company doesn't need an e-commerce/transactional Web site. Welch's has created a Web site, www.welchs.com, as one piece of a modern communications strategy and is working to understand how this element will evolve. The company has used it very successfully for promotions that involve some of the cartoon characters that it licenses for some children's products. But overall, it is more of a "wait and watch" for the Internet.

## The Future? It's All About R-E-S-P-E-C-T

I asked the people at Welch Foods one of my favorite questions: "How do you measure success?" I got a very interesting answer, one that uses a term you don't often hear. "We measure success in terms of both building and releasing grower value." Building value sounds familiar enough, but "releasing" value is a nice twist. Here is how they explain those two elements:

> Building grower value includes equity building, as measured by the better-than-competition rating, as well as other means of increasing grower value like new products.

> Releasing value is pretty obvious: Are we leveraging equity, and other elements of grower value, in such a manner to create a market for all their grapes, in both the short and long term? Are we creating demand that enables us to command the price premiums needed to give them a premium over other uses for the product?

It is worth it for you to read this quote several times and look for the way the brand equity and the ownership of the company underscore the thinking. The definition of equity building (the better-than-competition rating) is there, the attention to price premiums make the effort to grow the best product worthwhile, and the reinforcement that membership in the coop is a smart decision.

So how does this company see its future? Here is its vision statement:

> Welch's will be the best cooperative in the country by:

> Maintaining the most respected brand name in the industry.

> Providing quality fruit-based products while leveraging our grape core competencies.

> Being the most respected manufacturer/distributor in the categories and channels in which we compete.

> Growing twice as fast as the food industry average, achieving $1 billion in sales by early in the twenty-first century.

> Delivering the best long-term profitability.

> Attracting and retaining the most highly motivated and top-performing employees within a culture that promotes risk-taking and teamwork.

*© 2000, Welch Foods, Inc. Permission granted.*

Welch's envisions a future in which both the company and the brand name are respected. That respect is to be a chief contributor to financial success. The respect and the financial success contribute to the ability to attract and keep talented people, who will respect the brand and the company, and so on and so on.

Let's circle back to a question about brands that I posed at the beginning of this case study: Does age really matter? Brand new companies and categories have been the rage over the last few years because of the explosive growth in e-commerce. In Chapter 11, "Branding Inspiration: Information and Education Go Branded," we studied one of the hottest of these new companies, Media Metrix. And in the next chapter, we will study a company in the exciting world of entertainment.

If I asked you to choose one element that you think is the most important thing Welch's® has done, what would it be? My vote, and I will quote from what I said just a few paragraphs ago, is this: "It figured out how to get people into the franchise earlier and to stay there longer." And that is how brands stay fresh and relevant for more than 130 years.

What are the lessons here for you and your brand? Don't dismiss the question if your brand is hip-hop new and you can't imagine how it can relate to something so old. Really think about the lessons from the Welch's® experience, the sensitivity to brand equity, to quality, to respect, and to careful decision making in the midst of multiple priorities. Which of those things contains the germ of a good lesson for you?

If you have been thinking that there isn't a lot of learning for you in the co-op ownership element of this case study, please think again: The grape growers own the company, just like your shareholders own yours. These growers get closer to the heartbeat of the business than a bunch of strangers; but either way, the owners are your boss, and their concerns and their welfare, as measured by what you do with their brand assets, is what your job is all about. The respect for the stockholder is a vital part and, in some companies, a contentious part of the brand champion's job. There is a lot to learn from a bunch of grape growers.

---

### The Least You Need to Know

➤ Science is certainly the next frontier in brand marketing. Each year we get closer to understanding new elements of our environment, and mass media allows everyone to get involved.

➤ Education is moving toward adopting more brand marketing concepts. As parents and communities recognize the need for better learning programs, they focus more on differentiating one approach from another; public education can come in more than one flavor.

➤ All service businesses find themselves being evaluated more harshly by an increasingly demanding consumer. The healthcare field, in particular, is loaded with challenges for brand champions.

➤ The age of the brand has little to do with its ability to last and to grow. The real issue is the product line that carries that brand and what equity the target market sees in that image.

---

# Chapter 13

# Branding Inspiration: People and Entertainment as Brands

I am betting that you agree with me by now that Madonna and 'N Sync can be viewed as brands. That, you can buy. But one look in the mirror and another in your bank account makes it clear—you ain't no Madonna, and you can't dance like the guys from 'N Sync. My money still says that you can do a terrific job of creating Brand You and that you are capable of being an extraordinary brand champion, for yourself and the business you are working on.

When you first read about these ideas back in Chapter 1, "Living in a Branded World," you may have been thinking that I am a little off base on what is and isn't a brand. If ever there was a place to study the branding of an individual, it would have to be the entertainment industry. It has created many brands, in the form of net-works, stations, shows, and individual personalities as well. This is high-risk brand management at its apex. Why high-risk? Because these brands are built on a founda-tion of human beings, who cannot be programmed to deliver on time or to provide a perfectly consistent performance, as with a tube of toothpaste or a deck of cards. These brands are as volatile, changeable, and desirable as the people who create them.

Running an entertainment business, such as the radio station you will meet in our case study, is a juggler's delight. You need to build a brand that can drive loyalty, because loyalty brings in advertising, and advertising pays the bills. But the real power is the consumer barreling down the highway, or stuck in morning rush-hour, who pays nothing for the privilege of bossing you around. It isn't exactly the glamour job that many people assume it is, but it can be a lot of fun.

# Bam! It's a Good Thing, So Just Kick It Up a Notch

Television has created some indelible images of individuals who are better known than some brands in your local supermarket. You just read the headline for this section. Did you recognize that "Bam!" and "Kick it up a notch" are classic comments from chef Emeril Lagasse, and that "It's a good thing" is one of Martha Stewart's signature phrases? Katie Couric, Bob Vila, Chris Matthews, Ming Tsai, Larry King, Norm Abram, Kitty Bartholomew, Maria Bartaromo, Charles Gibson … I could list dozens of people. These are not actors playing a role, although I could put together a list of fictional characters who are practically brand names by themselves. These people come on our television stations and talk with millions of people each week. I intentionally mixed up that list to include news people, craft instructors, and great cooks. How many of them did you recognize?

**Heads Up**

Are these people all brands? Some may not have that kind of identity, but they all have an extraordinary presence. They have celebrity and the potential to truly brand themselves if they want, but that isn't enough to create a meaningful brand, as some celebrities have learned the hard way.

Katie Couric stars in both morning and evening news programs. She doesn't have a perfume line or a jewelry business, and she doesn't even make exercise videos. But did a nation ache for her when her young husband died of cancer? Yes, we did, because she is a unique entity in our minds; we see her as projecting a set of values and promises that we like. We have humanized her, although we will never meet her. The power of one person to build a unique presence in the minds of many is the platform on which personal brands are built.

It was hard to pick one celebrity to use as an example of personal branding because there are many to choose from. But I have to say, if ever there was a personality whose talents, fame, and fortune were intrinsically linked to the mass media, it is Emeril Lagasse. He has created a self-branded empire built on his skills as a performer and an accomplished chef, the strength of his personality, and his keen sense for marketing.

Emeril Lagasse is a chef who owns a group of very successful restaurants, has authored numerous books and has not one, but two cooking shows on television. Emeril (and I feel perfectly comfortable calling him by his first name, since warmth is a big part of his brand identity) is the living embodiment of a brand:

➤ **Identifiable entity.** You couldn't confuse him with any other television chef even with your eyes closed. To see him once is to remember him forever.

➤ **Specific promises of value.** Food is fun; you can easily learn to cook more exciting foods; work with me, baby, and we'll "kick it up a notch" in the kitchen.

What do you suppose the core values of Brand Emeril are all about? I would guess something like this:

➤ **Open the doors wide.** Good cooking is for everyone. Income and education don't matter.

➤ **The heart of the home.** Focusing on cooking and eating together builds the spirit of community among family and friends.

➤ **Cheerleaders have more fun.** Loosen up and relax—you'll like it. You cheer for me, and I'll cheer for you.

Emeril uses specific techniques to build audience involvement; from a brand perspective, that is like trying a new potato chip and deciding that you want to buy more. These involvement techniques work for the viewer at home as well as in the studio—a very nifty combination indeed:

1. Extravagantly adding ingredients that other chefs would shy away from, including lots of garlic, extra spices, and extra wine or brandy.

2. Making the audience the accomplice. Emeril is the guy with the twinkle in his eye who needs only a little encouragement to do exactly what the audience would want to do themselves.

3. Throwing out the rules and just having fun. Emeril takes the mystique out of great cooking and makes it look easy enough to try yourself.

4. Using key phrases and gestures: "Bam! Kick it up a notch! Yeah, baby." If you don't hear each of them as least a few times, you feel cheated. And, of course, he knows that the audience has been trained to yell "Bam!" when he cues them by picking up a pinch of "essence" seasoning—stepping back just slightly, he cocks his wrist and lets it fly. The audience knows it's coming and yet laughs every time he does it, like it was brand new.

Emeril Lagasse is a talented performer, and I mean that as a sincere compliment. He has married education with entertainment and makes learning fun. The fact that he has managed to attract such a broad demographic audience is a testament to the energy that he puts in and the talent that he displays.

So where is the "brand" here? It is in several different places. His name now has an equity of its own that has developed over the last few years. The fact that he is an identifiable entity, however, is just celebrity status; it is not enough to be a brand. The branding opportunity lies in what that equity is all about.

Without doing any market research, my guess is that two key elements make him so brandable:

➤ His *expertise* as a chef. He runs successful restaurants, and he sure looks like he knows what he is doing.

➤ His *teaching style*. He displays both ability and enthusiasm, making cooking fun and making it look doable.

What is critical to see in those two elements is this: Lots of people have expertise, but only some people can make that expertise accessible to a wide audience. Emeril trades on his expertise, but he sells his enthusiasm. His equity is something that you can build a product line around because it has a natural *elasticity*.

### Talk the Talk

**Elasticity** is a term that is used a number of ways in business. The most common is probably price elasticity, in which you analyze how much freedom you have in pricing something before the buyer says, "No way." Equity research estimates how much leeway you have to stretch the brand equity to incorporate new products or advertising positions and still make good sense.

Follow the logic of how Emeril's name has been used to create branded products. The Emeril name sells the television program to more and more cable providers. His name sells cookbooks. He just launched a line of cookware, Emerilware®. He just opened a restaurant in Orlando, Florida, at the Universal Orlando® theme park, a fun family destination. He does a promotional spot for Food Network™, which carries his shows. Who knows how many jars of "essence" he has sold? All of these product lines make sense within the overall equity of being a great cook and teacher. He has done only products and promotions that fit his expertise and his enthusiasm.

He has a series of product lines that carry his name, just like Chrysler® has a series of cars. I haven't seen him make a mistake yet. As the brand, he is in a tough position. His personal life could be a problem, if something went wrong. Many a famous athlete has seen that happen to a shining brand. But unlike an athlete's celebrity endorsement, this personal brand is more powerful and more complex.

An athlete licenses his name to an apparel company. The athlete has anywhere from little control to no control over the product, and the consumer doesn't expect more than the glow of fame. For personal brands such as Emeril Lagasse, this is different. *That person* is the product and the brand. The equity that the consumer ascribes to that brand is assumed to be 100 percent genuine what-you-see-is-what-you-get. High risk, high reward. Watch carefully how Emeril is handling that equity. He makes it look easy as pie.

# A Name Can Create an Instant Image

We talked a little bit about the difference between a celebrity and a personal brand. Now let's look at a few powerful images and see whether you think they have branding power. This is a fun exercise and a good way to get focused on thinking strategically about "the power of one."

I made a list of well-known names in the first column of the table. On the first line, I wrote in an example to follow. Now, just do these few steps:

1. Move right down the list pretty quickly, and put an X or check mark in the column labeled "Got It!" if you are positive that you know who or what this is.

2. Taking one at a time, decide whether you think people would buy something with that as the brand name on it. For the ones you say "yes" to, write a few key words on why it is brandable.

3. For just those same ones, jot a few words on what you think the name could sell.

| Well-Known Name | Got It! | Why Brandable? | Type of Product |
|---|---|---|---|
| Katie Couric | | integrity, good mother, positive outlook | children's books, inspirational books |
| Steven Spielberg | | | |
| Mahatma Gandhi | | | |
| Tom Brokaw | | | |
| *The Sopranos* | | | |
| Bill Moyers | | | |
| *Sex and the City* | | | |
| Bill Gates | | | |
| Robin Williams | | | |
| Jane Pauley | | | |
| *Nightline* | | | |

*Celebrity sale-a-thon.*

Now, why wouldn't you buy something from the ones with no notes? What does that tell you about your own feelings about celebrity status? What is missing or out of kilter in your image that just doesn't make this feel like a brandable entity? Now, go back over the list and ask yourself: Could some of these be used as a spokesperson or be tied in to a product somehow as an endorser, but not have their own names on it? Does that make a difference?

The power of a personal brand is entirely driven by the perceived "brand equity" of that person and what it can stretch to include. In fact, any of the people or shows on this list could be a branded line as long as they were matched up with the right product. Whether that brand would be a barn-burner success is another story entirely. That is what the other 25 chapters of this book are all about. Whether using Gandhi's name on a product line is tasteful is questionable to me (I can tell you my answer to that question really quick if you want …). And, just to be clear, I am not recommending that these celebrities start a product line, nor am I volunteering to head up the company.

## A Name Can Imply Lots of Things

If you want to know how to do first-rate home-keeping, I would have to say: Tune in to Martha. If you have a stunning, moving, emotionally charged movie screenplay to offer, I'll bet Steven Spielberg is on your list of people to find. Henry Kissinger and Walter Cronkite could make a meatloaf dinner sound important and significant, without ever stooping to comment on the quality of the entrée.

Rosie O'Donnell makes you want to hug her and your own wayward kids all at the same time. Sammy Sosa and Mark McGwire can play baseball like wizards and are great role models for kids, too. Oprah Winfrey makes you want to think deeply about how to live your life. Jerry Springer makes you want to … well, we'll leave that one out. And therein lies the message.

As we get to "know" our celebrities, we form opinions and images around them, and these can be far more emotionally charged than our opinions about tires or snow shovels, for sure. In fact, celebrities are just more famous versions of us. Out here in the noncelebrity bleacher seats are people who have as much talent as any of the famous names in this chapter, and that is no small statement. I am not suggesting that we rent a bus together and head for Hollywood tonight, but rather that you take a little more time to consider the Brand Called You discussion one more time. Remember your grandmother's old line about "bloom where you are planted"? Enough said.

All this talk about personal brands is to help you find marketing opportunities, to keep putting different ideas in front of you so that you will create a much wider range of options for yourself and your business. As you watch these celebrities on television or read about them in the press, do a quick check of how you are reacting to them. Ask yourself if they are brandable. These subtle little insights can build a first-class brand radar system inside you.

# Case Study: KISS 108-FM™ Radio

You met this station in Chapter 7, "Brand Equity: Like Money in the Bank," and heard that it has a simple three-part brand equity: the music, the fun, and "Matty in the Morning." You saw that these people take their equity seriously, with an ongoing commitment to research that may have surprised you. They listen to their associates, produce a first-rate product, and don't charge the consumer one cent for the privilege. Either these people are crazy, or they are doing something very right.

Having met a lot of them now, I can tell you the truth: They are like the perfect prom date—very smart and a lot of fun.

In 1999, WXKS-FM, fondly known as KISS 108, celebrated its twentieth anniversary. *Network 40™ Magazine* produced a tribute to them on the occasion of being the first inductee into the Network 40 Hall of Fame, and it is a lot of fun to read. This made them stand out in my mind as a great case study for this book.

The station thrives on being just exactly what critics say radio isn't: a dynamic, interactive medium. Whether listening in your car or walking through their office halls, you sense a rhythm and energy that is a real treat. The first time I visited the office, I figured that it was the fun nature of the business that created that buzz; the second time, I knew it was the mental energy and the positive attitude of the people. Such simple, old-fashioned qualities as these are what's behind a broadcast legend.

### Mentoring Memo

As a radio station using the public airwaves, KISS 108-FM™ cannot charge its users for the product, and yet the public is clearly the customer that the station serves. In this business, the paying customer is the company who buys advertising time and sponsorships of events. The station serves two very different customers every day. There is a terrific bit of strategic insight here: The customer who gets it all for free is 100 percent in control of how much the product is worth to someone else. Think about that one for a minute. How different is that from the business model that most of you are familiar with?

A radio or television station—and the same logic applies now to Web sites—needs to develop happy, satisfied, delighted, loyal customers, or else .... It is just that simple. Its ratings or shares determine the financial value of its product in a very direct way. This is much the same phenomenon as in the food business, where people say, "Sell it or smell it." That may not sound too glamorous, but it sure makes the point. The "product" is highly perishable unless it gets sold fresh, fast, and often.

## Engage the Audience Is the Rule of the Day, Every Day

So how does KISS 108-FM™ make its product fresh, fast, and fast-moving? Here's an analogy: These people don't KISS and run, they get engaged.

Their focus, every day and every hour they are on the air, is to engage the core audience in the music and the fun and the people they want to hear. When an on-air personality opens up his microphone, he says "No. 1 for 'Matty in the Morning' and today's hit music!"—even when the "jock" on the air isn't Matty. (Note: *On-air personality* is the politically correct terminology for what used to be called *disk jockeys* until records went into mothballs; "jocks" is a loving remnant of those old days and is so much faster to say. )

The core audience is women 25 to 44 years old, which covers a lot of different lifestyles, attitudes, and issues. The number of promotion ideas that you could dream up for a group this size and this diverse seems almost endless. The station is located in Boston, so it has a constant stream of event opportunities just by virtue of its location. So how does the station stay focused? I specifically asked for an example of a decision in which the brand equity clearly and directly influenced the outcome.

The general manager of the station is Jake Karger, and she gave me an answer that is so clear I want to pass it along to you:

> The application of what the brand means is more about the things we say "no" to than what we say "yes" to. We don't do anything that isn't going to be of primary interest to women 25 to 44. We only participate if we can find a way to engage our female listeners. That is the ultimate test. So we say "no" to virtually everything that is sports, for instance.

And yet, in June 2000, the station sponsored a celebrity charity event with Nomar Garciaparra of the Boston Red Sox. Why? For three good reasons:

➤ In Boston, the Red Sox isn't just a baseball team; it is part of the culture.

➤ Baseball is the sport with the highest involvement among women.

➤ Nomar Garciaparra is a celebrity whose image is bigger than baseball; he transcends the boundaries of his chosen sport because of his involvement in the community and his role model status.

What the station structured tightly fit the equity of the brand. The station's own entertainment director served as the MC, so he did interviews with the celebrities and gave away some free tickets to the upcoming KISS Concert, the hottest tickets in town. The event had a direct benefit to the audience because many women that age have young children who want to meet celebrities, and the adults want to win the concert tickets. It is a great image all the way around, and a good reason to break the rule.

The music plays all day, and it is always the big hits of the times. What meshes the music into a companion that you want to keep with you all day is the fun—and the fun is delivered through an ongoing stream of events and parties. KISS 108-FM™ does parties like nothing I have ever seen. The big hitter of all parties is the annual KISS Concert.

**Heads Up**

Do you think your company should break the rules and adopt an idea of yours that isn't an obvious fit? Prepare your pitch so that the benefits to the brand and the company are crystal clear. An idea that appears to have holes in it with a quick look can be successfully sold if you draw out *the links that make it work* and then build the program only around the best parts.

# KISS Concert: A Loyalty Legend

Every summer, this radio station hosts a major concert. That doesn't sound altogether different if you live in some of our major cities. But how many stations can pull together 20 or 30 performers for each of these events and boast names like this:

| | | |
|---|---|---|
| Celine Dion | Cher | James Taylor |
| Carly Simon | 'N Sync | Britney Spears |
| Backstreet Boys | Whitney Houston | Bon Jovi |
| k.d. lang | Kenny G | Chris Isaak |
| ZZ Top | Aaron Neville | Donna Summer |

I could go on for pages, but you get the idea. Tickets to the KISS Concert sell out each year *before the list of performers is announced.* Now that is customer loyalty. And, to show the station's loyalty to its listeners, the tickets are first offered to the members of The KISS Club. There are now so many Club members involved that the tickets sell out before there is a chance to offer them to the general public.

Membership in The KISS Club is a primary focus, and the station makes sure that the value of that membership is reinforced. Another example of the value, in addition to the concert tickets of course, is that only members can win special trips that are awarded weekly. Only members can win cash prizes if their name is called on air.

KISS 108-FM™ is in the entertainment business, but part of that package is information. The station is not trying to do economic analysis, mind you, but rather the kind of information that ties into the relationship that it wants to have with the audience. The station builds that relationship by what the jocks talk about in their

**Big Brand Insight**

Is membership in The KISS Club the only way to get listeners involved, and are concert tickets the only draw all year? From what you have read so far, you already know that the answers have to be, "No way." The station blends music and fun and personality all day, every day.

conversations with the listener and then reinforce KISS as the resource by providing two information outlets:

➤ KISS Cityline is a phone system providing contest rules, jokes, weather, access to concert tickets around town, background on the music and the performers playing on air, and many more resources.

➤ The Web site, www.kiss108.com, opens up the world of what you hear on air and lets the listeners spend as much time as they want browsing for information.

What kinds of promotions get this audience involved? KISS 108-FM does so many things that it is amazing, but let me just include a few of them here:

➤ **Camp KISS.** A weekend summer camp vacation in the mountains, with two of the jocks as counselors.

➤ **Acoustic KISSmas.** A charity fund-raiser with big-name performers such as Jewel and Alanis Morrissette. There is only one way to win a ticket—by participating in an on-air call-in.

➤ **ClubKISS.** Live broadcasts every Saturday night from one of Boston's hot nightclubs.

The portfolio of promotions is full and involves all the jocks. There is always something new to talk about, and there are always some classic elements to reinforce. But, all of this discussion leaves us with one last question.

## So What's with This "Matty in the Morning" Thing?

Matt Siegel, better known as "Matty in the Morning," is at the center of the promotion schedule, for sure. He is a fixture in morning drive time and is almost an icon for getting the day off to a great start. A cup of coffee and a big dose of Matty, and that traffic jam is manageable.

The importance of his daypart (that's media talk for just what it sounds like), his popularity, and his long tenure at the microphone make him the nucleus for a strategy that delivers against the promise of fun. There is always a Matty promotion going on, and these are planned and executed with style, flair, and a lot of laughs.

Want to go shopping with Matty? He took 200 listeners to New York for a day of shopping followed by cocktails. Do you want to *really* have breakfast with Matty, not just the bagel that you munch as you sit in traffic? Why not bring your children along? How about a fund-raiser breakfast during the holiday season with a show full of favorite children's characters? In 1999, the tickets sold out within minutes of the announcement on air and jammed the phone lines all morning.

I feel a twinge of guilt at this point for giving away so many of the station's promotions, so I need to stop the list right here. I fully recognize that imitation is the sincerest form of flattery, but these folks have put their hearts and souls and millions of dollars into building this exceptional brand, so I won't go on. If you are ever in Boston, though, just remember that it's KISS 108 for the music, the fun, and "Matty in the Morning."

Let me close this chapter on a different note. We talked earlier about personal brands and celebrity, and how when you are the brand, there is a lot of responsibility. There is also the risk of what happens to the brand if something happens to you. Right now, some of you have to be thinking what I was, so I asked the question: What happens to the station, and the brand equity, if something happens to Matty?

I like the honesty of the answer I got, because it wasn't the usual "Of course, we will sail right on" kind of nonsense that you hear too often. The general manager stopped for a minute, and her tone of voice changed significantly:

> "We would take a hit, there's no doubt about that. Matt Siegel is very important to us as a station, and so very important to us as people who care for him. It is hard to even think about that, but we know this much for sure: Our equity is not one-dimensional. The music and the fun happen all day long. Taking that hit would hurt our business and would hurt us personally. But it wouldn't hurt our equity, and the station would go on and eventually come back as big as ever."

---

### The Least You Need to Know

➤ Personal brands are intermingled with celebrity status to some extent, but they are not the same thing. By definition, a celebrity is an identifiable entity, but that doesn't mean that people would buy products with that name on it.

➤ Success in building a personal brand depends on what the person's image or equity is all about. When some type of expertise is part of that equity, there is a good foundation; fame alone isn't a base to build a business on.

➤ Radio and television stations are great examples of businesses that serve two masters: One enjoys the product, the other pays the freight. Only by keeping the audience very happy and very loyal can advertisers see the value.

➤ KISS 108-FM™ stands out in its industry for its commitment to building brand equity. The elements of this equity are non-negotiable guidelines for running the business, and that focus has paid off spectacularly.

# Part 4

# Building Your Brand Perspective

*Part 4 focuses on five major elements of your brand management strategy: target market analysis, channels of distribution, ways to identify your competition, how to set your pricing, and brand communications. Most important for you is that we will look at each of these from the brand perspective.*

*Part 4 leads off with a discussion of what I call a brand profile. A brand profile is a document that captures and clearly communicates many of the key decisions that you make about how the brand will be positioned and marketed. It is a great tool to help you clarify a lot of the thinking and analysis that you will do as you work through the following chapters. It is a very valuable asset when you need to get other people up to speed on the brand, and it's invaluable to keep in front of other people who also make decisions that impact the brand.*

*Part 4 has the longest chapters in the book, but don't let that deter you. Each of them includes lots of guiding questions, forms, and directions to help you see what is happening and then try out your own examples. Keep in mind that each of these subjects could be a book unto itself—and, in fact, in some of these areas you may want to study more. These chapters provide a very valuable ongoing reference for you to come back to over and over again.*

# Chapter 14

# What Is a Brand Profile?

---

### In This Chapter

➤ Capturing the brand's essence in a brand profile

➤ The brand profile guides decision making

➤ Identifying the brand's strongest benefits

➤ Merging the product and the brand

---

You have an awesome idea for a new direction in which to take your business. Or, you are one of those creative people who are always coming up with catchy phrases that could be great advertising slogans. Or, you really want to be an entrepreneur and get your own gig happening. Or, you are working on a branded business that is going nowhere and dragging all your life force, and maybe your career, down with it. We have some work to do.

One of the hardest, but most rewarding, disciplines of brand management is building a business plan that makes sense for the brand. That sounds so obvious. What people often miss is that to maximize the brand's value and potential, you need to look at every aspect of doing business from the brand perspective. Whether you want to create something new or figure out what to do with what you've got, you will need to put some hard work into sorting through the ideas that you have and finding answers to questions that you didn't even know enough to ask. And it is hard work.

Part 4 will guide you through the process of building your brand perspective step by step. This will help you build a brand profile statement to help guide everyone in your organization. First we will talk about what a brand profile is and do some preliminary thinking together. From there, Chapters 15, "Target Market Analysis: More Critical Now Than Ever," through 19, "Careful Communication: What's Right and Great About the Brand," will each take a major part of the profile and help you make good choices as to how you should take your brand to market. The question "What is in the best interests of the brand?" will come up over and over.

# Putting the Dream and the Reality Down on Paper

A brand profile is one of the most valuable documents that you can create if you are sincerely interested in building a successful brand. It is a thorough analysis of what the brand could be, should be, and then will be. "Analysis" really is the right word because this is a fairly rigorous process of looking at your dreams and hopes, tempering them with a heavy dose of reality, and then finding ways to put legs under them and making them march. It is a lot like boot camp in that regard.

### Big Brand Insight

The thinking that we are putting into creating a brand profile is a critical piece of the brand management process in large branded companies. Over time, pretty much all the senior management, no matter what department they come from, learn to think this way. It is not unusual for the chief financial officer to raise a question about whether some recommendation fits what the brand is all about.

Is all of this really necessary? Not absolutely, no. If you want to open a very small business out of your home, serving people in your town, you don't have to work through every element of this process, although I would still encourage you to do it. However, if your dream will require somebody else's money or sweat, you move into the camp of needing to do this analysis. If you are looking to a bank or a professional investor of some type, they will probably make you do at least part of it. If you are tapping into your parents' retirement fund, you owe it to them to do it. If you are mortgaging your own home, you'd better do this process right now.

A brand profile is similar to but different from a business plan. A full-blown business plan will include a section about the brand name, positioning, and a communications plan to develop that brand. If you are writing such a document, the work you do here will go right into your business plan. What is most valuable about doing the brand profile work first is that we are going to talk about lots more than the brand's personality and promises. We are going to go through the thinking process of how you make decisions, or how you translate what the brand is about, into a real business. It is almost guaranteed to help sell your idea in dozens of different ways, and it just might be the make-or-break piece of the puzzle.

How can I make such a broad statement? A thorough brand profile forces you to think very carefully about what the brand and the business have in common. It helps you think from the brand perspective in every aspect of your business. It forces you to figure out now, before you go any further, just where your dreams and realities intersect. It gives you backbone when tough decisions have to be made, and comfort when choosing between two good alternatives. It is a living document that you will turn to over and over again when decisions have to be made.

So what is our working definition of a brand profile? A brand profile is a document that captures and clearly communicates what the brand is about, why it is valuable, and how the brand will go to market.

The most important three words are right up-front: *captures* and *clearly communicates*. A brand profile is a written document. It can be as long or as short as you want. You can change the order of the elements, use paragraphs or bullets, include confidential data or not, and amend it over time.

The idea is to go through the discipline of really thinking about what the brand is and can be, what you have to work with, and then how you will go about marketing the brand *consistent with the profile that you say it has.*

Let's take just a minute to go through an example of what I mean when I say "marketing the brand consistent with the profile that you say it has." This is a good example of one of the subtle decisions—not the big, obvious, glaring ones—that can impact a brand name. Assume that you have a brand of men's clothing that is very high-fashion, premium-priced, and sold in chic boutiques and exclusive department stores. At the end of the season, you have some things that didn't sell, and you want to get rid of them. A number of companies take merchandise like this and resell it to discount operations.

A few months later, you are in one of the Palm Beach boutiques that sells your brand and overhear a customer telling the manager that he will never buy your brand again because obviously it is horribly overpriced. The story comes out that this man's assistant showed up one day wearing the same shirt that he had on and told this man that he got it at the Odd Lot Flea Market for $20, a rather substantial $70 less than original price. What kind of a problem is this? A complicated one.

This is a distribution problem that, if repeated too often, turns into a big, hairy brand-equity problem that turns into an ugly sales problem. A decision was made to let the product be sold/distributed in a very downscale venue. I can hear you screaming "No, I didn't decide to do that at all. We only sell to nice places." Yeah, right.

The real problem is that, in fact, the decision was not made at all in this case, which is even worse. You sold off the product to get rid of it for pennies on the dollar and never used your brand perspective to make sure that it went to a dealer that sells to places that are a little classier. You didn't pay attention to a distribution issue; you just made a financial decision, right?

Why would having done the work of a brand profile have made a difference? Because the full profile, as we will do it, forces you to address issues such as distribution and to set some guidelines. If you were out of the office the day that product was sold, whoever was making the deal would have known from the brand profile that you have standards for moving old merchandise just like you do for selling the new things. Make sense?

## Brand Profile Outline

When we finish this exercise, you will have a document that you can use with many different people and in lots of different ways:

➤ To show an investor that you are savvy and well-prepared.

➤ For orientation for a new advertising or promotion agency. (And will they be impressed—they hardly ever meet people this organized.)

➤ To take your own senior management through it to gain their support, and maybe more money (for you or the brand).

➤ To introduce to other people in your organization who need to catch the spirit of being brand champions. Why not use parts of this to bring them into the fold and generate input, enthusiasm, and commitment?

➤ To use as a great tool when you are training your own replacement because you are moving on to bigger and better things.

A brand profile provides answers to a lot of questions. When complete, it may run 10 pages long. Or, it may fit all on one page. If I can add my vote in here, I suggest that you let the longer version happen as you develop it. Review it and tighten it up so that it is clear. Then push yourself to boil it down to a one-pager, if possible. Imagine having a page like the following table over the desk of everyone who makes decisions about the brand. And imagine that where I show questions, you put the succinct answers.

### Your Brand Profile

| Answers | Questions |
|---------|-----------|
| Description | What exactly is this entity? |
| Benefits | What is good about it that has value to someone? |
| Target audience | Who should find the brand valuable? |

| Answers | Questions |
|---|---|
| Competitive position | What is different? Better value, more prestigious, more fun, and contemporary, best quality .... |
| Pricing | How does your pricing stack up against the competitors? |
| Distribution | What kinds of places do you want this brand sold? Is there somewhere that it should never go? |
| Positioning | What is the one thing that you will communicate over and over again until people "get it"? |
| Personality | If this brand really was alive, what would you want people to say about it? |
| Communications strategy(s) | How and where will you invest your communications dollars? What are the best places and situations for the brand? Will you work with promotion partners? If so, what criteria would you use to decide which ones? |

Imagine yourself being grilled by an investor or the president of your company. You would be asked questions like the ones shown on this table. That is why you need to have the answers.

Your turn: I strongly suggest that you get yourself a pad of paper now to keep with you as we go through the six chapters in Part 4. That way, you can jot down ideas that come to mind and have a good beginning point for developing your own brand profile. I think the easiest way to do it is to leave two or three sheets of paper at the front, and just label them "Background." That way, you have a place to scribble and cross out and make general notes.

Then plan to set aside at least one full sheet of paper, front and back, for each topic. When we get to pricing in Chapter 16, "Channels of Distribution: Getting from Here to There," you may need lots of scribbling room to try out some math problems, and a basic calculator to make it fast and easy. For the math-phobic people out there: Relax, I promise it will be simple and we will go step by step.

# First and Foremost: A Description

This should be simple enough. Start with the real basics. Is the brand about a product, a service, an idea, or a person? Now, get more specific.

Will this brand have more than one type of product (remember, this comes from the Five P's) under it? Some examples may help:

1. Mutual funds and individual stocks
2. Small business accounting and individual tax return preparation

**169**

3. Hardware and software

4. Minivans and sports cars

5. Seminars and books

6. Capacitors and accelerometers

7. Fitness center and personal trainers

Will there be combinations to work with of products and services, perhaps, or of ideas and persons? Again, some examples:

1. Networking devices and ongoing consulting

2. "Train the trainer" classes, and the workbooks for those internal trainers to use

3. Credit cards and the back-room customer service to support them

4. A Web site to visit, with software to download and links to other sites

Jot down a list of words that can describe the "what" of the brand. Include ideas for future expansion so that they get looked at in this analysis. When we are finished with all the elements of the profile, you should find it much easier to decide whether a new idea really could fit under this brand. Maybe it needs a brand of its own.

## Probe: What Have You Really Got to Sell?

Now that we are warmed up, I need to push you a little harder. What have you really and truly got to sell? The answers that I am looking for start to move us into what is strong and valuable and able to be communicated about your brand.

So now, what I want to know is how you can possibly look me right in the eye and tell me that this brand is worth my time and attention.

1. What is so great about it?

2. It isn't any different from the leading brand, is it?

3. Why should I believe you?

4. What is it going to do for me?

5. What are you going to do for me?

What am I trying to get at with these somewhat obnoxious questions? I want you to go beyond the basic facts of what the product is and move into what it can and should mean to the purchaser. I want to develop the promises that your brand can make.

What kinds of big things have you got to sell? If you own a Christmas tree factory, you sell a product that is convenient and reusable, that doesn't shed its needles, and that doesn't require a trip during a snowstorm to purchase. But do you know what else you have to sell? The mental picture of Christmas trees when we were little kids, the magic of transformation, the symbol of another year gone by ... I could go on, but mercifully, I won't. Those emotional things can end up being the motivator for many families to buy a fuller, more attractive, more expensive tree from you than that scrawny pile of plastic twigs from the other guy.

Want another one, if I promise not to get sappy on you? You make frozen vegetables and come out with a product that combines frozen vegetables, pasta, and sauce in one bag. The idea is that someone could cook it all up together and, in a matter of minutes, dinner is ready. So, what have we got for benefits? Convenient, great-tasting, fast, nutritious, and on and on. That is a good list full of nice benefits, you must admit. And they are all so obvious that this is a no-brainer to work on.

Do you know what else you have? Drum roll, please. *You have a solution* to a problem that plagues millions of families—alright, mostly women—night after night. "What will we have for dinner tonight?" What a great opportunity lies before us to use our creativity, show our loved ones how much we care, and use up all those little weird jars of stuff hiding in the refrigerator. That's a nice, warm, and cuddly image isn't it? Get real. When that question is asked, it usually comes out as a sad, plaintive wail. This is an audience looking for solutions, and they will listen really hard to what you have to say.

Your turn: Let's start to think about the value that your brand could bring, and let's do so in a multi-dimensional way. This often seems kind of elusive when you first do it, so let's look at the attributes or features of the product and then tie those things into value for the purchaser.

**Big Brand Insight**

Solution selling is the new name for what we are describing here. Rather than focusing exclusively on the direct benefits of the product, such as freshness, speed, or cost, the idea is to wrap those into the larger benefit of solving one of the user's problems. This is a very attractive and meaningful way to get people to listen.

## There's Features, Benefits, and Lots More

Mark off a section on your note page into four columns, and label them "Features" (or "Attributes," if you like that word better), "Benefits" (or "So What's," if that helps you), and "Value" (or "The Wow!" if that helps), leaving the last one blank for now.

Now, just think about your product (object, service, idea, person) as it exists, in reality or in your mind. If it already exists with a brand name on it, ignore that brand name for the moment. Just talk to me about the "what" of it. We will start off using just the first two columns.

In your first column, Features/Attributes, write down 2 or 5 or 10 or 20 things about this entity that are good to know, depending on how many you can come up with. Push yourself to list all the nice things that you can think of (remember those nutritious and delicious vegetables?). Remember to include easy-to-use packages, a convenient form, great taste, speed, all kinds of things. I hope you get at least 10.

In your second column, Benefits/So What's, put down next to each thing on the list a few words that answer one of these three questions: So what?, Why should I care?, and What's in it for me? Choose whichever of those elegant expressions makes it easiest for you to respond. If you have more than one "So What," write it in.

Let's look at a few examples of possible first and second columns of your table:

| Features/Attributes | Benefits/So What's |
|---|---|
| Prescriptions kept in database | Can check for potentially dangerous drug interactions and warn you. |
| Dry cleaning done on premises | Quicker turn-around; special four-hour service when needed; can fix problems right away. |
| Dry cleaning plus alterations | One-stop shopping for clothing; takes care of irritating little tasks such as mending. |
| Longer battery life | Confidence that item will work; won't run out for enough hours to do something (for example, fly cross-country with a portable PC). |

You get the idea. In plain English, what have you got to work with, and why should anybody care?

Now for your third column. Looking only at what you wrote in the second column, rank in order all these benefits from number one, what you think is the strongest, most appealing idea, all the way down.

After you have done that, answer one question: Are you the type of person most likely to want something like this? How valid is your ranking? Want to try it again with someone else's attitude and experience in your head? Good. At least try to become a working mom with three kids, a boss 30 years younger than her, a $10 bill in her wallet, and a run in her last pair of pantyhose. Put yourself in the purchasers' shoes for a minute and try ranking them again. If you think of something that you wish the product did, make a note of that and put big, garish stars around it. Then work on that possibility later.

Why is your fourth column hanging around all empty like that? Because I wanted to wait until you worked through the first three before I introduced too much bias into this. Here is the label for the last column: "Change My Life!" Looking over all the features and benefits identified so far, is there any really good, strong idea here? Maybe it is one thing; maybe the magic happens when you combine things. If so, make some notes in the fourth column, or perhaps put circles around the two or three things that you think might be the germ of a big idea. If nothing is jumping out at you now, just leave it blank and come back to it at the end of Part 4 of this book.

Want a few quick ideas to get your brain moving?

➤ A Web site that provides health information, from what vitamins and herbs are supposed to be good for avoiding a cold to the latest research on treating lung cancer. What is this selling? An information service, a confidential private investigator service, peace of mind, a means to being an educated consumer, or what?

➤ Here is an example off the list we just looked at. What if you owned the dry cleaning business in which the work was done on premises, and you offered alterations as a service. Could you round out the benefits and make them jump out by checking every item for missing buttons and torn hems? And, of course, would you then tell absolutely everyone in town that you do this as part of your commitment to being the best full-service cleaner for busy people who care about how they look? Now we are getting somewhere.

## Getting Initial Input and Feedback

I strongly encourage you to bring more people into this exercise, even though what we are doing at this stage is basically *grandmother research*. It is helpful to get other people's views, and sometimes they list something that you never even thought of. Just don't start calling venture capitalists after your neighbors fill out this form with glowing remarks.

When you are ready for some initial input, just make up a sheet of paper with the columns that we just talked about, and make a stack of copies. If you do this 5 or 10 times, you may be surprised by how much you can learn, but be sure to keep track of who gave you what input. We will be talking at length about defining your target audience in the next chapter. For now, just know that you want to put people's names, or some way to know who they are, on the sheets so that you can sort out the input later. The notation can be as simple as "men over 50" or "women who lift weights weekly," as long as it is helpful to you. Use the same instructions that I gave you. Ask them to not talk about what they think until *after* all the columns are done—not before.

**Talk the Talk**

**Grandmother research** is a common term for casual market research like this that has no predictive value. The sarcasm of the term assumes that if you asked your grandmother how she liked your idea, she might smile and tell you how smart you are, or, conversely, remind you that you were a horrible child. Neither input is particularly applicable to the subject at hand—although it may be absolutely true.

# What Do the Brand and the Business Have in Common?

So far, we have a much deeper understanding of the product that we have to work with, but we haven't talked about whether the brand fits with the product, and then where the branded product fits with the business we have in mind.

Now is the time to start thinking about what you know about the brand, if it already exists, and what the product says about itself and the brand. Remember that dry cleaning example? Let's assume that you liked the idea of combining the benefits of on-premises work, alterations, and the bonus of checking for defects into a full-service pitch to busy people. You make that your new plan to build the business around. Now play this out.

If you have an existing business, does this plan fit with the name that is already on the store? See what you think of these:

➤ Fast and Friendly Cleaners

➤ Value Cleaners

➤ The Concierge Corner

➤ George and Harriet's Cleaning Place

If each of these is what you had to work with, what would you do? Before you decide to change the name and make Grandpa George and Grandma Harriet roll over in their graves, push yourself to see if the new plan can fit the old name. Can you add a tagline or a positioning statement (remember Chapter 10, "The Powerful Duo: Brand Name + Positioning Statement"?) that pulls the two together?

Do you know what your customers think of your company now? Does your local newspaper run a "Best Of" survey each year? Have you ever won it? Do you know what questions are asked of the public? Would you put a short (and I do mean really short) questionnaire at the front desk and ask people to put the completed cards into a box?

If you are creating a new business, what benefits and "Change My Life" statements could be the cornerstone of your brand name? What feelings and beliefs do you want people to have about your brand name?

This process is one of sifting and measuring and tailoring. At this point in your analysis, what do your product and brand name have in common? Are you clear on the product's features, benefits, and potential to deliver really meaningful associations? That last part is the hardest, but we are nowhere near finished. The more we work through all the issues, the more likely you are to find changes and refinements that suddenly produce a truly great idea.

# Between You and Me: Do You Want a Business or a Brand?

Just between us, are you starting to get the message that there is a big difference between having a business and managing a branded business? It is a huge difference, actually. On a more personal note, and in the immortal words of Joan Rivers, the actress and talk show host, let's talk.

Getting business experience and brand experience is just like having a job and having a career. The first one is part of the second, but the second involves a lot more personal involvement. If you are tiring of all this talk about brand perspective and "Change My Life," it may be because you really are not excited about the branding process. That's okay. If you are sitting in a brand management position and you feel that way, get out of it and find a gracious way to move into a different part of the company. The smoothest way is to say that you want to develop a "broader perspective and appreciation for the hard work of the people in widgets, gadgets, and whatever." Managers love that kind of talk. But don't stay where you are unless you are fired up by all this branding talk. It is hard enough to motivate yourself some days, never mind being the cheerleader/brand champion for the whole company if that just doesn't interest you. On the other hand, if you are getting more excited about working brand management magic on a business near and dear to you, read on.

---

### The Least You Need to Know

➤ Developing a brand profile takes a lot of work. It challenges you to really think through every element of how you will handle the brand.

➤ The brand profile is an integral part of the overall business plan for the brand.

➤ The brand profile is a living document. It can change and adapt over time, but changes should be well thought out before they are executed.

➤ The brand profile should be on the desk of everyone who makes decisions that affect the brand.

---

# Chapter 15

# Target Market Analysis: More Critical Now Than Ever

## In This Chapter

➤ Understanding the size and dynamics of the market

➤ Identifying categories, segments, and niches

➤ Who wants what: demographics and psychographics

➤ Databases hold valuable behavioral data

Target market analysis is about finding the opportunities that put—and keep—your brand in business. Somebody, somewhere out there, is waiting for your product. Hopefully lots of somebodies. It seems like it shouldn't be so hard to figure out who they are and where they live so that we can go tell them about our wonderful products. In the old days, nobody worried about all this slicing and dicing of every category into perfect little packages of appeal. Today we do because our customers have so much more to choose from.

Have you ever walked through a huge shopping mall and tried to identify who each store thinks is its target audience—or who you think it is? That is a great exercise in strategic thinking, and it's very easy to do. Have you ever seen a TV commercial and wondered out loud, "Who in the world would buy something like that?" That is probably a good indication that the brand is not targeting you—either that or the ad agency for that brand is about to be fired because you are exactly who they want but are not going to get.

Choosing a target market sounds simpler than it is. But, do you decide who you want or figure out who wants you? You know, if we didn't have to deal with all these people issues, our jobs would be a lot easier.

# Do the Math First: Categories, Segments, and Niches

You may not believe this, but we are going to start talking about the target audience by doing some math. Sound a little inside-out, perhaps? How will you be able to tell me who your product is good for, whose wants and needs it can fulfill, and how big an idea this really is if you don't know where "the big idea" fits into the real world? That's why we are going to start sizing up the opportunity by figuring out where it fits and then finding out what kinds of things in that market people like most. Short of a crystal ball or doing 5,000 personal interviews, how can you find out what people like? There is almost always a way to get at that information from statistical data.

### Heads Up

Remember that old line, "Figures don't lie, but liars can figure"? The numbers may be honest and true, but with computerization, it is easy to make them say lots of things based on how they are grouped and manipulated. Start every analysis with how the numbers are organized. Understand what is the topmost line: dollar or unit sales, all ice cream or all frozen desserts, and so on.

Tearing apart the numbers is the what's what of business; it is being the surgeon general of market analysis; it is the who-done-it detective work of trend watching. Figuring out how a type of product fits into the bigger picture is fascinating. This is one of my favorite thinking exercises.

Whether you have a product that you are trying to find the biggest market for, or an idea for a product but no idea how big or small it could be, you need to understand how products are grouped and understood. Then you figure out where the opportunities for targeting are.

An example may help. Just so you know, I am going to make up all the "facts and figures" here, so don't go running to your brother-in-law who owns a bowling alley with this information.

You are thinking about buying a bowling alley in town because you really like bowling; think it is good, clean fun; and want a business close to home. You have some ideas for growing the business. You wisely decide that you should find out a little about how the bowling business in general is doing. The current owner hands you a report showing that bowling is on the increase, as measured by the number of lanes rented over the last 12 months. This is a national trend and makes all the owners in the industry feel great.

The report even says that the western United States, where you live, leads the growth trend. This definitely supports your own observations. While you are having this meeting with the current owner, your teenage son decides to be helpful and goes on-line to find statistics on bowling. He prints out a great report and gives it to you that night. You now have two pieces of research on bowling.

Let's see the numbers side by side:

| Column #1: What the Owner Gave You | | |
| --- | --- | --- |
| **Bowling Trends in the United States** | | |
| | **1998** | **1999** |
| *Lanes Rented* | 798,000 | 818,000 |
| West | 391,000 | 418,000 |
| % growth | | (+6.9%) |
| East | 407,000 | 400,000 |
| % growth | | (−1.7%) |

| Column #2: Son's Internet Research | | |
| --- | --- | --- |
| **Bowling Trends in the United States** | | |
| | **1998** | **1999** |
| *Lanes Rented* | 798,000 | 818,000 |
| West | 391,000 | 418,000 |
| % growth | | (+6.9%) |
| % U.S. share | 49% | 51% |
| East | 391,000 | 418,000 |
| % growth | | (−1.7%) |
| % U.S. share | 51% | 49% |
| *Lanes Rented by Type* | | |
| Candlepin | 41% | 49% |
| Tenpin | 59% | 51% |
| *Bowlers by Age as Percent of Total* | | |
| 5 to 12 years | 21% | 24% |
| 13 to 24 | 7% | 3% |
| 25 to 35 | 19% | 23% |
| 36 to 44 | 22% | 17% |
| 45 to 65 | 31% | 33% |

*Bowling by the numbers.*

*(Source: Nico's wild imagination)*

Column 1, the information from the current owner, clearly shows that more lanes are being rented this year than last. It also shows that bowling has grown faster in the western United States in the last year than in the eastern United States. He told you the truth. Good guy.

Column 2, the industry information from your son, also shows those two facts, which we have circled on both charts so that you can see them. But the information looks different here, doesn't it? There are lots more numbers, to be sure, but there might be other conclusions that you could draw than just those two.

Let's take the data line by line and watch the story unfold. Follow along with me as we move down the right column.

➤ The West did indeed grow nicely at almost 7 percent versus the previous year, while the East declined almost 2 percent. It's interesting to note, however, that both sides of the country are pretty evenly split, with each having about a 50 percent share.

➤ The two types of bowling, candlepin and tenpin, are pretty evenly matched right now, but that is due to a big jump in candlepin activity this past year.

**179**

➤ Teenagers and young adults seem to be turned off by bowling these days. The 13- to 24-year-old age group represents only 3 percent of bowlers.

➤ Young children are still into bowling and represent a big part of the business.

➤ The 25- to 35-year-old group is showing increased signs of interest in bowling. (I wish I knew if this was because they are accompanying the young children or coming on their own.)

➤ The over-35 age group is interesting. The 36- to 44-year-olds have gone bowling less in this last year, while the over-45-year-olds have increased and are now the single biggest group of bowlers.

Now that you see all of this, how do you feel about buying that bowling alley? That might depend on what kind of place it is.

➤ Candlepin bowling is growing rapidly. Your place is set up for tenpin bowling. Would you consider converting? Would that be all of the lanes or half? How much does each lane of conversion cost?

➤ The data says that the biggest growth in bowling is from adults 25 to 35 and children 5 to 12. That sounds like young families. Are there a lot of them in your area?

➤ There is also nice growth among adults 45 to 65, and they bowl more often. Maybe you should add cocktail service and pu-pu platters.

➤ If you add cocktails and hors d'oeuvres, the young families probably won't come. Or, maybe you can get them to come early and open the cocktail service only after 9 P.M. on weekends.

We started by looking at a bowling alley as a business opportunity, but we ended up seeing it as a lot of different things to a lot of different people:

➤ One element of total family away-from-home entertainment (market view)

➤ One bowling alley in a country full of bowling alleys (national category view)

➤ One bowling alley in the tenpin bowling segment (segment view)

➤ What may become one bowling alley in the adult/liquor specialty (niche view)

Depending on how you look at the situation, you can make very different decisions on how to advertise, decorate, equip, promote, price, and staff this place. The broader the view you take (the closer to the top of the hierarchy), the broader and less specific your target audience statement will be.

The simplest of questions are these:

➤ Who do you want to come into your bowling alley?

➤ Who is available to come into your bowling alley?

Do those two make sense together? Try this for logic. If your bowling alley is located in a good-size suburb right outside a major city, you probably have a pretty diverse group of people living within a 10-mile radius. So pick which ones you want, which ones the data says are most likely to come, and target them. In Chapter 17, "Who Is Your Competition? Are You Sure About That?" we will talk about defining your competition, and that will help focus your choices.

If your alley is in a small town, 50 miles from a good-sized city, you still have different kinds of people, but maybe not enough of any one group of them to set a specific target such as adults who want a cocktail and a string of bowling at the same time. That is a very specific target audience statement, and I applaud your ability to be clear and succinct, but it may not work.

Working the data is very important in target audience selection.

## The More You Know, the Easier It Gets

I am putting a lot of emphasis on having you understand how to identify and then dissect a category of products, for several reasons:

➤ It is critical to understand the larger environment in which your product exists. Our bowling alley can be looked at as part of several different categories: away-from-home entertainment, family recreation, children's recreation, adult recreation, sports activities … you get the idea.

➤ Once you see how the categories, segments, and niches line up, you can spot some easy ways to expand your product offerings. Other segments or niches may be just waiting to be filled and may take very little marketing effort to pull your customers into because they will seem like "natural" additions to your business.

➤ When you really learn to see your business in the context of many other similar but different things, it sharpens your ability to identify who and what your competition really is. We have a whole chapter coming up on identifying and dealing with competition, and it is firmly rooted in the ability to take a good, long look around you and see, clearly and completely, just what you really compete with.

**Talk the Talk**

A **decision tree** is a commonly used tool in problem-solving systems. It is a very simple device to help sort out an issue step by step. It was originally used to map out a process and the steps that went into it. It can also be used to map out the components or elements of an entity. That is how we will use it.

I want to show you a way to sketch out, and thereby figure out, what categories and segments you live within. This is a great exercise because it helps you to see that your product can fit into several or even many different market opportunities. Let's stay with our bowling alley example and do a *decision tree* format. In the interests of space, I will put in only a few of the many options at the first place our tree branches out.

*Where do bowling alleys fit? Weekend entertainment.*

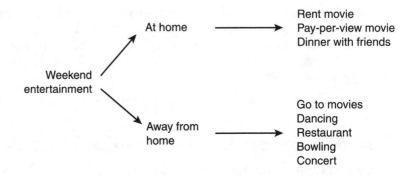

In the previous figure, we looked at bowling as one option within the context of weekend entertainment choices. We could have chosen to start with only family entertainment, or we could have started with indoor sports, family fitness activities, low-cost family outings, and who knows how many other starting places, and still ended up with bowling as one of the branches on the tree. It takes only a few minutes to sketch out another decision tree, and you may want to take five minutes right now to do one that starts with family fitness or adult entertainment. As you develop this broader view of where your product fits, it will give you ideas about who you may want to target or some benefits that you hadn't thought about before.

This is a great discipline and a terrific way to get your creativity flowing when you feel that you need some new ways to freshen up your product. Everything is part of something larger, and learning to think in both directions is invaluable when you are trying to figure out what benefits your product has that can be used to attract new users.

# Two Important Ic's: Demographics and Psychographics

Most people are accustomed to hearing *demographic* statistics quoted all the time because the news media uses them a lot. *Psychographic,* or *lifestyle,* comments come up all the time, too, but few people are used to hearing the term, never mind recognizing the comments as such.

A tremendous amount of demographic data is readily available for your use through the U.S. Government Census Office. If you go online to www.census.gov, you'll find a wealth of preformatted reports and the opportunity to find many, many different facts.

Psychographic data is not as readily available because it is not collected through the Census process. I see a lot of it in business magazine articles that are based on a company's experience and learning. However, just to give you some guidance, I went online to www.askjeeves.com, one of the popular search sites. I simply typed in "what is psychographics" and got to a number of sites that talked about it.

You can do two more things with Internet access that you should think about:

**Talk the Talk**

**Demographic** data refers to the facts and figures about the population of a specified area. These include age, gender, household size, and what percent of people own vs. rent their home. **Psychographic** data is often referred to as **lifestyle** data and reflects more about attitudes, beliefs, and personal choices.

➤ Be sure to check out the Web site for *American Demographics* magazine, at www.demographics.com. The site includes a wealth of great articles that will help many of you find good direction.

➤ Use the search engines to find industry information. In our bowling example, I just typed in "bowlers" and very quickly found the Bowling Proprietors Association of America. If we really wanted to buy that bowling alley, we should spend some time with these folks first.

# New Thinking: Which Is More Important, Attitude or Behavior?

Having just said how important people's attitudes, beliefs, and lifestyles are, let me go right ahead and sound like I am contradicting myself. If you asked me to choose which one set of information I want, either people's attitudes or their behaviors, 9 times out of 10, I will say behavior. That's because I have seen both, and almost always the behavior information is more actionable.

I have got to put a caveat in here. Attitudinal research can be very rich. It can generate wonderful and creative ideas. It can inspire new product benefits to talk about, new product ideas to develop, new sales techniques, and many other things. In the right hands, and used the right way, it is magical. I do not want to denigrate it in any way. But, tell me what people actually do, not what they say they will do or what they want to do, and I can usually make clearer decisions.

One of the great tools of advanced technology for brand management people has been the development of customer databases. The easiest way to think of what they are is the frequent flyer/frequent shopper programs that are so popular. The marketing goals of those programs are to encourage people to use that airline or store as frequently as possible. To help persuade people to do that, the program offers incentives based on how much of their service you use. Fly more miles, get more points.

The technology that tracks how many points the airline owes you also captures the flights that you took; that's how the airline can calculate how many miles it owes you. The technology involved in tracking this information got dramatically better in the 1990s. The improvements allowed more storage and better analysis. More storage means that you can have more people in your programs, keep track of favorite cities that they fly to, and hold on to three years of data instead of just one year. More data points, particularly when viewed over time, means that you can start to learn from the data, not just report on it.

A lot of the uses of customer databases are in the area of promotion, and we will talk about these at some length in Part 5, "Taking Ownership: The General Management Part of Brand Management."

### Talk the Talk

A **transactional database** captures the purchases or transactions of the customers and stores selected, pieces of that information about them for later retrieval. The amount of information that can be saved, and how long it can be held, is limited by the storage capacity of the computer system used.

The single biggest value of looking at this transactional data is that you are looking at what the customers actually bought, their real buying behavior. A *transactional database* is a deep well of learning just waiting for the right questions to be asked and the right tools to be used.

If your company has something like this, you need to sit with whoever is the keeper of the database and have that person tell you about the kinds of data collected and stored. You will then want to make up a list of questions, in plain English, that you want to find answers to and then go back and see how many of them can be answered. The process of pulling information out of the database is explained in detail in Part 5, so if you have access to something like this, I encourage you to study that section thoroughly.

What if you haven't got any kind of access like this, which is the situation for most people? You would be amazed how much you can ferret out from business magazines, newspaper articles, and Web sites. Where do you think they are getting their information? From companies who have run these programs and learned valuable lessons in the process, and who then let their stories be told. The business media people have extraordinary access and are delighted to tell everyone in the industry what these companies learned.

If you can get a data table out of an article or from a presentation, even something as simple as the one page on the right side of the "Bowling by the Numbers" figure we looked at, you can learn a lot.

The key is this: The numbers tell you what people actually did, what they spent their money on, and what they gave their time to.

Data doesn't get any more real than that. And that's why I like numbers so much.

# Putting It All Together: A Target We Can Find

Please don't tell me that your target audience is "women 25 to 54 years old" and expect me to say anything other than "that's nice." Which women in that age group? What is it about them that should make them interested in your product? Let's get much more specific in generating a target audience profile so that, even if we end up with a very broad age range like this, we hear women 25 to 54 who ....

We want to create a profile statement that helps you, and anyone who works with you, visualize the kind of people you believe are the best prospects for your brand. What we create can then help you make a lot of very pragmatic decisions, such as what kinds of advertising to buy, what kinds of stores or Web sites or agencies to use, and the kinds of promotions that will have the most appeal.

If you have already created a list of features and benefits for your product from our earlier exercises, this next step becomes easier. What you will see we are doing is sorting out those benefits into groups, and then figuring out which kinds of benefits are things we can use to our advantage.

Here are some different ideas of benefits that have functional, lifestyle, emotional, or value appeal:

> **Functional appeal:** Easy to use, ready to eat, easy open, all in one, fast, simple, doesn't clog-run-drip-smell-tangle-rip

> **Lifestyle appeal:** Convenient, modern, traditional, variety, family-oriented, entertaining, age-appropriate

> **Emotional appeal:** Safety, security, reassurance of quality, stability, excitement, calm

> **Value appeal:** Best value, smart choice, select/exclusive, lowest cost

Now start to compose the target audience statement by filling in these blanks, using only the ones that make sense for your product:

> People who are _____ (adults, children, male, female, ages, ethnic groups, religious affiliation) ... and who use or want _____ (type of product) ... and who want _____ (type of lifestyle, functional, or emotional benefit) ... and who value _____ (type of value benefit).

If we had a bowling alley in a suburban neighborhood and wanted to target women 25 to 54, figuring that they are the entertainment decision makers for families, adult couples, and adult groups of friends, then we have a lot going on, but let's see what the list might look like:

➤ Women 25 to 54 years old, looking for local entertainment that is healthy, fun, and easy to learn; that encourages friendly fun; and that is easy on the budget

➤ Women 25 to 54 looking for group fitness activities that welcome people with a variety of fitness levels, and who feel strongly that ideal choices must be reasonable in cost and easy to learn

➤ Women 25 to 44 who organize entertainment for their own families and outings specifically for their children and friends, and who value clean atmosphere, reasonable cost, and the option to have birthday parties within the facility

What you are looking for is the cross-section between what your product has to offer and what people do and want that could make your product a good fit for them.

# Now What? I Know Who I Want, but Where Are They?

When you spend time scouring every data source that you can think of and you are through adding ideas and subtracting dead ends, you have a pretty good idea of what kind of customer you want. After doing all the work of describing your product in terms of its characteristics and benefits (see Chapter 14, "What Is a Brand Profile?"), you also have a language that you can use to now talk about what is so good and so right about your brand.

**Mentoring Memo**

Hang in there if this seems a little overwhelming. At this point, you actually have more to work with than you may think. The language that you developed by building the benefit statements is the basis for your message; the target customer that you identified is the bull's-eye. There are lots of arrows that you can use.

We will talk at length in Chapter 19, "Careful Communication: What's Right and Great About the Brand," the final section of Part 4, about different ways to communicate what your brand is about. I am holding off on addressing the advertising issue right now because, until we go through the upcoming chapters on distribution and competition, you really aren't ready to make advertising decisions. But, after spending all this time trying to find out who makes sense for you to target, it would seem a little abrupt to not even address the issue of how you can reach them.

Many people think that the only determinant of which brands use television advertising is the size of the wallet. While I am the first to tell you that is a *huge* factor, not just a big one, it obviously isn't the only one. There are so many ways for a brand to communicate today that every budget can find something to work with.

Some of the things you want to be thinking about now are these:

➤ Where is your product available ("in distribution" is the correct phrase)? What kind of geographic pattern does that create for a communications strategy?

➤ If you are an Internet-based business—just clicks, no bricks—then you essentially have no geographic boundaries. You also don't have the luxury of rounding up all your customers in the Baltimore/Washington, D.C., area with local television, radio, or mail.

➤ The cross-section of finding your target audience is where the people you want live—that's the who and the where. In this case, the word *live* needs to be understood as where they can be found, not where they sleep at night or leave their dirty laundry. People can be found geographically if they sit in front of their televisions or read their mail. They can be found by lifestyle if they go to concerts or movies. They can be found electronically if they read e-mail or visit Web sites. They can be found by occupation if they go to college or attend industry conventions. They can be found spiritually if they are involved with an organized group, or philosophically if they support certain causes or charities.

Finding who you want is really not as hard as you may think.

# New Technology: Targeting Is Tough—Let Them Do It Themselves

An interesting outcome of the development of the Internet and so many other pieces of related technology is that information systems are now much more flexible—so flexible, in fact, that a lot of us average users of technology can do all kinds of whiz-bang things with just a few mouse clicks.

We can even take a load off the shoulders of the marketing people by doing our own target marketing ourselves. That's right—using technology, we can take control of the sales pitch and make it tell us exactly what we want to hear about. This is definitely the self-help movement at its apex.

You don't remember doing anything like that? Have you used a search engine lately? Cruised an online store anytime? Looked up any news or stock quotes or memorable quotes? Researched any travel Web sites? Then you have done this kind of self-targeting.

The extraordinary flexibility that can be built into a good Web site lets it act as the biggest of big stores, with untold variety and selection, but there are virtual golf carts to take us around so that we don't have to get worn out getting to the department we want. Maybe a better analogy is that you just think of where you want to go, and you get "beamed up" and dropped there. No walking, no crowds, no long lines.

### Big Brand Insight

A simple way to see the mechanism of self-targeting in action is to go into a retailer's Web site like Gap.com. This is obviously a big brand name, and the company has merchandise for babies to grandpas. At the home page, you can walk right to the men's department or do a quick check of what's on sale all over the store. It's kind of like walking into one of the mall stores and seeing sale signs all over the place.

If you operate a sports apparel and equipment store, whether a real store or a Web site, lots of people with very different interests can come through your door. They don't want to walk around in archery gear when they are looking for bowling shoes. On the Web site, millions of people can come through the door and, with one click, pick the name of the sport they are interested in, and off they go. How many one-second clicks does it take to find all the bowling shoes available?

➤ Find Web site.

➤ Click on Bowling.

➤ Click on Equipment (not Apparel, the other choice).

➤ Click on Men's (not Women's or Children's).

So who is the sporting goods store's target audience? If the store had to sum it up in a sentence or two, I don't think the word *bowling* would be in there. The store is looking much further up the ladder to a market definition of total sporting goods apparel and equipment, of which bowling is a segment, bowling apparel and equipment are two subsegments, and bowling shoes is a niche.

### The Least You Need to Know

➤ You need to understand where your product fits in the architecture of the category, segment, and niches. This helps you see the size of the opportunity and may give you ideas for new products that you could add very easily.

➤ Put considerable effort into finding as much statistical and behavioral information as you can. You want to generate a pretty dynamic look at the kinds of people who should want your brand.

➤ Use simple sketching techniques to help you see where your product fits into the larger framework of reasons that someone might want what you have. Try the decision tree technique to generate ideas.

➤ There are many ways to reach your target audience. Do not fall into the trap of believing that you don't have the budget to advertise or promote your business.

# Chapter 16

# Channels of Distribution: Getting from Here to There

---

**In This Chapter**

➤ Distribution as part of the selling process

➤ The relationship between the brand and the place

➤ The distribution chain's three key links

➤ Channels of distribution: options and conflicts

---

Distribution has the unfortunate reputation of being a dry, dusty topic, full of equations and train wrecks and tractor-trailers driving in the wrong lane, which, of course, is whatever lane you are in. The stuff of our lives magically shows up where we need it most days, so many people don't think much about how it gets there. How much are we conscious of the distribution chain, which is the *process* of distribution or how something gets from here to there? Do we even really think about the channels of distribution, the *where* it actually is, unless we really need to?

Distribution, also called logistics, which doesn't make it sound any sexier, is one of the subjects that I really disliked in graduate school but found that I thoroughly enjoyed in real life. In fact, the whole area of operations, from manufacturing to moving the product through to the end point, turned into an ongoing fascination for me. I always grab the chance to tour a manufacturing or warehousing facility, a truck depot, or a processing plant.

Distribution is not well-understood by a lot of people. This chapter includes an in-depth description of the process itself before addressing the brand-specific issues. I like the area of distribution and logistics, and I think that it is very important for students of brand management to appreciate it. It is very logical, it appears to be woefully dogmatic, and yet it requires and thrives on creative thinking. I like the apparent paradox in that. It builds good thinking skills to sort through tangles like these, and distribution issues, for all their old-world, dusty imagery, are at the heart of the new Internet e-commerce economy. Hint: Remember the holiday shopping season of 1999 and the trashing of certain Web sites that didn't deliver the goodies on time?

# Get the Brand to the End Users, and Get Them to Your Brand

Distribution, in its simplest form, is the basic work of getting your product into the hands of the *end user,* the person who actually wants or needs it. What is often not seen initially is that part of the work of distribution is getting the end user to the brand. Isn't that the job of sales and marketing techniques? A good part of the job certainly is the advertising and sales programs that build awareness. But the point at which the user and the brand actually meet is part of the distribution process.

**Talk the Talk**

The **end user** is the final point along the line, the person who will actually use your product. Very often, but not always, this is also the person who pays the end cost for the product, with all the cost of goods and handling costs factored in. The end user may be an individual person, such as George, or an organization, such as the George Company.

We usually think of distribution as transportation, but that is only one of its functions. A different piece is how the product is made available, or where the product and the end user finally meet up. Think of it this way: You are walking through a hardware store and suddenly spot the display of cordless drills. At that moment, you start giving serious thought to getting one. You recognize the brands from some advertising, but until you see the products, you don't act on the advertising. The hardware store itself is part of the distribution process. This would be called *retail distribution;* the product is seen and bought in a retail outlet.

Or, you are on an airplane reading the magazines in the seatback. You see a suitcase that is just what you want. When you get home, you call the 800-number and place your order. The catalog and the truck that will deliver the suitcase to your home are both part of the distribution process. This is called *catalog distribution.* Distribution of all types is central to the sales and marketing process.

The term *distribution* refers to the handling of the product, but it needs to be seen in a broader context. Keep in mind that the bigger goal is to get the right product to the right end user at the time when that user wants it, and it takes a lot more than a few good trucks to make that happen.

Before we can ship a product out the door, it needs to be sold to somebody. Where are we sending it? And, by the way, the folks in accounting want to know who is paying for this and when they are sending us the money for it.

So, before we can ship the product, it needs to be manufactured or processed somehow, which also means that somebody needs to forecast that we will need it; it needs to be sold to somebody; and along the way we need to get paid for it. And somebody (this means you) had better be thinking about who we are selling to and how this is getting to the end user, because there are a lot of people and resources going into just getting it there.

As with each element of the puzzle, we want to look at distribution both as a function and as part of your brand strategy. The more you understand each step in the process, the easier it is to find both cost-saving ideas and new opportunities. I am always delighted when I hear someone raise questions such as, "Since we are already spending money to get to X point, can we use that to service Y more inexpensively?" or, for a different twist, "I know we can service Y pretty cheaply, but is that the right place for the brand?" They are thinking about distribution as a strategy, as the point where how we move the product and where it goes comes together.

Distribution strategy is a hot topic. There is a lot of opportunity to waste—or, conversely, save money—by carefully thinking through where the product needs to be, how fast it needs to move, and the best ways to make that happen. Distribution costs can become astronomical as more stops are added and more handling happens. This applies whether the product is an object or a service.

To pull your thoughts together for the distribution section of your brand profile, let's focus first on the elements of the *distribution chain*. I have broken them down into three steps, or points, along the chain: disbursement, contact, and delivery. After that, we will start to factor in how your distribution options fit with your brand; those two things together form your distribution strategy.

**Talk the Talk**

The **distribution chain** is the series of stops that a product makes from when it leaves the manufacturing/processing or creation point until it gets to the end user. This may be a direct route or may require a series of stops along the way. The "chain" analogy reflects the fact that the whole system is only as good as each link along the way.

## Step One: The Point of Disbursement

It would be so easy for me to tell you that all you need to know about the three steps in distribution is that a product starts where it is created, it gets sent somewhere, and then somebody opens it up and uses it. On the surface, that is pretty much what happens. However, what the product is—meaning its physical properties or its sensitivity to atmosphere or criminal neglect—make the system much more complicated than that.

The distribution system technically begins at the point of creation and then follows a path to reach the end user. Let's follow one easy-to-understand example and look at it in some depth. Then I will add other quick examples to broaden your understanding of how distribution works with very different products. Our easy example is a physical product, a can of Welch's Frozen Concentrated Grape Juice. I have purposely chosen the frozen form instead of a bottle of grape juice because it adds a little twist that is worth seeing.

The product is prepared and sealed in one of Welch's processing plants, where it is put into a special deep-freeze unit. Because the product needs to be kept frozen from this point on to protect the product quality, it requires *special handling*.

The cases of frozen grape juice need to reach thousands of different locations, and this will be done almost exclusively by truck. But stop and think about that: The product is frozen solid while it sits in the production plant's freezer and cannot be allowed to thaw. Because it will require special trucks, it only makes sense to send each one out filled to the maximum weight level.

A full truckload of frozen juice is more than 1,000 cases. Large supermarket chains and warehouse club stores can often handle a full truckload of frozen product in their warehouses; smaller stores obviously cannot. That means some of the product must be kept in storage at a secondary warehouse so that 5 or 10 cases can be sent to a store when needed.

**Talk the Talk**

**Special handling** issues show up in many product categories and need to be identified as critical steps. Temperature control issues exist with certain pharmaceuticals and home delivery of fresh pizza. Sanitation issues come up in laboratories and food preparation. Can you think of a few others? How about astronauts in space capsules and credit card transactions over the Internet?

Here are some other examples of points of disbursement:

| Product | Point(s) of Disbursement |
| --- | --- |
| Music CD | The CD may be produced and assembled at one facility and then sent to a music distributor's warehouse for disbursement to stores. |
| Consulting project | The office of the consulting company produces the documents and then distributes them to the client via e-mail, snail mail, or personal delivery. |
| Flu shot | Getting the shot in your arm means that the place (doctor's office, clinic, pharmacy, town hall) is the disbursement point; the liquid inside the syringe was disbursed from the manufacturer's processing plant out to some forward location (hospital, medical supplies distributor). |

It becomes quite easy to think through any distribution chain after a while. That is one of the nicest things about this whole topic; it is remarkably logical. Now, let's keep moving forward in the chain to the next link, the point of contact.

# Step Two: The Point of Contact

Looking at distribution as a three-step process may seem confusing when you look at this subject from your viewpoint as a consumer. I chose to use a frozen can of juice from one of the oldest brand names in America to make it easy, and you may be wondering how it can sound so hard to just go buy the thing, bring it home, and enjoy it. The fact that it is so easy for you to do so says the distribution system is working. You can go get the product pretty much 24 hours a day in a store near you and not have to wonder who might sell it or how to find it.

Stay with me on this one, and I promise not to lose you. Step 2, the *point of contact* and step 3, the *point of delivery*, may be the same or quite different. Until you look at each case, you also don't know which to call the *point of sale*, which is a phrase a lot of people use casually to mean either of those things. It isn't really all that clear anymore.

If we all shopped at the old general store that we see in ancient cowboy movies, this differentiation would all be unnecessary. But we don't. We shop 24 hours a day, 7 days a week, from catalogs and Web sites and 24-hour grocery stores. And we pay when we order in some situations, and at other times we pay when we actually get our hands on the product. Sometimes we don't pay until after that point. There is a big difference between giving a credit card number to a catalog operator, giving a $10 bill to a gas station attendant, and sending a check to your plumber. As a consumer, you don't think much about this, but as a businessperson, you do.

A quick run-through on the differences in these terms makes sense before we go any further. Read each of these phrases, putting the words "the point of" in front:

> … contact is where the brand and consumer meet.

> … delivery is where the consumers get their hands on their own piece of your product.

> … sale is where the payment is made, which could be before or after the delivery (for example, giving a credit card number over the phone and then getting delivery).

Let's get back to our cans of frozen grape juice, which right now are all sitting in a frozen warehouse somewhere, and move them closer to the consumer. The product has been pulled out of wherever it has been stored and put into the retail store's freezer section. Most of the time, for products like this, the point of contact and the point of delivery are the same: the supermarket, convenience store, or warehouse club store, for instance. The end user sees the product and decides to purchase it (point of contact). In a split second, she puts it in her carriage (point of delivery), pays for it at the checkout (point of sale), and takes it home. The one store played a lot of roles. It is pretty straightforward like this for a lot of our transactions.

That was, of course, until the last few years. Today, the point of contact may be Streamline.com, for instance, a Web site through which users can order supermarket-type products along with a wide range of specialty items and services. If the end user ordered the grape juice through this Web site, that is the point of contact. When the Streamline.com truck pulls up to her home, that is the point of delivery. Technically, the point of sale was back when the grape juice was ordered because that is when a credit card account was authorized to pay for it. This used to look simple didn't it?

**Talk the Talk**

A **class of trade** is one type of outlet. Supermarkets, drug stores, and restaurants are three different classes of trade. You may also hear this expressed as three different **channels of distribution.** Department stores and discount outlets are different classes of trade. Bookstores and airport shops are different classes of trade even though they both sell books.

As a businessperson who wants to maximize sales, your first inclination is to get as many points of contact set up as possible. As a brand champion, you modify that goal to be as many *positive* points of contact as possible. Think back to the example of the exclusive men's clothing line whose end-of-season items ended up at a flea market in Chapter 14, "What Is a Brand Profile?" That is not a positive point of contact for the brand if the manufacturer wants to continue selling on Rodeo Drive in L.A. and Worth Avenue in Palm Beach.

When you can identify a whole *class of trade* or *channel of distribution* as a positive contact point, like all supermarkets would be for Welch's grape juice, then, yes, you want every one of those individual points. But, if you are a brand of very high-end, imported, hand-squeezed, organic juices selling for $10 a quart, a lot of the supermarkets in this country simply don't make sense.

What are some other not-so-obvious points of contact? Catalogs, Web sites, direct mail pieces, radio and television shopping shows, and radio and TV direct-selling advertisements. These last two raise all sorts of interesting questions. Aren't they really advertisements? But then again, they create the moment when the brand and the end user meet. History would say they have proven to be both, but from a distribution standpoint, they absolutely count as points of contact. They are the "place" where the decision to buy is made.

## Step Three: The Point of Delivery

Finally, let's get to the people. The point of delivery is what it sounds like, the final destination for the product. Well, yes and no. They are often the same thing. It would be way too easy if they always were.

Our easy example is the frozen can of grape juice. We already saw that the points of contact and delivery are the same when it is a supermarket transaction, but they are different when ordered online and delivered to the home. But at least the point of delivery is still the home freezer. That is where it needs to go and where it will be used up.

Let's take a giant step away from a simple physical product like that and go to a hybrid product/service: the creation of a television commercial. Let's stay with Welch's so that we don't get too far astray. This time, let's look at Welch's advertising agency as the company gets ready to launch a new campaign.

The agency works with the brand group and senior management to develop the ads, get legal clearances to produce them, do the actual filming and editing, and get ready for the final unveiling. They will take a copy of the finished commercial to Welch's headquarters, the agency's point of delivery for approval of its work. Everybody says "yes," and the deed is done, right? The approved product has been delivered. Well, yes, but, a TV commercial on the VCR in the board room is not the same thing as a commercial on a hit TV show. The true final, final destination is all the TV stations, or networks, across the country chosen to air the spot.

This "finished" delivered product now starts up another whole cycle of distribution. It needs to be copied and disbursed to the facilities that will get it on the air. The creation of the commercial was one cycle; the airing of the commercial is another. Cycles, or layers of distribution, are very common as products pass from one hand to another. Your definition of the distribution process may just be for your share of its total life span, but it may move from your company right into someone else's distribution process and start at the disbursement stage all over again.

# Points and Percentages of Distribution

I want to cover a phrase that is very commonly used in so many industries that it really needs to be addressed here. I have held off on using the term *points of distribution* or *percent distribution* until now because I didn't want to mix usages of the word *distribution*. We only used it to mean the whole system of moving a product from origination to final destination. But you need to be familiar with these terms and the way they are commonly used.

"Points of distribution" sounds like a simple enough term in itself, but some people mean percentage points and others mean the number of different store or location points. And most often, it is really more like jargon because it gets used in so many different contexts that you need to be psychic to catch the drift. When you are new in an industry, it can be extremely confusing.

See the differences between each set of these statements:

➤ We have 75 percent U.S. retail distribution on our brown leather wallets.

➤ We have 75 percent store distribution in Macy's on brown leather wallets.

The first bullet says that the wallets are stocked (in retail distribution) in stores that account for 75 percent of all sales in the United States. This is a *sales volume* number.

The second says the wallets are in 75 percent of the Macy's *stores*, which may generate more or less than 75 percent of Macy's sales volume. This is a *store count* number.

And here's another set:

➤ So far, 75 percent of the Supermarket ACV (all commodity volume) has ordered the new juice item.

➤ So far, we actually have 52 percent retail distribution.

➤ So far, we have 65 percent of the stores in stock.

In the first case, we hear that supermarkets, which in total represent 75 percent of all sales in the United States, have ordered the new juice. *ACV* is a term commonly used to mean total volume of sales, distinct from the number of stores. Think of it as market share, and find out what terminology is used in your industry.

In the second bullet, we hear that it is "in retail distribution" (meaning in the retail store and available for sale) so far at stores that total only 52 percent of total sales. (Note that 75 percent *ordered*, but the product hasn't arrived everywhere yet in this scenario.)

The last bullet says that, in fact, the product is in stock/in distribution in 65 percent of the *stores*. Hang on just 10 more seconds, and we will do some very quick math and see what is being said here.

Assume that there are 100 stores in the entire United States, and let's say what our three bullets are telling us: We know that 65 percent—therefore, 65 stores—actually *have* the product.

Those stores represent only 52 percent of the total sales in the country, so that means they are probably the smaller stores. (Note: If all stores were equal, 65 stores should produce 65 percent of sales volume.)

We know that a large group of stores have ordered the product, but we don't know how many. We just know that when you put together all the stores that have ordered so far, they generate 75 percent of all the sales in the country.

The key question when you hear *points of distribution* or just *distribution* being used is to clarify *what kind of distribution is being counted* because these are not the same measurements:

➤ 65 percent store distribution (store count = 65 percent of total stores)

➤ 65 percent department store (or drugstore or record store or office supplies store) distribution (volume count = stores selling 65 percent of total volume in that class of trade)

# Does Your Brand Belong Here?

Now that we have done all the heavy lifting of distribution, let's sit back and ask ourselves if we did all that work for the right outcome. You got my message already about wanting to put your product into the right points of contact—the right stores, so to speak. This cannot be emphasized enough.

I recently read a good article on this subject in *Forbes* magazine (May 2000), entitled "Luxe.com." The article talked about the luxury-goods Web site Ashford.com and a number of the premium-brand products that it sells, or wants to sell. In the article, you can read both the Web site's perspective on building a premium-brand image for itself, and the manufacturer's caution in making sure that its products will be treated appropriately. Neither side is cavalier. They see each other as vital elements of brand strategy. Ashford.com only wants to distribute the right brands, and the brands only want to be distributed in the right venues.

So, as brand champion, you need to look at each opportunity to put your product into a new distribution chain with questions like these:

➤ Will the point of contact provide a positive environment and image for my brand?

➤ Can the brand be maintained with integrity all through this distribution chain? If a fancy gourmet store doesn't have carefully controlled freezer space, your cocoa truffle ice cream bar won't taste good when it is bought, and the consumer may think that your brand isn't up to snuff.

➤ Considering how much intermediate handling may be required, will the final selling price for my brand make sense competitively?

We will talk extensively about the relationship between place and price in Chapter 18, "'What's the Price?' Has No Easy Answer."

# Prioritize Your Selling Opportunities

In addition to the image/positive environment issues surrounding where you decide to place your product, there are some other marketing and financial things to consider. The basic questions involve which products go where to maximize total value, and can we afford to be everywhere?

An announcement that I thought very smart was to sell Vapor and Reflex only on the Web. Who are they? Correction, *what* are they? The Volkswagen New Beetle, that friendly reminder of rainbows, daisies, and endless summers in the 1960s and 1970s, came back with a splash in time for the millennium celebrations. In May 2000, two new colors were added to the lineup: Vapor, a soft, light blue, and Reflex, a very bright yellow. What is so interesting about that? The only way you could get one of these cars was to order one on the Web. The cars would be "distributed" only on the

Web, meaning the point of contact in this case, because they were delivered into the real world.

Why does this make sense? The company has invested a lot in its Web site, allowing buyers to get a new kind of personal involvement with their purchase by tracking its movement through production and delivery. So that means you aren't just buying a car from them—they are making your car for you. Nice touch. Want more people to visit your Web site and get involved with your brand? Give them a reason—and why not create a terrific public relations opportunity while you are at it? Every newspaper will carry the story. Smart, very smart. See what I mean about distribution being a creative exercise?

**Talk the Talk**

When channels of distribution overlap too closely, it is called **channel conflict.** One channel feels threatened by the other; is the brand still fully committed to this channel? Expensive watches sell in exclusive department and jewelry stores. When they show up on the Internet, it is a new channel that can draw sales away. When they show up there at a lower price, it can start a war.

## Channel Conflict: You Need Good Manners and Good Sense

The car story and the Ashford.com story have a second issue wrapped up inside them. They represent recent examples of *channel conflict,* which has been around for a long time but is gaining steam because of the Internet.

Channel conflict comes up in the clothing business all the time. Think of the very popular Liz Claiborne brand of women's clothing. This brand is sold in department stores all over the country. In addition, the brand opened its own stores. Overstocks and end-of-season merchandise is found in discount stores all the time. And now you can walk into an outlet store operating under the brand name in many places. How do you suppose the department stores feel about all this competition, particularly the stores with the brand's own name on them? These are very sensitive issues, and for good reason.

What about someone who bought a franchise and two years later finds out that a "corporate store" is opening in the new mall five miles away. A corporate store is one operated by the owner of the entire franchise. Is it going to be any different than all the others? Maybe not, but maybe it will be. Maybe the product will be the same, and hopefully the pricing will be, too. But what if that store is used to test new promotion ideas that will be introduced to all the franchisees in the future? A higher level of promotion activity—and probably more exciting ideas—could seriously hurt the franchisee. It is bad enough his sales territory has been effectively cut just by opening this new store; now the company is going to make him look non-competitive.

What could be done? What good manners plus common-sense options could be identified in this situation? The franchise contract may spell out that it is absolutely legal for a corporate store to open anywhere the management wants, so forget about a lawsuit as the first line of defense. Does the franchisee deserve some type of compensation for lost sales? Where do you draw the lines on fair competition versus market manipulation? What is in the best interests of the brand? That last question needs to come up over and over again, and it should guide the decision-making process.

## Can You Afford to Play Here?

The question of whether you can afford to play in certain channels is a strategic question as well as a financial one. The easiest way to see the strategic question may be to turn it around into "Can we afford not to be here?" For many brick and mortar companies, that has been the driving question about whether they need a Web site. If they do create a Web site, what should it do for them? Remember back in Chapter 4, "E-Commerce Makes Branding Hotter Than Ever," we talked about what role the Internet should play? Should the Web site be informational (recipes, archives of magazine articles, government regulations) or transactional (sell shoes, insurance, or cosmetics)?

Similarly, if you own a clothing line, you do want someplace to get rid of your extra product at the end of each season. But you also want to protect your brand name and relationship with your stores. Can you strategically afford to let your overstocks go to the highest bidder?

There are two different financial aspects to whether you can afford to play in certain channels of distribution: Can you afford to get in, and can you afford to stay? They both may involve several different types of costs.

In some industries, there is a fee, which could be cash or its equivalent in free product, to get into distribution. The argument is that the customer taking in the product has costs to set it up in his systems and must set aside warehouse space (if applicable) to hold it. These fees may be fairly small or may run into tens of thousands of dollars per customer. If you cannot afford to pay all these fees, you will need to prioritize which customers are most important to you and go there first. As your budget permits, you then add other customers.

The critical question when choosing which customers to approach is whether you really believe your brand can prosper there. If the cost to get in

**Big Brand Insight**

Can your brand prosper in this environment? That can be a tough question to answer objectively when you are pushing to build your points of contact. To be excruciatingly clear, the question is meant to determine whether your brand can sell enough so that the customer is happy with his volume and profit and that you can make a decent level of profit yourself.

is low but the customer's expectations of how much advertising and promotional support you will provide is way out of line, is it really worth going there at all?

Once you are in the door, and you believe this is a good relationship for the brand, you face a more subtle issue, one that many people don't prepare for because they don't even see it coming. Do you have the technology and the systems to stay? That's right, are your computer systems and your customer service functions compatible with what the customer needs and demands? Many industries are pushing hard for computer-to-computer ordering, eliminating as much paper and human error as possible. Is this where your company is? Is this where your customers are?

Here's one more example of a cost that can be a killer. In the opening of this chapter, I mentioned the holiday shopping season of 1999, the first really big Internet shopping time. By definition, the online stores had computer-to-computer ordering, they had lots of product information and descriptions, many had great pricing and promotions, and the only thing they couldn't do was handle the orders and the deliveries. Oh, that's all? The "cost" of being ready to be in business all the way—not just selling the idea, but delivering it—is a structural cost that the jazziest of advertising slogans and the most charismatic of CEOs won't let you wiggle out of. You still need to deliver the goods.

Whatever your product, you should spend some good time thinking through your options in getting from here to there. Many types of products have multiple opportunities to choose from. You may not be able to afford to do them all, and frankly, probably shouldn't anyhow. As a brand champion, you need to identify the right places and the best ways to get your brand into your users' hands.

---

### The Least You Need to Know

➤ The process of distribution is often called the distribution chain.

➤ Three major links, or points, exist in the distribution chain: the point of disbursement, the point of contact, and the point of delivery.

➤ Your distribution strategy is the combination of how you will get your product to market, where it will be found by the end user, and which places make the most sense for the brand.

➤ From the brand's perspective, the most critical piece of distribution is getting the right points of contact. Making sure that the product is delivered properly and on time is becoming a very big issue with catalog and online sales.

# Chapter 17

# Who Is Your Competition? Are You Sure About That?

## In This Chapter

➤ Identifying a competitive set

➤ Using data to spot competitive opportunities

➤ Questioning to find hidden competitors

➤ Anticipating new competitors

This chapter may surprise a lot of you. I feel strongly that a deep understanding and a thorough, open-minded analysis of competition is one of the best general management disciplines around and one of the least appreciated. There is a myopia, a near-sightedness that afflicts a lot of us when we are busy building our businesses. We keep our noses to the grindstone day in and day out, and one of those days find ourselves staring at an "overnight sensation" that is stealing away our most valuable customers. It is insulting if this new kid on the block turns out to be your oldest competitor; it is terrifying when it turns out to be some "virtual" invader.

There is a real benefit to keeping an eye on your competition that is often overlooked. The more you understand what is out there in the marketplace, the easier it will be to look at opportunities for new products or new ways to refresh your brand's image. You can find advertising positionings and promotion partners and even acquisitions by doing your competitive homework. In this way, the discipline of really staying on top of the competition strengthens your strategic thinking.

A different and kind of frightening reason to keep your eyes open is to learn to spot competition before it sabotages your brand in ways that you are totally unprepared to battle. This has been the greatest lesson of the Internet revolution for traditional companies. Whether you are a bricks or a clicks business, or both, there are stealth bombers out there silently headed your way.

# Take Another Look at the Obvious and Always-Been-There Crowd

Some days it seems like all we do in business is worry about our competitors. Worse still, it seems like there is a new one every time we turn around.

You need to get a good handle on what and who you are really competing with. You need to understand this for the obvious reason, which is to know what other kinds of product values your target market is being offered, what promises these other brands make, and how they stack up on pricing next to your brand.

### Talk the Talk

**Competitive set** is the group of brands or product types that a user can choose among. Recognize that your brand can have different competitive sets in different distribution channels, and be sure that you look at each of them separately. A can of spray paint in a craft store may have very different competitors when it is in a large home and garden center.

You also want to know what else those competitors of yours *could* be up to. A good competitive analysis includes an examination of the existing brands in your *competitive set* and the companies that own them. Those companies represent a potential threat many times greater than what you know about today.

Why analyze the owners? If you had already sunk lots of money into people and systems and some sort of production facility (whether for widgets or insurance plans), you would probably be very interested in new products that could utilize a lot of that investment. That situation probably describes at least half, if not most all, of your major competitors.

Companies that have sunk investments like this want to generate as much productivity per dollar invested as possible. They have a built-in radar mechanism and a big motivation for spotting ways to spread the overhead costs across more products.

Look at it from the view of a manufactured product. One of the great ways to get more efficient usage out of a production line is to create a new item that requires only minimal *change parts* and *down time* to convert between one product and another. If the company has enough extra time on one or two production lines, it makes sense for it to actively look for new ideas to bring those lines up to efficient production capacities.

It is a similar story in a service-oriented company. Let's say that there's an information products company that aggregates and sells reports on some industry. The company realizes that once the very hard work of data collection is done, its massive computing power can spin out dozens of different reports, each a product. Each viable new product generates an income stream, much of which can be pure profit.

**Talk the Talk**

**Change parts** and **down time** are manufacturing terms. Think of a production line that ran only three days a week to produce the needed quantities. If it could be adapted to handle something similar, with just an hour or two of time to switch a few parts and clean it down, it could run another one or maybe even three days of production each week.

So, many of your existing competitors have a financial incentive to move into new areas, whether you do or not. And, the classic reason for them to seek new ideas is that they are a lot like you: They want to grab as much of the action as they can. Like you, their brand champions are pushing to make the company's brand and its products the most attractive to the purchasers.

Never assume that a sleepy competitor is out of the picture. You never know when a change in management will shake things up. And you never know when someone from your company may walk in and announce that he is defecting to the other side.

Give some serious thought to organizing a few brainstorming sessions with five or six different people from your company and maybe outsiders, such as a trusted ad agency or consultant. Each time, be sure that you draw people from different departments, with the goal being to finish these sentences for each of your top five competitors:

➤ "If I owned (name of competitor brand) I would work like crazy to make _____ happen."

➤ "If I owned (name of competitor company) I would want to protect _____."

➤ "If I had the _____ (facilities, such as plant or equipment; computer systems; 1,000 employees; offices in 12 countries) that (competitor) has, I would want to leverage them to _____." (This helps flush out what the people in your company see as the competitor's strengths at the same time.)

➤ "If I owned the brand equity that (competitor) has, you couldn't stop me from _____."

Now you are thinking like a strategist. You are also facing up to the fact that it is easier to understand the enemy you know, and it's a lot more painful to be trumped by him than by a total stranger. Now for my one caveat, painful and painfully true: You need to keep the outcome of these sessions highly confidential. As much as I am a proponent of collaboration and sharing, I have learned the hard way that a thorough report after a few of these sessions is virtually a business plan ready to go—right to the competitor. This is a serious ethical issue. It is also impossible to control once copies of a report are sent out.

# Now, Look Under Rocks, Behind Doors, and Inside Brains

We've got our usual list of suspects under the microscope now, and we will get much more insightful about anticipating what kind of threat they could be to us.

Understanding competition is often looked at as part of war maneuvers, or the military strategy side of business. It is important to understand who the competition is and what they are doing that could draw people away from your brand. But too often, business people are blindsided and end up feeling betrayed and under attack when unexpected competition "suddenly" shows up.

We just talked about learning to anticipate competition from the most likely sources, and that is certainly the first place to begin. But the world of business has changed so dramatically in the last decade that we need to develop new skills, more akin to being equipped with radar instead of a pair of binoculars.

I call these skills "smart sleuthing" because they really are detective work. They are highly intelligent and sophisticated detective work, at that.

Smart sleuthing needs to be part of every brand champion's skill set. Frankly, it can also be one of the most enjoyable parts of the job if you like and are comfortable with mental juggling or pieces-parts puzzles.

Bringing your competitive set to life, making them real brands and real threats coming from real smart people, is right in line with our whole philosophy of being a brand champion. When you see your own brand as alive, as vital, as needing guidance and discipline and creativity, it is much easier to see your entire business that way—yes, even the dreaded and the slow-footed of your competitors. They didn't get that way without human interaction. There is either a bunch of smart people steering the ship or the possibility of a revolt, with one captain walking the plank and another on his way to glory.

Let's work through five different facets of smart sleuthing, each of which involves asking questions and listening really hard for answers—and then thinking really hard to figure out what the answers really mean.

# Smart Sleuthing 1: Find the Source and Get the Facts

This is the easiest part of your smart sleuthing assignment. Between libraries, bookstores, telephone books, magazines, and now the Internet you can find numbers on almost anything.

The hardest part may well be identifying exactly what you really need to know and not getting lost along the way. I would suggest that you start the mission this way: Write down a simple goal statement and then 5 or 10 questions that are as clear as possible and are the minimum that you need to learn. What kind of a goal statement? Something like, "Identify the market size, major segments, and top five competitors in the golf club category."

Your questions would then include things such as these:

1. Who are the competitors?
2. What are the brand names they manufacture under?
3. What are the market shares by brand and total company?
4. How is the category segmented? For example, woods, irons, specialty items such as putters and sand wedges, graphite versus steel shaft. (If only I could hit straight, I would look like I actually understood this game.)
5. What are the growth trends of each segment?

Pull together a separate list of questions that would be great to find out but that won't ruin your day if they stay under wraps. Like what? Well, how about what percent of Titleist golf ball users are forecasted by some guru to defect to the Nike brand because Tiger Woods changed affiliation? This is only a forecast, but it is an interesting comment on the power of celebrity branding and will be something very interesting to watch over the next two years.

Do some searches through the online archives of major business publications looking for articles about your industry or competitors. You may pick up a lot of very good information that is sitting right there in the public domain for everyone to read. Often the best part is when you get statistics that come right out of a piece of research that somebody paid a half million dollars for, or when the CEO of your competitor is bragging about his expansion plans.

**Big Brand Insight**

Big brands often have big research budgets to go along with them. It is interesting, however, to see how much of the "news" on competitors or possible new product ideas comes in from the people in the company. The big research projects provide data that you can feel confident in using for projecting the size of a market or product. The people provide the emotional appeal of a market or product.

If you are looking at statistical data, you can work with it and feel as comfortable as any of us can that it is accurate. If you pick up things that are opinion (forecasts) or pomp and circumstance (the CEO's soapbox speech) just be sure you keep it in context. It may be a clue or a caveat instead of a conclusion.

# Smart Sleuthing 2: Ask the Industry and the Players

Sometimes we humans overlook the obvious things in life. It is another form of myopia. And, if you work in a department where constant interaction with your buying customers isn't part of the program, you can really lose touch with this little gem.

If you want to know what's going on, what your competition does better than you, and what is most likely to happen next, why don't you go talk to the people who spend their whole day thinking about that kind of thing? If your business is up and running already, then somebody has been buying your products. Unless you sell direct to the end user, you are going through some type of third-party *distributor,* and whether that is a retail store, a broker, or a clearinghouse, that distributor is in a good position to help you. And quite possibly, you have been sourcing some types of materials or services. That means you have got both distributors and suppliers, and if they work with you, they just might work with some of your competitors, too.

Here's a simple suggestion:

➤ To find out what the suppliers are seeing, start with whoever has responsibility for that relationship in your company. What do they hear? What suppliers are most tightly involved in the whole industry? Are they planning a visit with a good supplier anytime soon that you could sit in on?

➤ To find out what the distributors think, do the same thing. Someone in sales probably handles those relationships. Ask the same type of questions; try to get into the meeting.

**Heads Up**

We are using the term distributor here to mean the channel of distribution in general, not just companies who call themselves distributors or wholesalers. Refer back to Chapter 16, "Channels of Distribution: Getting from Here to There," for questions on the many different channels of distribution available.

Do you have an industry association of some type? Most do. Those folks are usually outstanding at pulling together research and task forces and customer share groups. Call up and make a new friend. Some of the best friendships I know came out of business beginnings, and I can personally attest to the dedication of a large number of these association people.

What is the bottom line? Get help figuring out what is going on around your brand. Lots of people are involved all along the way and can be very valuable.

# Smart Sleuthing 3: What Do the End Users Have to Say?

Are the people purchasing your product buying what you think they are? Say what? Are they purchasing a flood insurance policy or a security blanket? Are they buying a blood pressure pill or a good night's sleep? Are they buying a cemetery plot or less stress for their children and a better eternal view of the pond?

What business are you really in? Are you sure? Because if you're not, your customers are. And if you don't understand just what it is they are buying, you have absolutely no idea who your competition really is. And this is how companies get blindsided.

You have to know the "reason why," the motivation for people to buy this kind of product. And that means you need to listen and read and watch with exquisite skill and grace.

A few months ago, my college-age nephew told me about a marketing project he had just finished for school. The assignment was to develop a marketing communications campaign for a racetrack. The work required writing radio, television, and billboard advertising. As complicated as that sounds, the hardest part was figuring out what to say about a racetrack that would make the fictitious new owner happy. In the case study, the owner wanted a classier image and felt sure that he could bring in a nicer group of people than in the past.

We hear what the owner wants, but how do consumers look at a racetrack? Is it a gambling place, a spectator sport with cocktails, a relatively "safe" place to go slumming? What could it be? What "categories" could it fit into? In the end, the nephew chose to position the racetrack as exciting entertainment and a different, out-of-the-ordinary, and very nice Saturday night option. He targeted couples who want a nice dinner and some fun entertainment. Too bad it was only a class project. It would have been fun to see how it worked.

In the real world, decisions like this need to be made all the time. Those people who actually use products like yours are chock full of opinions and ideas, and, boy, do they like to tell companies what to do. So, why don't you let them?

Can you figure out some type of forum where real users are able to tell you what they want and think and wish they could find? One technique used very often is a focus group of about 10 people with a professional moderator to guide the conversation.

I have been in hundreds of focus groups as a listener or as the moderator. This is the moderator in me speaking: Please do not waste everybody's time and money doing the same old boring, tightly constrained, repetitive nonsense I see too often. Use a professional if you can possibly afford it, and find one who wants to really get people talking, not answering the same 20 questions. Then listen hard for the message. It takes more attentiveness from you, but it is worth it.

If you cannot afford your own focus groups, what about approaching your industry association to see if it might want to share the cost with you so that it can learn, too? What about looking for another brand in your company to share the cost and the attention. A lot of times, it is quite easy to talk about two different products with the same group of people.

**Heads Up**

Okay, what are these five bullets really all about? These are possible value statements that would fall under the "Change My Life!" column in the discussion on brand profiles in Chapter 14, "What Is a Brand Profile?"

So, back to where we started this discussion. If you sell blood pressure medicine, you might really be in all kinds of businesses:

➤ The peace-of-mind business

➤ The medical-miracles business

➤ The I-am-a-proactive-consumer business

➤ The forever-young business

➤ The death-don't-darken-my-door business

If you worked at a pharmaceutical company, what would you do with such conflicting inputs? You would tailor your advertising message. You would align yourself with marketing partners that play up these aspects of your business. You would choose what magazines and Web sites to advertise on. You would set up your own Web site to let consumers pick their own version of the story, clicking their merry way to what they want to hear.

That last one is a beauty isn't it? Be sure you read about self-targeting in Chapter 15, "Target Market Analysis: More Critical Now Than Ever." It is a brave new world out there.

## Smart Sleuthing 4: What Do They Say and What Do They Do?

Who is the "they" I am referring to? It is your competitive brands, the distributors that you use, and the end users of your product. And for all of them, you need to separate what they say and what they do if you want to see the whole picture.

Remember back in Chapter 16 on target market analysis, when we looked at transactional databases, where actual purchases are captured? The great power and opportunity of those databases lies in the picture that they give us of actual behavior. People say lots of things, and quite often they mean what they say. But there can be a world of difference between what people say and what they do.

As an example, the director of marketing from your biggest competitor confides to you over drinks after a trade show that he is disgusted with his company for not putting any emphasis on new product development. In fact, he is thinking of leaving to find a more aggressive place to work.

➤ Wow, great input. Send an e-mail message and follow up with a voicemail right away to the President, all the VPs, and the head of R&D at your company. This competitor is toast when you launch those new widgets.

➤ Yeah, right. So how come the CEO of his company is over in the corner slapping the back of that big new products consultant hired two months ago? And by the way, this turkey has dribbled his cosmopolitan martini on your new shoes.

Or, you finally get in to see Lucille, the VP of purchasing at your biggest distributor. The meeting goes great. This lady really knows her stuff and is very open about what she sees happening in the industry. She encourages you to look at some new technology and gives you a discreet—and ethical—heads-up on some things that just *might* be in the works. You two are going to be friends, you can see it happening. You each share thoughtful criticism of your own organization's struggles and a vision for a different future.

➤ Get the IT (that's information technology) guys on the horn right away. Lucille says this new whatsis is where the leaders in the industry are all migrating. We need to migrate there, too, and, furthermore, we need to go there. (Yes, I really did write it that way.) One more thing—send Lucille a huge basket of flowers as a thank you.

➤ Or, Lucille never gets the flowers. Lucille shows up in your office the next Monday morning. Lucille is your new boss. Lucille now knows that you tell outsiders the company's business.

I could go on, but then again, you get the idea. Listen to what they say and then match it up with what they do. Remember, Americans are always on a diet, but we always order dessert. We spend millions on health clubs but think that the dumbbell is the guy next door.

# Smart Sleuthing 5: Where Are the Stealth Bombers Lurking?

They're out there. Silent. Invisible to your radar. Maybe.

They could be competitive companies or new technologies. They could be from around the corner or around the world. In some brand management organizations, the stealth bomber could be sitting next to you, going out to lunch with the president to quietly update him on New Improved Whizbang, which will render good old

Whizbang, your pride and joy, totally obsolete. Don't worry. As soon as you clean up all the odds and ends, there will be another job for you somewhere in the organization. Maybe.

If you had to guess, what or who are the five most frightening competitive possibilities on the horizon? Think hard. Ask questions just like that all over the company. And don't fall into the trap of just thinking about new products.

➤ What if a business process changed?

➤ What if two of your competitors merged?

➤ What if one of your competitors merged with a technology company?

➤ What if the majority of people grew to trust Internet transactions within the next three years?

➤ What if your two biggest distributors merged? Or what if these were your two biggest suppliers?

One of the great business sayings that I have heard repeated endlessly this last year is attributed to Andy Grove, the CEO of Intel, Corp.: Only the paranoid survive.

---

### The Least You Need to Know

➤ Your competitors may have even stronger reasons to launch new products than you do, and they may be aggressively pursuing ways to leverage investments that they have already made.

➤ Smart sleuthing is a five-step plan to learn more about your competition. It involves rounding up factual data, talking with industry insiders, listening to end users, watching for differences in what people say and do, and keeping your eyes open for brand new competitors.

➤ Encourage associates throughout the company to send in magazine and newspaper articles, direct mail inserts, and notes about television, radio, or Web site mentions about your competitors.

➤ A thorough, open-minded analysis of the competition is one of the best general management disciplines.

# Chapter 18

# "What's the Price?" Has No Easy Answer

---

## In This Chapter

➤ Calculating gross margin and markup

➤ Targeting your everyday selling price

➤ Figuring discount structures and feature prices

➤ Price promotions that support your brand goals

---

This chapter is the longest in the book, but I don't want you to skip it. Just know up-front that the two best ways to use this chapter are to have a calculator and some paper at hand, and to take your time, coming back to it at different points until it all makes sense. Probably no other element of brand management has caused more anxiety and arguments than setting price structures. If you work in a company where sales, marketing, and finance are all different people, you can count on confusion, frustration, and disagreements until each of you understands where the others are coming from and what calculations you are using. It is worth learning.

Pricing can go through just one stage or many stages and changes, so it is critical to understand, whether you sell direct to the end user or through a reseller of some kind, such as a store, a Web site, an agent or a distributor. Most importantly, your pricing absolutely must be consistent with the promises of value that you choose for your brand. Just quickly imagine trying to convince consumers that a super-premium, organic, hand-sliced, only-top-grade corn chip is really all that special if it sells for only $.59 a bag. The price and the promise are out of sync.

We will look at how our original pricing decisions impact the final selling price and the implications that they have when we offer discounts and incentives to sell more product. Why worry so much about all this? After all, if your product is good, it will sell, right? No, not really. It may get into distribution, but you may be in for a rude shock when you see the final price set for it. And worse still, you may be astonished when you are told that your re-sellers are discontinuing your wonderful product after only four or five months because it "just isn't selling." It can happen to you as it has to too many others.

# Understand Gross Margin vs. Markup Once and for All

*Markup* and *margin* are completely different things. You would be amazed how many educated people still don't know the real difference between these two pricing systems and how to calculate each of them. We are going to change that for you in this chapter.

**Talk the Talk**

**Markup** is simply a *percentage added on* to the cost of the product. A $1.00 product marked up 50 percent is then $1.50. **Margin** is the *penny difference* between the two prices. The same $1 product, sold for $1.50 generates $.50 in margin. The confusion comes when this penny margin is expressed as a percentage. Let's hold that part for later.

Margin is what you need to be focused on. Margin, the money generated by selling something, is what you need to support and grow your business. This needs to be tattooed, embossed, or somehow emblazoned onto your memory forevermore.

Here is part of the confusion: Both markup and margin are usually expressed as percentages. Both of them loosely refer to the difference in dollars and cents between what the product costs you and what you charge for it. Markup is a casual "rule of thumb" figure. Margin is the actual number used in calculating profit and loss. So, when you hear markup being used, just know that it is not a number that is likely to show up in the annual report. And, as a businessperson, you need to stay focused on margin.

To see the difference, let's talk about a jar of peanut butter that we manufacture. Let's say that we sell it for $1 a jar and have been told that "the store takes another 25 percent." What will the store sell it for— $1.25, $1.33, or $1.45?

The right answer? Well, that depends on just what it is the store "takes." If the store takes a 25 percent *markup*, the answer is $1.25. If the store takes a 25 percent *margin*, the answer is $1.33.

Is 8¢ really important enough for me to be making such a big case out of this? Yes, it is, and here are two reasons why:

➤ You need to understand where your product will be priced relative to competition. If you do the math wrong, you could end up way out of line.

➤ When you are presenting your product, most buyers will ask you what retail/resale price you think is right and what kind of margins they can expect. How bad do you look if you crisply answer these questions, buyers check your math and then tell you to get out of the office because you clearly don't know anything about the business if you don't know markup from margin?

Before you read any further, you need to understand the differences between the *original selling price,* the *resale price,* and the *retail* or *final* price.

Assume that you make it through the sales pitch to the buyer for a group of small convenience stores. The stores don't have much warehouse space, so they get their product from a wholesaler or distributor, who holds the product for them. You sell your peanut butter for $1 a jar to the wholesaler, who then resells it to the stores. Watch what happens to the final retail price when you think everyone is taking a markup and instead they all look at margins. We will review the formulas to do these calculations in just a few minutes:

> **Talk the Talk**
>
> The **original selling price** is the price you charge for your product. It may be expressed per unit, case, ton, yard, hour, or gigabyte, whatever is appropriate to your business. The **resale price** is the price at which your product is sold to another company in the distribution chain. The **retail/final price** is the price at which the product is sold to the end user.

| | Original Price | *plus* | Resale Price | *plus* | Retail Price |
|---|---|---|---|---|---|
| 30% markup | $1.00 | $.30 | $1.30 | $.39 | $1.69 |
| 30% margin | $1.00 | $.43 | $1.43 | $.61 | $2.04 |

What if this happened to you? You knew that the most popular peanut butters were selling in convenience stores at around $1.59 and, using your markup calculations, felt like you were close enough with $1.69. You proudly walk into the store to admire how good your product looks and see your brand way out of line at $2.04. I can tell you that in the convenience store business, being 45 cents higher than the competition, which is a 28 percent premium, can be a really big deal.

Find out if markup is commonly used in your industry. If it is, you will need to keep both concepts in your head. Most people work with margins. When in doubt, always use margin calculations. It is the more professional and universal tool.

## When to Use What: Markup and Margin

Let's look at markup first, and you will see why it is more a rule-of-thumb figure. Think of markup as answering the question, "About how much more could we sell it for?" The clothing and furniture industries use the term markup regularly. It is also common to hear markup used when discussing wine prices in a restaurant, You may hear that furniture, clothing, and restaurant wines are usually marked up 200 percent to 250 percent.

In the case of wine, the comparison is between two different retail establishments: what you would pay in the liquor store near home versus in a restaurant. You can expect to pay 2 to 2.5 times more for the same bottle of wine in a restaurant than in a retail liquor store. It does not mean that the restaurant is making a 200 to 250 percent profit, as we will see later. In furniture and clothing, the reference is to the difference between wholesale prices (what the storeowner pays) and retail prices (what the consumer pays). The term *markup* is more often used between people within an industry than as a hard-and-fast financial measurement.

The formula for calculating markup is just the base price multiplied by the percent markup. So, a bottle of wine that costs $12 in a liquor store would be marked up 250 percent in a restaurant: (Note: Markup is always written as a percentage.)

Base price × Mark-up percent = New price

$12.00 × 2.50 = $30

To clarify, using just these three numbers we can look at the "profit" on this bottle of wine that just got marked up 250 percent:

| | |
|---|---|
| Selling price | $30.00 |
| Cost | −12.00 |
| Profit | $18.00 |
| Profit % | 60.0% |

Be careful assuming that markup and profit are the same thing. By the way, the $18.00 isn't really profit, it is margin, which we are about to discuss.

Margin, on the other hand, is short for contribution margin and is a very important number for every businessperson to understand. Think of contribution margin as answering the question, "How much do I have to sell this for if it costs me this much?"

## Margin Is the Way to Go

Let's start at the beginning. Contribution margin is the difference between your selling price and your cost. So, a jar of peanut butter that you sell for $1 and that costs you $.30 to make will have a contribution margin of $.70, or 70 percent. Easy enough. The reason I am putting so much emphasis on it here is that as the brand manager, you are the one who needs to decide that $1 or some other number is *the right selling price.* You need to understand *how much margin you need* and what happens to that margin.

Contribution margin becomes extremely important because whatever amount you have in there is all the budget you have to work with for advertising, promotion, marketing research, new product testing, and, hopefully, profit. Everything sold by your company must carry some contribution margin on top of the cost to produce the product, and it isn't as simple as tacking on a profit number that sounds good. You also need to anticipate that each company that buys and resells your product has expenses also, and they will be factored into the final selling price.

Let's stop here and take a look at the Peanut Butter Simplified P&L/Profit and Loss Statement here. We will make four assumptions:

➤ We will sell 100,000 jars of peanut butter.

➤ Each jar will cost us $.30. This is the cost of goods, or COG, for short.

➤ The competition all sells to the chain stores and wholesalers between $.90 and $1.10. The leading brand sells for $.95.

➤ To be successful in the long term, we believe that we need at least $60,000 a year for advertising, promotion, and other expenses.

Here is the challenge: Which of these selling prices would you recommend, and what level of contribution margin, or CM, for short, would you then have?

## Peanut Butter Simplified P&L

| Measurement | Formula | Option 1 | Option 2 | Option 3 | Option 4 |
|---|---|---|---|---|---|
| Selling price | | $.90 | $.95 | $1.00 | $1.05 |
| Units sold | | 100,000 | 100,000 | 100,000 | 100,000 |
| Total sales | Price × units | $90,000 | $95,000 | $100,000 | $105,000 |
| Cost of goods @ $.30/unit | Units × $.30 | $30,000 | $30,000 | $30,000 | $30,000 |
| Contribution margin $ | Sales – Cost of goods | $60,000 | $65,000 | $70,000 | $75,000 |
| Contribution margin % | Contribution Margin ÷ Total sales | 66.7% | 68.4% | 70.0% | 71.4% |
| Expenses projected | | $60,000 | $60,000 | $60,000 | $60,000 |
| Profit | Contribution Margin – Expenses | $0 | $5,000 | $10,000 | $15,000 |

Looking at this table, let's do five things:

1. Choose at least one of the options, follow down the column, and do the calculations yourself to make sure that you know how the numbers were derived.

2. Look at how different the profit numbers are by making 5¢ increments in pricing.

3. Think about your competitive situation. Which prices do you think could work?

4. Do you really need $60,000 for expenses or can you cut back?

5. What combination of price, expenses, and profit would you choose if this were your brand?

Stop and think about how important the contribution margin dollars and percentage lines are to your entire operation. This is the way to think about pricing from now on: Good pricing creates margin, and margin builds businesses.

You need some quick formulas. First I want to give you what I think of as the Master Formula. This simple formula has saved me on many, many occasions, and I strongly advise that you memorize it, post it over your desk, and put it on a sticker on the back of your calculator.

**The Master Formula:**

>  (Selling price – Cost) ÷ Selling price = Margin

Notice that there are three different elements in this formula: selling price, cost, and margin. You will need to be able to find any one of the three at different times, so we will end up with three different formulas in total. Remember sixth-grade math? Remember how they taught you to "solve for" the different elements in the equation? Well, lots of other smart people don't remember any of those details either, so all three formulas are written here.

If you want a quick formula to calculate what the margin will be on any item *when you know the selling price and the cost,* use the Master Formula.

**How to Find (Solve for) the Margin:**

Try it yourself with peanut butter selling for $1 and costing $.30:

>  ($1.00 – $.30) ÷ $1.00 = .7 = 70%

As a brand manager, you need to go one step higher with the mathematical formulas. You need to know how to take this basic formula and, just like in sixth grade, pull it apart to solve for other variables. Sound vaguely familiar? Why am I making you do this? Because you need to be able to figure out what selling prices would result from various margin requirements. What would you do if someone asked you to price the peanut butter at a 78 percent margin? Suddenly the formula we just looked at doesn't solve the problem. It has all the right components, but you don't remember how to turn it around to make it work. You need to remember one very small detail from sixth grade: The inverse of a fractional number is the amount that you would have to add onto it to equal 1. So, the inverse of .25 is .75; the inverse of .30 is .70.

**How to Find the Selling Price:**

Cost ÷ Inverse of margin desired = Selling price

Try it yourself with peanut butter at a 70 percent and a 78 percent margin. Remember, the inverse of .70 is .30, and of .78 is .22, so here goes:

$.30 ÷ .30 = $1.00

$.30 ÷ .22 = $1.38 Higher margins = higher prices

**How to Find the Cost:**

Selling price × Inverse of margin = Cost

Try it again for peanut butter:

$1.38 × .22 = $.30

Note: In this case, you must multiply, not divide.

## Making It Easier on You

I know that all this inverse stuff, and when to multiply versus divide takes some getting used to. Make your life much easier.

➤ Memorize the Master Formula.

➤ Write all three formulas on a sign over your desk or a sticker on the back of your calculator.

➤ If all you can remember is the Master Formula, simply use a dummy example to figure out the other two. Think of it this way: If I sold something for $1 that cost me $.75, what margin am I getting? Just plug in the two numbers you know, find the third, and voila—you have a way to figure out all three equations because you now know the selling price is $1, the cost is $.75 and the margin is 25 percent, right?

$1.00 – $.75 ÷ $1.00 = 25%

From this point on, we will talk only about margins—yours and those of any resellers in your distribution chain.

# Price Points: Targeting Your Everyday Pricing

Now we are ready to decide on your pricing levels, which set the stage for your competitive positioning and play an enormous role in how you structure promotional offers. Your pricing needs to be consistent with the key elements of your brand profile, so this is a very important step. We will work through a five-step pricing process to look at everyday pricing first and then to identify opportunities or pitfalls for special deals and discounts.

You need to make two starting decisions:

➤ Where would you like your price to fit relative to your competition? Will you be the lowest-priced? Do you want, and can you support, a premium product/ premium price strategy? Do you just want to be competitive within a reasonable range around the midpoint?

➤ Will your product be sold directly to the end user or go through some kind of reseller (retail store, Web site, or original equipment manufacturing [OEM] for example)?

If you sell direct, you need to go through only one stage of pricing analysis. If you sell through another company, you need to project the final price that the end user will see.

Let's talk about the kind of pricing decisions that you will need to make and then use our margin calculations to analyze your options. We will work on setting our *everyday price* first and will go through three steps:

1. Look at the competitive pricing situation and the margin requirements of your resellers (if applicable).

2. Calculate a range of pricing options to choose from.

3. Check that your favorite price is consistent with your brand positioning.

Then we will take that pricing and, using steps 4 and 5, look down the road:

4. Create a *promotional price* and simple, price-based promotion proposal for your buyer that opens a conversation on what options you have.

5. Make price-based promotions fit different strategies.

**Talk the Talk**

The **everyday price** is just what it sounds like, the price that your product sells for most every day. The **promotional price** is a "special" providing extra value through a bonus or discount.

Most products and many services have both an everyday price and a promotional price. Sometimes the promotional price is just that, an obviously different price for the same product. The peanut butter that usually sells for $1.49 is on sale this week for $1.09. At other times, promotions are structured so that the price of the item or service is not the center of attention, but instead some other aspect of value is being communicated. Say what?

Look at these examples of things you see all the time:

➤ Peanut butter may have a bonus pack of 12 ounces for the regular price of 10 ounces. The price on the jar is the usual 10-ounce price, but in fact this is a 20 percent discount because you get an extra 20 percent more product.

➤ Cellular and digital telephone services may offer one free month of base service when you sign a one-year contract. This is the same as a $\frac{1}{12}$, or 8.3 percent discount.

➤ Restaurants send out coupons for $5 off on their famous $15 steak dinner. This is a 33 percent discount on that dinner, although you will need to buy another dinner at full price to qualify. Assuming that the second dinner was the same price, you now have a 16.5 percent discount on your total dinner bill.

Before you can get creative with promotional offers like these, and we will discuss each of them later in this chapter, you need to establish your own everyday price for every product that you sell.

Let's do the three steps to establish your everyday selling price.

## Step 1: Competitive Pricing and Margin Requirements

You need to work through some basic questions to assess the right selling price for your products. First, let's look at the prices of competitive products/services. You will need to look at their final pricing and, if applicable, any unit pricing comparisons that a buyer might make.

For instance, the prices on Brand A peanut butter, sold in small, medium, and large sizes, might be $1.19, $1.49, and $1.89. You need these numbers and also a cost-per-ounce comparison. If you sell laser printer paper, you need to analyze pricing for 1 ream, 5-ream mini-cases, and full cases of 10 reams. You would also have to look at paper weight (20 lb. vs. 24 lb.) and brightness (86 vs. 90).

Which characteristics do you need to analyze? To find out, just answer this question: When consumers shop for (your product type), what information do they check to decide which is the best product for them? Now write those characteristics in the spaces here, and then rank order them for importance, with number 1 the most important:

_____    _____

_____    _____

_____     _____
_____     _____
_____     _____

Now, let's look at the competitive pricing analysis formats here. You can easily customize them for your own business.

1. List your competitors by brand.

2. Insert a description of some type, such as the model number or size (something to identify the exact item you are analyzing and to differentiate between similar items under the same brand name).

3. Insert the price for that item.

4. Use another one to three columns to identify specific characteristics from the previous list and to calculate the "cost per." In this example, I am using peanut butter and showing the price for each jar size and a cost per ounce.

5. Consider creating a master list like the one that follows so that you have a good overview of the competition. Then sort it, like the second one, to look at specific issues.

## Competitive Pricing Analysis—Master List

| Brand | Description | Price | Per Ounce |
|-------|-------------|-------|-----------|
| Brand A | 8 oz. chunky | $1.19 | $.149 |
| | 8 oz. smooth | $1.19 | $.149 |
| | 12 oz. chunky | $1.49 | $.124 |
| | 16 oz. chunky | $1.89 | $.118 |
| Brand B | 8 oz. smooth | $1.25 | $.156 |
| My Brand | 8 oz. smooth | | |

## Competitive Pricing Analysis—by Size

| Size | Brand | Price | Per Ounce |
|------|-------|-------|-----------|
| 8 ounces | Brand A | $1.19 | $.149 |
| | Brand B | $1.25 | $.156 |
| | Brand C | $1.29 | $.161 |
| | My brand | | |
| 12 ounces | Brand A | $1.49 | $.124 |
| | Brand B | $1.55 | $.129 |
| | Brand C | $1.61 | $.134 |

When you have the information collected, you may want to see it visually. Simply draw a line, mark it proportionately, and write in where various brands fall in pricing. You can do this on a general basis, noting where brands are relative to one another, or specifically on a size or count basis. For instance:

*Brands relative to one another (basis: 12 oz. size by brand).*

The last piece of this step is for those of you who will sell through some type of re-seller. You need to identify two things:

➤ Once your product is sold by you, how many more times is it likely to be resold?

➤ What margin requirements does each reseller require? Note: These may not all be the same.

Create a simple chart like this to capture the reseller information, inserting the correct names and margin requirements for each reseller in the chain. This one says: We sell to a wholesaler, who takes a 10 percent margin and then sells to a retailer who takes a 25 percent margin.

*Capture reseller information.*

## Step 2: Identifying Your Pricing Options

Before we go on, let's do one small but important brain-shift. We have been talking about what your selling price is so far. Now we need to turn around and, as obvious as it sounds, think about *your selling price* as *your customer's cost*. If you sell direct to the end user, that's all there is to it. However, if your product is handled through a re-seller, there will be a new selling price that factors in what the reseller paid you for it and what his costs are to handle it.

Let's take our different pricing options and project them forward using the chart that follows, "Estimating Final Selling Price." Why do I call it "estimating"? Because, unless you sell direct to the end user, you cannot control the final selling price that a reseller will charge.

➤ Take one pricing option at a time.

➤ Write in the margin requirements of the first reseller.

➤ Using the formula for finding the selling price, calculate what the first reseller will likely resell it for, and put that in the third column, marked "Resale Price." Reminder: That formula is: Cost/Inverse of margin = Selling price.

➤ If applicable, repeat this step for second or third resellers, using their specific margin requirements each time.

➤ Go back and fill in the exact amount of margin dollars that each reseller is getting to sell to support your product. While you don't necessarily need to ever know this number, it is smart to understand how much or how little your business contributes to the financial health of your resellers.

### Estimating Final Selling Price

Assumptions: First reseller requires a 10 percent margin; second requires 25 percent.

| Starting Price | Reseller A 10% Margin | Resale Price | Reseller B 25% Margin | Final Price |
|---|---|---|---|---|
| $ .90 | $ | $1.00 | $ | $1.33 |
| $ .95 | $ | $1.05 | $ | $1.40 |
| $1.00 | $ | $1.11 | $ | $1.48 |
| $1.05 | $ | $1.17 | $ | $1.56 |

You are ready to look hard at where your products will fit competitively. Go back to the "Competitive Pricing Analysis" charts that you created earlier, and see where each of the final prices that you calculated would fit. You are almost ready to choose your selling price.

## Step 3: Are Price and Positioning Consistent?

In Chapter 6, "Brand Champion—Your Toughest and Most Important Role," we talked about the importance of being a brand champion and said that your focus must always be on building and defending your brand. Central to that challenge is making sure that any decisions on how the business will run must be consistent with the core benefits and positioning of the brand. That means always asking two critical questions:

➤ Is this in the best interests of the brand?

➤ Does this decision make sense with what we say the brand is all about?

Earlier in this chapter, I referenced the idea of creating a super-premium corn chip product but then pricing it at a bargain-basement $.59. The positioning, or promise, is all about a carefully prepared product and the best ingredients. The price is all about being cheap. They don't make sense together.

To check for positioning and pricing consistency, ask yourself these questions:

1. What are the two most important promises/benefits of my product?

2. Where do the competitors stand on those promises?

3. Do those promises really warrant any price premium over the competition? Do these qualities actually cost more to produce? Is it believable to the end user that they would cost more?

4. Have any competitors been able to successfully price themselves above the norm? If so, what are they promising?

5. How much choice do I have, given my costs to produce and sell this product? If it is expensive to make, can I cut any other expenses so that I will not need to take as big a margin?

# Trade Deals and Discounts

Most industries use some type of discounting structure to encourage bigger or more frequent purchases. Car manufacturers advertise rebates and low-interest-rate loans. Phone companies offer 5¢ a minute on weekends, and grocery stores advertise Thanksgiving turkeys at 69¢, or even 49¢ a pound to get you to do your whole holiday shopping with them.

These discounts are all part of a promotion plan. Because of its importance, we talk about promotion in a number of places in this book. In this chapter, we focus on the pricing side of promotion. This section emphasizes the hardest part of the game: working through a reseller to get what you want and need for your brand. Because you cannot directly control their final selling price, you need to structure your promotion to work smoothly into the reseller's policies and preferences. If you sell direct to the end user, you may want to skip ahead one section to "Feature Pricing and Special Deals—What Are Your Options?" There, we talk more about the strategy of using price promotions.

## *Step 4: Creating a Price-Based Promotion Proposal*

Let's start with some information gathering about what your resellers do to generate increased sales:

1. How do they communicate a special offer: newspaper, television, package inserts, direct mail, newsletter, flyers on windshields, radio, Web site banner ads, and so on.

2. How do they structure the special value: lower price, multiple purchase pricing (two-month membership for $25.00), 20 percent off, BOGO (buy one get one free)?

3. How long does a promotion usually last? This is actually a trick question. You need to know two things:

> ➤ How long do you need to make a promotional price available to the re-seller?

> ➤ How long does the promotion last for the end user?

A good example is a mass merchandiser or drug store where feature items are advertised for one week, but you need to make the price available for perhaps four weeks. Why the discrepancy? The reseller needs to buy in advance of the sale week to have inventory on hand and then wants to replenish his stock at that good price.

4. What is the reseller's promotional philosophy? This may be the toughest one for you to answer, but it is the most important. Don't hesitate to call and ask that question. Most people will be delighted that you want to understand it when you tell them that your goal is to structure promotions that will work hard for them.

Now, using our peanut butter example, let's create a promotional pricing proposal structure that addresses the needs of the resellers in this scenario (grocery stores, convenience stores, and mass merchandisers) and will be very similar for many other industries. We will use these guidelines:

➤ This will be a 12-ounce size promotion; the selling price is $1/jar; and we can afford only a 15 percent discount.

➤ The product is sold in cases of 12 jars, so the case price is $12.

➤ We are selling directly to the retailer, who will require a 30 percent margin to then sell it to the consumer/end user.

Here's the math and a simple format for you to adapt to your needs. Note that the format I am giving you handles a number of issues simultaneously:

➤ Identifies the exact products being discounted.

➤ Specifies a limited time period for the special pricing.

➤ Puts the everyday buying terms of a 2 percent discount for quick payment right on the page.

➤ Shows both unit and case pricing side by side because that is what the buyer will need to do. In this situation, he buys in cases but sells in units.

➤ Shows both dollars and percentages.

➤ Recommends a feature price for the reseller to consider.

*Promotional pricing proposal.*

*Product:* My Brand Peanut Butter, 12-ounce size only, Smooth and Chunky
*UPC numbers:* (or model numbers or other identifier in the reseller's computer system)
*Case pack:* 12/12 oz. glass jars
*Promotional purchase dates:* All purchase orders received between January 1, 2000, through January 31, 2000, calling for delivery by February 15, 2000.
*Terms:* 2%30/net31

|  | Unit | Percent | Case | Percent |
|---|---|---|---|---|
| Regular Retail | $1.43 |  | $17.16 |  |
| Regular Cost | $1.00 |  | $12.00 |  |
| Regular Margin % | $ .43 | 30.0% | $ 5.16 | 30.0% |
|  |  |  |  |  |
| Promo Discount | $ .15 | 15.0% | $ 1.80 | 15.0% |
| Promo Net Cost | $ .85 |  | $10.20 |  |

*Feature price optons:*

|  | Unit | Percent | Case | Percent |
|---|---|---|---|---|
| a. Hold margin | $1.21 | 30.0% | $14.52 | 30.0% |
| b. Margin reduction | $1.19 | 28.5% | $14.28 | 28.5% |
| c. Margin reduction | $1.09 | 22.0% | $13.08 | 22.0% |

*Recommendation:*
Feature My Brand Peanut Butter 12-ounce Smooth and Chunky @ $1.19 week of January 16, 2000, generating 28.5% margin.

All we had to do is show the regular pricing and margins, the exact amount of the discount offered, and the promotional selling prices that should be considered. I included three promotional prices for the buyer to look at:

➤ The promotional price that would result from holding the margin. This is a good reference point, and often it is not a particularly enticing number because it is odd-looking.

➤ The nearest more attractive price (sales items often have promo prices ending in 9—for example, $.99, 1.49, and so on).

➤ One more step lower to see if the buyer will consider dropping his margin to potentially sell more product or have a more enticing price point for his ad. You never know what you can get unless you ask, and a creative suggestion such as one offered by the accompanying "Big Brand Insight" sidebar just might make it feasible to recommend and get the better pricing for your brand.

# Feature Pricing and Special Deals—What Are Your Options?

You have a lot of options when it comes to structuring special deals. It all comes back to being true to your brand profile, choosing those strategies that are consistent with what the brand is all about, and costing out each promotion idea that you have. Back in the section called "Price Points: Targeting Your Everyday Pricing," I gave four different examples of promotional pricing. Each of these is a different way of offering a pricing incentive to the end user. Let's review each of them to give you some ideas for promotion offers that you might use.

1. **Peanut butter bonus pack: 12 ounces for the regular price of 10 ounces.** The price on the jar is the usual 10-ounce price, but in fact this is a 20 percent discount because you get an extra 20 percent more product.

   ➤ Giving away a real product has a known value that is immediately obvious to the purchaser, and bonus offers create incentives to purchase without tinkering with your price perception.

   ➤ Bonus offers are a good way to load up your consumer if a new competitor is in the market. They may not try the new brand if they have enough of your product on hand to last a while.

2. **Cellular and digital telephone services offering one free month of base service when you sign a one-year contract.** This is the same as a $1/12$, or 8.3 percent discount.

   ➤ This is a classic loyalty technique. The phone company now has you signed up for a full year, which is very valuable to the company in terms of cash flow.

   ➤ Your costs are the lost revenue for a free month for everyone who takes the promotion. Assume that the monthly fee is $25. You may be charged the full $25, or your company may choose to charge back only the actual cost to provide one month of service, without overheads or profits attached to it. This is a company policy issue.

3. **Restaurant coupons for $5 off a $15 steak dinner.** This is a 33 percent discount on that dinner, although you will need to buy another dinner at full price to qualify. Assuming that the second dinner was the same price, you now have a 16.5 percent discount on your dinner bill.

   ➤ This is a classic transaction-builder technique. By requiring that two dinners be purchased, the total revenue value of feeding you has been raised, and the bottom line impact of a high-value offer has been lessened. Again, the value is easy and obvious to see.

   ➤ Look at doing this versus putting the steak dinner on sale for $10. This way, the restaurant ensures a larger total dinner spend and eliminates turning this into a 33 percent discount with a single diner at a table.

## Step 5: Make Your Promotion Match Your Strategy

Choosing how you promote your product can be very creative and lots of fun. Choosing the right way to use price to promote it requires a steady hand and a cool head. I encourage you to brainstorm regularly for promotion ideas that are unique and interesting, that add lots of extra value, and that stretch your budget. However, when pricing becomes one of the tools you will use, you need to go back to the brand champion's key question: What is in the best interests of the brand?

A promotion that is fun to execute or that makes your resellers deliriously happy may not be the right thing to do necessarily if it undermines your brand's value perception, confuses your end user, or bankrupts your budget.

Remember that super-premium organic corn chip we talked about? What if in this case it had a regular selling price of $2.49, clearly way above the rest of the competition, but supported by a strong message of being pure, organic, and somehow better for you. One of your largest resellers wants to include it in a big, splashy One Dollar Sale advertisement that it is running and to feature it at $1. What an opportunity for you! Should you do it? Is it in the best interests of the brand? You will probably sell a lot more products than usual, and that means people trying your brand for the first time. You may be able to convert some of them away from their regular brand and onto yours. That would be outstanding.

But, what happens when they come back to buy it next time and see it at $2.49? Will they make the leap of more than $1 above their usual brand and $1.50 above what they paid last time? What will it cost you to participate in this great sale? Oh, you didn't think you were getting this great deal for free, did you? It will cost you plenty to get down to that $1 price point, even if the reseller gives in on lots of margin points. How much might it cost? Let's do one more round of math:

Assumptions:

➤ The retailer agrees to lower his usual margin requirement of 30 percent, but he doesn't specify a new level, waiting to see how good a deal you will offer him.

➤ You want to put together several options, hopefully enticing him to give you as much as possible:

| | |
|---|---|
| Regular retail price | $2.49 |
| Regular margin | 30.0% |
| His regular cost from you, given the preceding is: | _____/jar |

Here's the formula and thought process:

In this case, we need to find the cost at which the buyer will buy, since we know the other two. So here's what you do:

Retail price × Inverse of margin = Cost

Try it yourself:

$2.49 × .70 = $1.74

To prove it works, plug these numbers into the Master Formula:

$2.49 – $1.74 ÷ $2.49 = .30

Now we know that you usually sell the product for $1.74. That's right, the usual price you get is already $.74 higher than the buyer wants to retail it for. This will take some serious discounting, so here goes:

|  | **Regular Price** | **Special Price** |
|---|---|---|
| Retail price | $2.49 | $1.00 |
| Regular cost | $1.74 | |
| Regular margin | 30.0% | |

Promo Options—If the retailer agreed to take these margins, how much would you have to discount your product?

|  | **New Cost to Retailer** | **Discount Needed from You** |
|---|---|---|
| a. Margin of 0 percent | $1.00 | $.74 |
| b. Margin of 10 percent | $ .90 | $.84 |
| c. Margin of 20 percent | $ .80 | $.94 |

We don't need to go any further to see how crazy this becomes. For most businesses, the excitement of a promotion like this is far outweighed by the cost to execute it and the downside of tinkering with the end user's value perception. The big picture here?

If you sold 1,000 cases of 12 bags each:

| Sales @ regular selling price of $1.74 unit/$21.00/case | = $21,000 |
|---|---|
| Discount needed @ $.74 unit/$8.88 case | = 8,880 |
| (lowest-cost option for you) | |
| Net sales generated | = $12,120 |
| Discount as percent of sales | = 42.3% |

This is the kind of promotion that you will most likely have to pass on for all the right reasons.

# A Pricing Worksheet to Use Every Day

We have done a lot of math in this chapter and have dealt with pretty complex issues of finance and strategy. In most businesses, these go hand in hand all the time. Once you understand the logic however, you can create a simple worksheet to check out pricing options.

The format I am giving you here for an everyday pricing worksheet can be set up in a spreadsheet or printed up to make copies for working on when away from your computer. It starts with your own internal margin needs to arrive at a price and then works through the reseller's impact.

To make sure that it is clear, I am using some of the My Brand Peanut Butter numbers we have seen before. That way, you can work with the numbers and be sure that you know how each line was calculated.

There are several different uses for this worksheet:

➤ If you have your own costs settled and are preparing for a sales call with a reseller who uses a different margin than you are used to using, just run the numbers through here, and you are ready to create your proposal.

➤ If you are at an early stage, don't yet know what margin your own business needs, or are considering a new product, plug in some guesses and use this sheet to do some "what if" scenarios.

You will learn a lot about what your options are within just a few minutes. If your competitive analysis tells you that you need to hit a retail price of about X, plug that in, estimate the margins the resellers will need, and see how much you can sell it for and what margin that gives you. You may find out that there wouldn't be enough margin for you to advertise or promote, never mind pay yourself a salary.

## Everyday Pricing Worksheet

|  | Unit Basis | Case/Pack Basis | Total Sales |
| --- | --- | --- | --- |
| Selling price | $1.00 | $12.00 |  |
| Quantity sold | 12,000 units | 1,000 case |  |
| Total sales |  |  | $12,000 |
| Contribution margin $ | $.70 | $8.40 | $8,400 |
| Contribution margin % | 70% | 70% | 70% |
| *Reseller Pricing* |  |  |  |
| Cost | $1.00 | $12.00 | $12,000 |
| Less promotion allowance | $.15 | $1.80 | $1,800 |
| Net price | $.85 | $10.20 | $10,200 |
| *Final Price Options* |  |  |  |
| Margin of 30% | $1.21 | $14.52 | $14,520 |
| Margin of 25% | $1.13 | $13.56 | $13,560 |
| Margin of 20% | $1.06 | $12.72 | $12,720 |

What else can you do with this chart? Add more columns and try out different levels of promotions to see how much they will cost you and how much impact they are likely to have on your final selling price to the end user. For instance, look at 10, 20, and 25 percent discounts in comparison to the 15 percent example shown. What final price points might you get with a different discount? Do you have any sense of whether this would increase sales?

### The Least You Need to Know

➤ Margin is the method to use when doing pricing calculations.

➤ Everyday and feature pricing must both be consistent with your brand profile.

➤ Price promotions have to be evaluated in terms of their ability to move the product and to fit within the brand's basic positioning and budget.

➤ There are many ways to structure price incentives. Finding the ones that support the brand's positioning and goals is the responsibility of the brand manager.

# Chapter 19

# Careful Communication: What's Right and Great About the Brand

> ### In This Chapter
>
> ➤ Building brand awareness and image
>
> ➤ Advertising for attitude or action
>
> ➤ Ten types of brand communication besides advertising
>
> ➤ Advertising and promotion ideas for every budget

You can't wait to tell the whole world: Your brand and your products are the best and the brightest around. It is very exciting to have a business filled with creative opportunities, and going out to tell anyone who will listen is a natural urge.

You know that if you are going to build the brand equity you want, you will need to communicate clearly and often, and to the right people. There are a lot of ways in which the brand story is told, and each of them needs to be thought through.

Brand communication starts with the brand manager/brand champion, and the burden of responsibility rests on your shoulders. The public elements of what you say about the brand and how you say it are what keep you up at night working through one idea after another. The more private communications, between the associates in the company, between the company and close outside vendors, are what have the power to accelerate creative and strategic thinking or to slowly sap its strength. As brand champion, you are the role model.

# Advertising Is Great—Got the Message and the Money?

A fundamental truism of building a brand is that people need to know the brand exists. You need to create *brand awareness.* Powerful brands are built on repeated impressions, also called *frequency,* that reinforce the core benefits and promises, or the *positioning,* in a way that the target audience can hear and understand. The big guns of advertising have traditionally been television, radio, magazines, direct mail, and newspapers, plus the combination of locales rounded up by the phrase "outdoor advertising" (think billboards, bus signs, ball parks, blimps over football games). The advent of the Internet brought new techniques such as banner ads and e-mail ads.

### Talk the Talk

**Brand awareness** has two parts: First, do people know your brand exists? Second, do they have "top-of-mind" awareness? The second part means that, if asked to name brands they know in a category, would they mention yours right off the top of their mind? Or, would they need to be prompted before they say "oh, sure, I know that one." **Frequency** is how often someone hears or sees your brand advertised or at least mentioned. **Positioning** is what the brand chooses to say about its promises and value. **Implied endorsement** is when the listener assumes that the celebrity spokesperson believes that the advertised product is good. Celebrities are very popular and very well compensated for endorsing brands. Branded companies put a lot of time and effort into choosing the right person to represent them.

Television advertising has always been the gold standard for brand marketers. It has enormous reach and the sensory powerhouse combination of visuals and audio; it engages at least two of your senses simultaneously. It lets you "see" cleaner clothes and cleaner casserole dishes. It lets you see how nice you will look when your wrinkles fade away and your pot belly evaporates. You can even see into the future and how comfortable your retirement will be if you start saving now. That is some crystal ball.

Radio, the theater of the mind, engages the ear and the mind simultaneously. There are some masterful radio spots that let us "see" sandy Hawaiian beaches; tall, cold iced teas on a hot, humid day; and the sizzling burger waiting for us at the next intersection. The on-air personalities will sometimes get involved by doing a "live" spot, reading it during the show, or taping the spot themselves, so you get a little local celebrity flair. Some of the best radio advertising that a brand has ever gotten is when the on-air personality comments on the brand, which then stretches a 30-second spot into a minute or maybe much more. There is a halo effect of *implied endorsement* when a celebrity gets involved.

The hallmark, the true gold standard of all implied endorsement radio spots, can be heard when Paul Harvey, a legend in the radio business, does his own unique news program in which he comments on the happenings of the day. The products advertised during his show are talked about, not advertised. You may well hear that Paul himself tried Brand X and, sure enough, it works just like they say it does. This takes implied endorsement up to a certified, verifiable stamp of approval. If Paul Harvey says it works, then lots of people feel that is good enough for them.

Magazines, direct mail, newspapers, and outdoor advertising each have their strengths and weaknesses, just as television and radio do. What is great is that each of them has good solid data on the ability to reach certain audiences, and that makes it easier to decide which of them is right for your brand.

The Internet is the hot new medium that thousands of people are trying to figure out. Banner ads are pretty much everywhere, trying to build awareness for Web sites other than the one you are on at that moment. They are analogous to TV, radio, and print advertising such as magazines, newspapers, and outdoors. The hope is that they will have a "billboard effect" and be highly noticeable. E-mail ads function more like direct mail. They drop into your mailbox and get sorted through just like regular mail.

Whatever type of advertising medium you choose, you will have a few different things to consider:

➤ Your budget will probably dictate some decisions because one TV ad could be equal in cost to X radio spots, which is equal to X + Y banner ads, and so on.

➤ Even though the budget seems to overwhelm everything, the first thing to talk about is where best to reach your target audience. The classic example of a group that is hard to reach is working women. Everyone says they are missing them: daytime television because the women are working; evening news shows because the women are making dinner; morning news shows because the women are getting themselves and their families out for the day; and prime time because the women are asleep in front of the TV. Is that absolutely true, that TV can't reach them? No, but it is tough. How would you find them with your message?

➤ Does your message lend itself to one medium better than another? Some products really need the visual element. Others need more time to explain their benefits. These are very important elements.

# So Tell Me Already: What Do You Want Me to Do?

The role of advertising, or any brand communication, is to build a relationship between the person and the brand. At first, that may sound like a touchy-feely statement; the word *relationship* isn't what comes to mind first when we think of wastebaskets, shoes, and computer chips. But *relationship* is a good word.

A quick look through your home helps to make the point. What brand of computer do you have? Did the brand of computer or the brand of operating system matter most to you when you bought it? What about your blue jeans, deodorant, magazines, cold medicine, laundry detergent, and ice cream? Which of these things are brand purchases rather than category purchases, meaning that you don't even have to think which one to pick up? This sentiment, whether it is trust, a simple preference, or an image that feels right to you, is what your relationship to those brands is all about.

So what do you want consumers to do when your brand communicates with them?

➤ **Awareness:** Become aware of the brand and its promises.

➤ **Trial:** At least give the brand a chance.

➤ **Repurchase:** Display loyalty; buy the brand a second time.

➤ **Reposition:** See the brand in a new light; hear the brand's new promises.

➤ **Reintroduce:** See an older brand as relevant to today.

Here's another question: Are you trying harder to create an attitude or an action? When you think about it, all advertising has as its endpoint the purpose of getting the target audience to do something, right? But if you push harder, you can get closer to the real outcome desired.

**Talk the Talk**

A **promotion** is an incentive to purchase the product. Promotions can take many different forms, such as cash savings ($5 off dinner for two), extra/bonus product (32 ounces for the price of 24), free gift (free mascara with any $20 purchase) or extra benefits (room upgrades, executive concierge service).

What do you want, attitude or action? Want a good, simple exercise to check this out? Over the next week, tear out every magazine ad for any product that you can relate to at all. Assume that you were in the market for this type of product right now, even if you just bought a car, a computer, or the green beans in the ads. Put the ads into piles based on whether they get you to the inspiration, consideration, or action point. Then look through all the ones in the inspiration pile and figure out what information they gave you that made you put it in that pile. Do the same for the others.

What did the advertiser choose to do in that ad that got you to think of it as one of these three descriptors? What would the ad have had to say to get you further down the line? Was it a message about the product that motivated you or a *promotion* for the product?

# Ready to Talk: Ten Other Types of Brand Communication

I remember well how exciting it was to meet the big Madison Avenue ad agencies that worked on my brands. I was surprised how different their personalities were, how open some senior partners were to us lower- and middle-level brand people, and how others wouldn't even acknowledge our existence. We weren't the final decision makers, so who needed us, seemed to be the message.

In the early days of my brand management career, I thought that they, the glamorous ad agencies, were what advertising was all about. I never stopped enjoying the commercial "shoot" (that's agency talk for the actual filming or photography for the commercial) or the taping (radio talk for same).

In my mind, I clearly separated these events from most everything else we did in the brand group. The next closest thing in creativity was the development of a coupon layout for a free-standing insert (FSI), that coupon section that is delivered in your Sunday newspaper. That had an artistic component, since it included some type of artwork, but it was still only a promotion piece (note the tone of second-class citizen here). Advertising was when you talked with people about the brand, and promotion was when you tried some maneuver to get them to buy it. Things have changed since then, certainly for me, but also for the realm of advertising and promotion.

## *Watch Out! Your Advertising Is Leaking*

The reality is that your brand is being advertised all the time; the problem is that quite often, a lot of it is sloppy, silly, or downright stupid.

That is a harsh statement isn't it? I could write this section as 10 cheery suggestions for better brand communications, but I have elected instead to write it straight and honest. This is a serious issue, and just about everyone I know, including myself, has messed up on one or more of these over the years because we just didn't think things through this carefully. I want you to do a better job.

I will take the role of the bad guy here, the hyper-critical new CEO who is looking around the ship that she just signed onto and is not a happy sailor. So here are 10 not-so-obvious places where brand communications "leak out" all the time. There isn't a radio or TV comment in this whole

**Mentoring Memo**

The message has to be about the brand, not about you. Smart businesspeople quickly figure out how smart you are by the way you handle yourself and the brand. The handsomest people working a convention booth are only as valuable as how good they are at building the brand. It is just like pretty packaging that hides the best-quality product behind a too-cute facade.

list, so do these things really count as leaky advertising? Do they ever. Anytime the image, value, and reputation of the brand are being communicated, you are advertising something; the question is, what?

## 1. Convention Booths

I had to address this one first because it is just so easy to attack that it acts as a warm-up for all the rest. There are three main elements in a convention booth: how it is set up, the interaction within the booth, and the follow-up after the fact.

➤ **Physical setup of the booth.** Most people do a very good job today of the obvious things, such as having a big, readable sign with the brand or company name on it, so I am skipping any graphic design lessons here. Only one comment on signage: If the name of the company has little or nothing to link it with the brand name, be sure that the brand name(s) are prominent.

➤ **Interaction within the booth.** The biggest issue is the interaction that happens once the show is open. The worst problem is the behavior of the people inside the booth. I am going to sound like a schoolmarm here, but this is not the company picnic. Your job is to reach out in a professional manner and draw people into a conversation about the brand. The dress code should lean to the conservative side (as CEO, if you make me get any more specific than that, my blood pressure and your career are both going up in flames). Always assume that someone is watching you. Paranoid is good in this situation. Pick the right people to work the booth, based on knowledge and ability to present. And that leads to the second piece of this puzzle: the materials used in that conversation.

A one-page overview, often set up as Q&A (question and answer) is great. Having a few extra one-pagers that address specific issues (technical specifications, market research, that sort of thing) is also great. That way, you can pull out one or two of them that address questions or provide you the opportunity to bring up key selling points. Sometimes a video is okay, but most of the time it is not. They are boring and take too long to watch. Sometimes a computer demo is great, and sometimes it is horrendous. When deciding what to put into the booth, ask yourself: What elements will help me build a strong relationship between the brand and the customer? If your computer demo will let someone really see the zippy insight that you promise, that is terrific. If it is a canned demo, it will be too long for the nontechies to weed through and too wimpy for the techies to like.

➤ **Follow up after the fact.** Promise me that you have a box or basket in which you are collecting every business card. Promise me that if a person needs a specific follow-up, you either write the question on the back of his or her business card or, better yet, have a short form that you can staple to the card with instructions for follow-up.

## 2. Selling Materials

In a nutshell: what in the world were you thinking when you printed up all this stuff? Or worse still, what makes you think I like sitting almost in your lap to see the tiny screen on your laptop? If we have to do it this way, at least let me hit the Enter key so that I can make it move faster.

To get this point, all you have to do is change places. I am sure that every one of you has had to sit through a presentation of some type, where you had to really control yourself to not shout "I'm dying here." So please, decide what we really need to talk about, focus on that, present it simply, show me the data so that I can see the important numbers, answer my questions, and let me buy what you are selling. Then get out before you lose the sale.

## 3. Packaging

There are two basic components of packaging: functionality and graphic design. If your product is something I can see and pick up, such as a razor or shaving cream, both of these are very important. In the store, I want to be able to pick it out of a crowded section, and it should convey the image of its promises, such as high tech/ latest tech. When I get it out of the package, I need it to function well. In the case of a razor, it needs to feel both comfortable and secure in my hand, for obvious safety reasons.

Both elements of packaging need to support the brand promises. Label design needs to be clear and easy to find. Avoid typefaces that torture, such as curly italics; remember that my eyes want to find something to focus on, so avoid clutter and cuteness, unless for some horrible reason that is part of the brand image that you want. When the image in my head doesn't match the image that I see on the shelf, scientists call it dissonance. Consumers call it a headache they don't need.

## 4. Press Releases

Most press releases are very carefully written by public relations (PR) professionals. However, two things can happen:

➤ There is no PR person, so you write them yourself.

➤ The PR person, under the time gun, inadvertently says something that doesn't come out right, maybe because that person didn't know about something going on. It creates suspicion or laughter.

You would be better off with no press release than to invite the press to criticize you. This is a very tough area; consequently, you need to be sensitive to what each of these says about the company and the brand. Beware brash statements or predictions of impending overwhelming success. Don't trash the competition. Use good grammar. Use correct legal symbols such as ® for a registered trademark and © for

**239**

copyrighted material. Why? IT IS IN WRITING. If you need to defend your ownership of the trademark someday and you don't use it properly yourself, good luck. If you say something nasty, untrue, or libelous, you have just handed your enemy his proof to show the judge. Please, at least make your brand's enemies work harder than this.

## 5. Promotion Incentives

What do you say about your brand if you run a sweepstakes with a trip to a casino, $10,000 in cash, all the liquor you can drink, and a personal bodyguard to keep you out of jail? This may be right on target for the Party-Hearty Motel, but it might not provide quite the right element of contemporary appeal for Nana's All Natural Butterscotch Pudding. This is an exaggerated example, for sure, but what about all the times you, as a consumer yourself, have thought, "What does *this* have to do with hammers (or bicycles, waffles, a magazine subscription, and so on)?"

The structure of the incentive sends a message about the brand. The structure may be what we just talked about or, going back to Chapter 18, "'What's the Price?' Has No Easy Answer," may be a special price deal that makes people wonder how your brand can be sold so cheaply one day and so expensively the next. And that is a very good question.

The image generated by the promotion is part of your brand image. Isn't that why you ran it? Oh, it isn't? You just wanted to generate some excitement? Be careful what you wish for.

## 6. Promotion Partners

Oops, that casino trip won't be repeated again, but your nice new partner, that magazine subscription service, didn't deliver the goods. Or, you put together a deal to co-promote, meaning to do a joint promotion, with another brand to share the costs. If the partner you chose has an image that is out of sync with yours, or if it fails to deliver on its end of the bargain, it can taint your own brand image.

These partnerships are entered into with all good intentions. But sometimes the subtleties of image similarity just don't work out. It is embarrassing to have to tell a potential partner that you will not go through with the deal because you don't think his brand is good enough for yours. But I would rather you have that conversation at the early stages than when contracts are on the table or, worse, already signed.

## 7. Brand Talk

You know, this job is sounding more and more like being a prison guard. Can't you ever just relax a little? Sure, you can. Just be careful what you say around the proverbial water cooler, which today is better known as e-mail, voicemail, lunch meetings, gripe sessions, and sales meetings. Word does get around, and anything you say about the business will be repeated if it smacks of insider attitude, never mind insider information. This is why your ancient Uncle Harry told you to keep your business life and personal life separate. We should all have listened to Harry years ago.

## 8. Interviews

No, not the kind *you* are thinking of going on. On second thought, yes, even then. Interviews with people outside the company, whether media, customers, or prospective new employers for you, are easy to dazzle with your depth of detail. These people are also loudmouths, competitors, newshounds, and gossips—some of them, that is. Some are terrific, smart, creative, and great fun to talk with. The problem at first is that you don't know which is which. Act accordingly.

## 9. Letters to the Editor

This can be so small that it fell off this list twice already. Then last week I read two "bombs" in different places, and I finally put it back on, promising myself only one paragraph. It must be fun to see your name in *The Wall Street Journal*. Call Mom and Dad, and tell them to buy 10 copies for the family archives. Please, please, remember who you work for and what their interests are before you put words to paper or e-mail forms and then send those succulent bits of sophisticated and stunning sounding statements to the press. Please.

## 10. Social Events

Again, a quick one. Remember that guy in Chapter 17, "Who Is Your Competition? Are You Sure About That?" who spilled his cosmopolitan on your shoes while coaxing juicy little bits of confession and chaos out of you? See all these nice people at this cocktail party? Some of them aren't nice.

# The Math of Two for One

I have another thinking exercise for you: Do you still have last Sunday's newspaper around the house? I want you to do three things with the major newspaper in your area:

➤ Look through the inserts that come in the middle of the newspaper. Sort them into two piles: advertising and promotion.

➤ Read through the rest of the paper and identify, even cut out, at least 20 things that count as advertising or promotion.

➤ Find at least three things that the newspaper itself does that count as advertising or promotion for the newspaper.

**Talk the Talk**

**Promotional advertising** combines the best of both worlds. It utilizes a powerful advertising medium to generate as much awareness as possible, and then it delivers a message specifically designed to create a purchase behavior. The content, or language of the ad, will tend to be much more specific on benefits. Quite often price and a limited time that the deal is available are featured.

What you see in front of you may be two piles, as directed, or three or even more for some of you. What did you do with the pieces that seemed like a cross between advertising and promotion? Did you force them one way or the other, create a third pile, or create two more piles because they weren't all really the same thing?

A lot of what is in front of you is what I call *promotional advertising,* a pretty simple concept.

# Promotion and Advertising Ideas for Smaller Budgets

One of the great frustrations of brand managers everywhere is the lack of funds to do big advertising campaigns. When you believe in your brand, you just know that you could grow it so much faster if you could let more people know about it. Believe it or not, this frustration even exists inside big brand marketing companies. There are usually a few big "star" brands in each company that get the deep-pockets hug from management, and a lot of others get small or non-existent ad budgets.

So how do you stretch your budget? You do two things:

1. You start to chant "partnerships, sponsorships, events, and acid indigestion." You don't think this is going to be a Top 40 hit, do you? Don't be so judgmental just yet.

   ➤ **Partnerships.** Think hard. Who wishes they had what you've got, and has what you wish you had (namely money)? Think retailers and suppliers and big businesses that want the same kind of people you do. Use your target audience as the starting point so that you don't end up wasting time and money with potential partners who make no sense.

   ➤ **Sponsorships and event marketing.** Lots of local events rely on sponsorships and create all kinds of advertising packages in exchange. For the next month, make a point of listening to a different radio station every few days. Keep moving around the dial until you get a sense for what each station is about and what kinds of events each is involved with. Radio stations are almost always involved with any major events in town and do a lot of work to bring sponsors together. If you read about an event being organized, find out who is in charge and call that person. Find out what the deal is. Ask if there is a TV station, newspaper, or radio station involved. If so, be bold. Call, e-mail, or write the sales manager and say that you want to talk about Event X. Let her know that you are very interested in finding a creative way to work your product in. And read on to find out more about a delicious way to maybe make that happen.

➤ **Acid indigestion.** No, this isn't the delicious idea I just talked about. That's coming. When you have a small budget, skip over the nice-to-know, touchy-feely, image stuff, and go for the throat. Tell people why they need you, and make it so real that they have acid dripping into their stomachs as they stress out over getting you into their lives fast enough.

2. As strange as it may sound, figure out how much of that budget is cash and how much is sweat. Yes, sweat, perspiration, the outcome of exerting yourself. And then, before any flights of creative fancy get going, figure out one of the most important things of all: What are you holding behind your back that you can trade with? Whaattttt?

➤ **Cash.** This is obvious, kind of. My only comment here is to be sure that you look at the timing of the money needed. It may be that you can make a "down payment" out of one pocket and pay the final bill out of next quarter's pocket.

➤ **Sweat.** What kind of work can you put in that won't require a cash outlay? If you own a bakery, will you and your two brothers spend a Sunday making 5,000 brownies to barter with? If so, your only cash is for the flour and other ingredients. I feel obligated to tell you that an accounting book would make you estimate the cost of lights, gas to heat the ovens, and the cardboard trays to put the brownies on, but I don't work for the IRS, and you are probably willing to ignore those costs.

➤ **Trading cards.** You know those brownies …. Well, you have the brownies to barter with, and you have that fabulous reputation for making the best, richest, most enthralling brownie in the county. And those two things make your bakery a valuable promotion partner. What else could you have behind your back and up your sleeve? Here are five more ideas to inspire you:

    a. Your car wash has discount coupon books for frequent customers. What are they worth to a promotion partner? What is your real cost?

    b. Your flower shop buys vases by the dozen, pays the floral designer by the hour to stay there even when you aren't busy, and always has extra flowers left over. What is it worth to a promotion partner to have a bouquet delivered, in its name, to five lucky winners, once a month, for a year, in lieu of cash up front from you?

c. Some big company has agreed to sponsor a charity event. It can afford the sponsorship fees, the booth, and plenty of people, but it needs a nice "hook" to generate donations. You know those sinful brownies of yours? I'll bet lots of people would gladly donate $2 or $5 each, or, if it is a swank event, $10 each, once they are told these are Bob's Bold & Bodacious Brownies. Your brand name, prominently displayed and advertised by the big guy, is the hook.

---

### The Least You Need to Know

➤ Be clear on what you want advertising and promotion communications to do for your brand. Are you looking to affect an attitude or push someone to purchase your products?

➤ Brand advertising can "leak out" in a lot of ways that can be harmful. Be conscious of all communications and events.

➤ Promotional advertising combines the power of a media-driven message with a strong pull to get the customer to buy.

➤ Every budget can handle some advertising and promotion programs; you just have to work harder as the dollars get smaller.

# Part 5

# Taking Ownership: The General Management Part of Brand Management

*We have been through a rigorous program in the first four parts of this book. We have created a brand manager orientation program for you and then loaded you up with projects and issues that need to be resolved.*

*You have created a brand profile and seen how difficult that process can be. It requires clarity and a rigorous appraisal of every element that impacts the brand. You have taken responsibility for how your associates look at the brand and have encouraged them to treat the brand like the valuable asset that it is.*

*After all that hard work, we are going to give you some more. This time, we are moving you up to a senior management position so that you can see even more of the big-picture impact of operating in such a fast business environment.*

*This part of the book is well-suited for quiet contemplation. If you aspire to senior management, it is terrific preparation. You will find things to discuss from a strategic standpoint that can help you stand out in a field of candidates. If you are going out on job interviews, it will feed you some terrific questions to ask.*

# Chapter 20

# Analysis Without Paralysis: Learning to Love Those Numbers

I teach a management development program called "Thinking Skills for the Data Overloaded," and every time people hear the name of that course, they grin, roll their eyes heavenward, and groan, "Boy, do I need that." I can almost predict what the next 10 minutes of conversation will be. They will tell me about the amount of data they have access to, the daily piles of reports that get stacked on their desks or e-mailed to them, and the tiny amount of it that they use at all. And then the guilt pours out.

The worst part of having this scene repeated so often is the frustration that I hear. These are smart people. They want to do a good job. They are excited about how much they *could* know. They are angry about how little they *do* know. And after a while, most of them will tell me that they have made enormous efforts to really use some of this material, and then they found that it took so long to figure out how to read it that they ran out of time and patience and simply gave up.

Why is there a chapter on working with numbers in a book on brand management? Because every brand manager needs to keep a close eye on how his business is doing and needs resources for good ideas and insights. Data analysis is a critical skill. Many people think that they cannot admit that they don't really know how to use some reports. It seems as though when you start a new job, you get a week to ask all your "beginner" questions, and after that you are expected to fly solo. So, six months or six years later, how do you admit that you don't know how to do something so basic? Take heart. Most of us were never taught how to read data tables, and even fewer of us were taught how to turn the data into information. Let's stop and do that right now with a few of the techniques that I teach in that course.

# Data Overload Is Here to Stay

It is reasonable to assume that computers are going to stay around, that the World Wide Web will continue to increase in size and scope, and that all of our companies will generate more, and more dynamic, data reports. There will simply be way too much information available and not enough time to do much of anything with at least half of it.

What is my goal with this chapter? Two things:

➤ I want you to end this chapter with the skills you need to integrate at least two important reports into your weekly activities starting right now. Pick reports that would make a big difference for you. Pick reports that you are embarrassed to admit you don't really understand. Pick the two that you hate the most, and let's get it over with. If you spent one quiet hour with one report, no interruptions, could you learn how to read it and find at least five things that it says? My money says yes, you can.

➤ If you have people reporting to you, I want you to know that some of them are struggling with this issue. I want to encourage you to find a way to introduce these skills to them without embarrassment. Could you start to work in a little teaching during your team meetings by going through a report together? What can you do to bring everyone's comfort level up a few notches? Your business needs insightful analysis. What are you going to do to encourage this?

I suggest that you adopt two goals with data reports. These are good long-term goals and are absolutely critical in the short term, when you are trying to dig out from under a mountain of paper:

➤ **Prioritize ruthlessly.** Separate the "must know" from the "nice to know." Remember that the information you rank as middle- or low-level importance for you is someone else's top-dog report. If you need a specific piece of data, can you call someone? If you are part of a group, does it make sense for all 10 of you to be focused on the same reports, with not one of you looking at the other things? Could you each take just one of the "other" reports each month, write up five bullets on what it says, and send that by e-mail to everyone else?

➤ **Plan to find conclusions, or don't bother at all.** When you approach any report, really go after it; go looking for things to learn. It isn't a novel, even though it has a story to tell. Try the process that I outline in this chapter, and see if it makes your time much more productive.

As you start working with a report, what are you looking for? What you want is the story hidden between the columns.

# Tell Me a Story

"Every page of numbers is a story waiting to be told." You have now heard the opening line to my "Thinking Skills" class. I like that sentence a lot because it sums up an attitude, a process, and a reason for the page to exist. It is fair to say that a lot of reports could be improved dramatically if they were formatted better; it would be so much easier to figure out what the page is supposed to be doing for you. Are you willing to take the time to draft up a new format, get some input on it, and then take it to the powers in charge? Lots of people have done this very successfully.

Have you ever used the line, "So, what's the story?" Well, that is exactly how you want to approach a report. And, conversely, if you want to *design* a report, ask yourself, "So, what do I want *this story to tell me?*"

Why do I talk about stories and not about numbers? If all I need is a number, I don't need you. It is the "why" of the number, the "what if" and the "relation to" of the number that is the human value. But aren't stories long-winded and complicated answers to simple questions? Only if you make them that way.

> President: "Sue, how is the Midwest doing this quarter?"
>
> Sue: "They're at 42 percent (the unspoken "of quota" is assumed)."
>
> President: "Mary Ellen, how is the Midwest doing this quarter?"
>
> Mary Ellen: "They're at 42 percent of quota with only 30 percent of time elapsed. The new sales manager has everyone ahead of pace, and we are projecting a finish of around 110 percent."

This is the president of the company asking the question. Who is he going to turn to next time? My money is on Mary Ellen.

I want to focus on helping you use the reports that you really need to get your job done. And then I want to see you shine, so we will talk a little bit about turning the story that you find into a presentation. I am going to use two different reports, with different levels of complexity.

> ➤ The first report is real data that measures the activity levels of the Top 20 Web sites in the Health category for the month of April 2000. Media Metrix supplied the data to us. You will remember this company as the pioneers in Internet usage analysis that you read about in Chapter 4, "E-Commerce Makes Branding Hotter Than Ever," Chapter 7, "Brand Equity: Like Money in the Bank," and Chapter 11, "Branding Inspiration: Information and Education Go Branded." The format is straightforward and easy to read. The information that you can pull out of this one report is fascinating.

➤ The second report is one that I have made up that is intentionally a little more complex and that probably looks a lot like one in your business. The purpose of using a spreadsheet with so many columns is to show more of the analytical shortcuts that you can use, as well as a more robust set of observations and conclusions.

Each of these reports is full of information and could spawn a series of presentations. We will work through each one in two steps: First, understand the format, and second, find the story. Let's look at what is happening on the Internet first.

### Top Twenty Health Sites
#### Source: Media Metrix April 1998, 1999, and 2000

| | April 2000 | | April 1999 | | April 1998 | |
|---|---|---|---|---|---|---|
| All Digital Media: World Wide | 77,883,000 | | 64,968,000 | | NA | |
| Web: | 74,796,000 | | 61,128,000 | | 53,922 | |
| | Unique Visitors (000s) Home/Work Persons 2+ | Reach (%) Home/Work Persons 2+ | Unique Visitors (000s) Home/Work Persons 2+ | Reach (%) Home/Work Persons 2+ | Unique Visitors (000s) Home/Work Persons 2+ | Reach (%) Home/Work Persons 2+ |
| **Sites** | | | | | | |
| ONHEALTH.COM | 4,797 | 6.4 | 449 | 0.7 | 88 | 0.2 |
| WEBMD.COM | 3,707 | 5.0 | ... | ... | ... | ... |
| MOTHERNATURE.COM | 1,972 | 2.6 | 277 | 0.5 | ... | ... |
| DRKOOP.COM | 1,920 | 2.6 | 926 | 1.5 | ... | ... |
| NIH.GOV | 1,629 | 2.2 | 1,537 | 2.5 | 1,206 | 2.2 |
| THRIVEONLINE.COM | 1,572 | 2.1 | 748 | 1.2 | 948 | 1.8 |
| PLANETRX.COM | 1,366 | 1.8 | 235 | 0.4 | ... | ... |
| DRUGSTORE.COM | 1,361 | 1.8 | 562 | 0.9 | ... | ... |
| BABYCENTER.COM | 1,272 | 1.7 | 602 | 1.0 | 188 | 0.3 |
| MORE.COM | 968 | 1.3 | ... | ... | ... | ... |
| EDIETS.COM | 876 | 1.2 | ... | ... | ... | ... |
| MAYOHEALTH.ORG | 859 | 1.1 | 592 | 1.0 | 437 | 0.8 |
| MEDSCAPE.COM | 753 | 1.0 | 273 | 0.4 | 273 | 0.5 |
| DISCOVERYHEALTH.COM | 653 | 0.9 | ... | ... | ... | ... |
| HEALTHCENTRAL.COM | 618 | 0.8 | ... | ... | ... | ... |
| INTELIHEALTH.COM | 580 | 0.8 | 741 | 1.2 | 362 | 0.7 |
| HEALTHSCOUT.COM | 572 | 0.8 | ... | ... | ... | ... |
| SELFCARE.COM | 567 | 0.8 | ... | ... | ... | ... |
| COSTCO.COM | 564 | 0.8 | 288 | 0.5 | ... | ... |
| FAMILYMEDS.COM | 472 | 0.6 | ... | ... | ... | ... |
| **Total** | **27,078** | | **7,230** | | **3,502** | |

... = Insufficient sample size. Monthly minimum reporting standard is 200,000 unique visitors.

**Media Metrix Definitions:**

Unique Visitors: The estimated number of total users who visited the Web site once in the given month. All Unique Visitors are unduplicated (only counted once).
Sample Size: More than 50,000 individuals throughout the U.S. participate in the Media Metrix sample.

*(Source: Media Metrix © 2000)*

1. Joe Jones has now earned one free CD of his choice, up to $15 in price, by purchasing 10 CDs in his first year of membership. Joe is sent an e-mail announcing this, and his membership file is amended to note that he has a $15 credit waiting for him.

2. Joe is also reminded that in his second year of membership, if he purchases at least 15 CDs, he will get two free CDs.

3. Joe's tastes in music can now be analyzed. It is clear from the product ID numbers that Joe is an oldies fan. When Joe signed up for the club he indicated that he wanted to receive special offers, so he will now be sent the "Oldies but Goodies" weekly e-mail newsletter. The next time the local oldies radio station does a promotion with the record store, Joe will get a special invitation to the party, a 20 percent off coupon, and first crack at buying tickets to an oldies concert sponsored by the station.

4. The Main Street, USA store outpaces all the others in the region for sales of oldies and punk rock. This information is matched against the demographics of the area and seems to correlate well. Families heavily populate this town, with age skews favoring 45- to 55-year-olds and 12- to 17-year-olds. This looks like Baby Boomer parents with teenage children. What promotions should this record store be running to maximize sales with these groups?

5. The Main Street, USA store's transaction data indicates that 70 percent of all purchases are made in conjunction with a club membership. That is a full 14 percentage points higher than the national average. We need to find out what the manager and the sales staff are doing so right in that store.

6. We can now look at Joe's purchases over the last year and assess where he fits in our *best shopper* profiles based on the *frequency, recency,* and *profitability* of his purchases.

**Talk the Talk**

Who are your "**best shoppers**"? Each company sets its own guidelines, but it is usually some combination of **frequency,** how often someone buys; **recency,** how recently that person bought; and **profitability,** how profitable that person's purchase history has been.

We did all of this without ever peeking into Joe's closet or his wallet, without interviewing his boss or even meeting his mother. This is a passive system; it is not invasive or intrusive. It is entirely voluntary on Joe's part, and he is now seeing the value of having signed up.

With this kind of information, we can create promotion incentives that make sense to Joe, and we can communicate them through the cash register, e-mail, or mail to his home.

# Who's Got the Cards?

According to the latest data from ACNielsen, it seems like just about everybody's got a frequent shopper/loyalty card. The term "frequent shopper" is almost generic at this point because it is the most commonly used term to define programs of this type. In its Fourth Annual Frequent Shopper Survey released in April 2000, ACNielsen studied the usage of frequent shopper programs in supermarkets. The survey's findings are very interesting. In 1999, 70 percent of all U.S. households participated in some type of program, double the number recorded just three years earlier. That certainly says that those retailers have hit on a big idea.

Here's another piece of data from the same study: 59 percent of these households belong to two or more programs. So that means they really like these cards, right? Yes. It also means that they are "loyal" to more than one store. These customers are playing hardball, aren't they? Look at the data in markets across the United States:

| Market | Percent Shoppers with Card | Market | Percent Shoppers with Card |
|---|---|---|---|
| Chicago | 97 percent | Phoenix | 96 percent |
| Los Angeles | 92 percent | Charlotte | 92 percent |
| Denver | 91 percent | New York | 73 percent |
| Buffalo/Rochester | 89 percent | Houston | 51 percent |
| San Antonio | 20 percent | St Louis | 17 percent |
| Columbus | 14 percent | Miami | 6 percent |

*Frequent Shopper Cardholders by Geography—Source: ACNielsen, Fourth Annual Frequent Shopper Survey. © 2000 ACNielsen. Permission granted.*

Think about some of the other kinds of "frequent shopper" programs you see: airlines, rental cars, video rentals, shoe stores, bookstores, and so on.

Does your bank reduce or eliminate fees if you keep certain balances in your accounts? Does your local bagel or donut shop give you a free product after 10 purchases? Does your drugstore have a rebate program, does your carwash or gas station have a year-end bonus, and does your credit card give you mileage points or gift certificates? All of these are forms of frequent shopper programs. They are also examples of promotion at work, encouraging you to buy more products from these companies.

# The Evolution from Mass Promotion to One-to-One Marketing

Technology has absolutely been the driver behind a very significant shift in how promotion incentives are considered and delivered. In the last 10 years, the promotion business has moved through many steps in evolution. I can think of six different terms that were "the latest thing" in the last decade alone, and that is a lot of change in a short time period. What is interesting about these six names is that in many cases, they really were just quick, mental adjustments from 50 years of mass marketing and the ultimate goal today of personalized marketing, one to one.

Mass marketing was the excitement created by radio and television many, many years ago. Just to be able to find a way to get at the purchaser and send your message was very exciting. There were also magazines, newspapers, and billboards to use, and this created the glory days of advertising. Coupons and advertisements were the major tactics used, both of which send out the offer to far more than the real target audience. The idea was that the people who were interested would see the message and respond. The rest of the people, who saw the message but didn't care were referred to as "waste" (nothing personal here).

Airlines and credit card companies were early adopters of database marketing. The idea was to use the database of names and addresses, which the companies had to collect anyhow to do business, to help them create competitive differentiation: It gave the marketer direct access to talk with the target audience. The people in the database were, by definition, people who used credit cards or took airplane flights. These programs have always relied heavily on delivering mail to the home or office because that was the most efficient way to reach the audience. In the case of these two examples, the companies had to send statements anyhow, so the additional cost to include messages and special offers was not out of line.

When scanning became widespread, it created the opportunity to take database marketing into many more industries. The computer that recorded the sale of a hammer in a hardware store had almost all the information needed except the one big thing: who bought the hammer. Think how different this is from a jet engine in a huge manufacturing plant being delivered to an airline. In that case, the sale information was complete: The customer name, address, and what was bought was all in one place.

It was the consumer end of the business that couldn't tie things together until a system was created to identify the purchaser so that the transaction information could be tied into their names. The name "frequent shopper" really came into use at this point, because these programs were mostly found in retail store settings. While this term is used generically today to mean almost any promotion program like this, the term actually faded out fairly quickly among professionals involved in creating the programs. The

**Heads Up**

Some of you may be thinking that database-marketing techniques don't apply to the business you are in. Consumer-oriented products and services are easy to understand here, but the same thinking can apply to more technical or component-driven products. We all want profitable repeat business. How can you learn more about doing that?

reason for the change in terminology is very interesting, and it shows how quickly the thinking matured and developed.

Let's go back to our music store example and follow a real fast evolution. Here are a few scenarios—see what you think:

➤ Our chain of music stores was running a frequent shopper program, so we defined our "best shopper" as someone who shops/purchases often, as defined by the trends in the industry (maybe 10 purchases a year). After a year or two, we looked at the data and saw that only 20 percent of our card-holders fit the best-shopper profile, and yet the industry data showed that more people were buying more music.

➤ When we analyzed the data further, we discovered that half of the club members bought only items that were on sale.

➤ When we did some research among club members we learned that almost all of them had a membership with at least two music stores.

➤ That same research showed that our members routinely watched the sale ads and went to whichever store had the best price that week on the music they wanted.

What happened here? Our music store learned that "frequent" shopper is a misleading term in many businesses. What it really wanted was loyal shoppers and profitable shoppers. And that is how "frequent shopper" became "loyalty marketing," which became "relationship management" and is now trying to become "one-to-one marketing."

These last three evolutionary steps are very similar, each a refinement of the previous thinking rather than a departure from it. The basic tenets of loyalty marketing are to do the following:

➤ Find out what the customer buys.

➤ Identify which customers shop most often, spend the most money, buy the most profitable mix of products, and spend the biggest percentage of their dollars with you.

➤ Identify which customers are most "valuable" overall, and sort them into groups.

➤ Try out a variety of incentives to get them to maintain a profitable loyalty to your company.

From here, the concept deepens into relationship marketing: looking at a customer as a true asset of the company/brand. What do you do with assets? You think what your investment strategy should be, you start to think about what kind of return you want on your investment, and you rethink the cost and value of the programs you offer.

The ultimate goal is called one-to-one marketing, which is highly personalized and virtually directed by the customers themselves. In a perfect world, none of us would ever have to wade through a pile of mail each day, throwing away half the envelopes. We would get only the mail that we want (you will still get the bills, of course); the offers would be only for items that we need or are considering.

As e-mail now takes on a lot of the communications work that regular mail previously handled, we are starting to deal with the same issues of dumb, irritating, mailbox-clogging junk. E-mail has enormous power to move one-to-one marketing to the forefront, but for now it is more of a goal than a reality for most companies.

The vital concept for brand managers to understand about one-to-one marketing is that the customer must be allowed to opt in or opt out of participation. Say that again? Ever gone into a Web site and been asked to "register"? Most of the time these days, there will be a box that you can check if you want to receive mail from this Web site and its "affiliates" (that's code for advertisers and the people who want to send you promotional offers). If you say no, that should mean no; you have "opted out," or, used your option to say no.

One of the very interesting pieces of database analysis is what is called the lifetime value (LTV) of a customer. That's right. It says: Look at how much money you think this person could reasonably spend on the products that you sell over the next 5, 10, or 20 years or so, and figure out your profit margin on that. Deduct from this what it would cost you to go find another customer if you lost this one (advertising, wooing them with promotions), and figure out what a loyal customer is worth. This is very different thinking than when I was a brand manager!

# The Top Ten Problems with Loyalty Marketing Programs

I spent some time talking with Ann Raider, senior vice president of SmartSource Direct. Raider is one of the pioneers and a recognized leader in the area of relationship marketing. She co-founded Consumer Card Marketing Inc. (CCMI) in 1991, which was then sold to News America Marketing in 1999 as part of its SmartSource Direct business.

Raider gave me her perspective on the 10 biggest problems that she sees today with loyalty/relationship marketing programs:

1. **Effectively communicating the *right* message.** What do customers really want to hear about? It has to be what is important and relevant to them. A classic example is sending promotional information on dog food to people who don't own any pets.

2. ***Efficiently* talking to consumers.** Raider says that all you have to do is realize that the average person gets 8,000 "messages" a day to realize that you need to reach people when and where they want. Things such as "opt in" e-mail messages are perfect.

3. **Linking loyalty to category development.** If you are a retailer, you need to look at things like this: If you put Brand A on sale at a great price and 50 percent of your best shoppers don't buy it, what's wrong? Link the learning between the database and what you carry in inventory.

4. **Mark-down promotion analysis.** Raider's example is crystal clear: You can sell bananas for 29¢ per pound and sell lots of them. You can sell them for 39¢ pound and sell some amount less, but potentially with more overall profit. And, with the database, you can see if all the 29¢ price did was bring in people who just are "cherry picking" your best sale items. They will never be profitable customers.

5. **Market segment/opportunity (category voids).** Your very best shoppers buy lots of Category D. Your second and third levels of best shoppers buy lots of Categories E through H. What can you do to draw each market segment into the other categories?

6. **Analyzing share of wallet.** Using government statistics, you can get a sense of about how much a household at any given income level will spend on types of products. How much of that is being spent with you?

7. **Product relationships.** A simple example helps here. Look at who buys bread, and then cross that with who buys peanut butter and jelly and butter. Are their any opportunities to cross promote?

8. **Developing customer profiles and clubs.** Can you identify a specific group of customers, maybe senior citizens, and create a "club" idea in which you promote special values to them? These could be things that you sell or another business that you partner with.

9. **Linking loyalty to e-commerce.** Raider says this is still virtually untapped but likely to grow fast in the coming years. An example would be enticing a customer who buys your products to visit your Web site. Within your Web site, that customer is able to get even more value (by deepening his relationship with you) through special offers available only through you.

10. **Manufacturer tie-in programs.** Manufacturers and retailers have mutual interests. It makes good sense for them to work the database together, looking for ways to bring the brand's customers into the retailer's stores. Both sides are happy when the customers buy more of Brand A and spend their dollars at Store B.

# Learning to Say "Please, May I?"

We talked about the idea of letting a consumer "opt in" or "opt out" of promotional offers. That is quickly becoming a golden rule of promotion. It is the equivalent of asking, "Please, may I contact you?" This desire on the customers' part is born of exhaustion from a constant barrage of offers that they don't want and a real sensitivity to letting too many companies know too much about them. What is "too much"? Whatever they think it is.

You don't need to look far to find stories of consumers being devastated when their credit card numbers were stolen. And the nightly news shows now regularly run segments on people who have experienced *identity theft*. We all watch these shows and think, "How awful." When it happens to someone in our families, we think, "This can't be happening."

Identity theft is when someone pretends to be another person by using that person's unique identity numbers, such as Social Security, credit card, driver's license, and bank account numbers. Somehow, the thief gets hold of this information and operates under the assumed identity, running up debts and leaving a trail of bad news. The injured party probably knows nothing about it until denied a mortgage or bill collectors come calling.

Things like this have made us very sensitive to privacy issues. As stories of computer hackers crop up every month or two, the anxiety level goes higher still. It is true that computerization is a core component of the problem. However, turning off the computers isn't any kind of fix.

The burden of responsibility is falling more and more on the marketer. It is up to us to respect the desire for privacy, to accept that everyone has a sense of personal "space" that they don't want invaded. How will your company handle this?

# The Privacy Wars: Everyone Wants to Know Who Owns the Info

If you are serious about using database information on your customers to help build a loyal, profitable relationship, you need to become very sensitive to privacy issues. In our music store example earlier in this chapter, I made this statement:

> We did all of this without ever peeking into Joe's closet or his wallet, without interviewing his boss or even meeting his mother. This is a passive system; it is not invasive or intrusive. It is entirely voluntary on Joe's part, and he is now seeing the value of having signed up.

I believe that is a fair and accurate statement. Now, see what you think about these scenarios:

➤ If Joe had ordered these CDs from a Web site, he would have given a credit card number that could also be stored in his club member file.

➤ If we asked Joe to tell us his birthday so that we could send him a "special gift," we would know how old he was.

➤ If Joe stopped to pick up a prescription at the pharmacy next door to the music store, should he be concerned about whether his name will be given to a pharmaceutical company who wants to send him valuable information about his medical condition?

At what point do we go from "not invasive or intrusive" to "over the line"? The power of this whole class of database marketing techniques has now got to be matched with a powerful commitment to think long and hard about how you will capture and control any information that you collect. You need to look at exactly what questions you ask people—what information is critical, and what is "nice to know" and therefore should be optional? What safeguards are you prepared to invest in and defend, defend, defend?

As I write this, a bankrupt Web site, Toysmart.com, has become the lightning rod for this issue. As part of the bankruptcy proceedings, the company put its customer database up for sale. That data contains customers' personal information, including credit card numbers, which were generated voluntarily because, obviously, the consumers were willing to give it to get delivery of the toys. However, as I understand it, the consumers were given a privacy guarantee on the Web site. Now this information is up for sale to the highest bidder. This promises to be a landmark legal ruling, and we should all watch these cases very carefully.

## *Your Five New Promotion Rules Explained*

At the opening of this chapter, I said that you probably should start thinking of your promotional activities and behaviors as similar to a good houseguest. The analogy works very well.

1. **Develop the art of conversation.** Talk about what your host is doing and what is important to them these days. What are your customers' plans? Let them guide the conversational topics. Learn to listen instead of talking about yourself all the time.

2. **Show good manners.** It is always a good idea to remember to say "Please" and "Thank you." A thank-you note will never go out of style. If someone introduces you to a friend, go out of your way to be gracious and accommodating. Make your hosts look good for knowing you. Make their friends glad that they met you, and make them look forward to seeing you again.

3. **Pitch in and help with the chores.** How about asking, "What can I do to be helpful?" instead of just saying, "Holler if I can help." Do you hear the difference? Give a few specific suggestions of things that you could do for them. Quite often people draw a blank on what else they need when they are rushing through busy lives, and they only later kick themselves for not saying, "Yes, I could really use a ----- right now."

4. **Mind your own business.** Don't ask awkward, embarrassing questions that you don't really need to know anyway. If they want to and they trust you, they may open up and give you some information. If you handle that well, they may give you some more.

5. **Don't gossip about any little things that you overhear in their homes.** You don't really need to tell the neighbors that George snores like a freight train and that Martha has cellulite, do you? Or that they are concerned that their kids may be having some "substance abuse" problems and are desperate for information and guidance. And for sure, you don't need to tell anyone on this planet about the contents of George and Martha's medicine cabinet. Why don't you bring your own tube of toothpaste so that you won't have to go looking for theirs?

As promotion gets more intimate, there will be times when you will wonder how to handle certain situations. Think about this idea of being a houseguest and act accordingly. Good manners in business may get you even further than good manners at home.

---

### The Least You Need to Know

➤ Database technology has revolutionized promotion. More powerful scanning devices, coupled with vast data storage and more flexible software tools, make databases storehouses of marketing knowledge.

➤ Frequent shopper/loyalty card programs are very popular. The airline and credit card companies built them, but now many industries use the techniques.

➤ Loyalty and profitability are the cornerstones of a good customer relationship. These are better measurements of a customer's value than frequency.

➤ Customer privacy is a critical issue. It deserves careful planning and a company commitment to defend it.

# Chapter 23

# Revolution and Relevance: The Future of Brand Management

As we end this book, let's focus on some of the major themes that look like they will influence the future of brand management and, by extension, influence the opportunities there for you. I have pulled together five issues for you to consider.

A common element through these five issues is technology. A lot of different pieces of technology promise to change the business landscape over and over again. For some of you, the technology itself will be what your brand is about. For just about all of you, technology will be something that you use to help sell your product. As we interact with our customers in more sophisticated ways, how much of the magic will be technology? How much of the message is a function of the technology that delivers it?

Brand management will have to grapple with an interesting paradox: Our customers will have ample opportunity to walk away to any number of our competitors, and yet they seem to crave a stable relationship with a "brand of choice." This idea of having a relationship with a brand will be your biggest opportunity, your greatest challenge, and the new definition of a competitive "barrier to entry." So let's start there.

# Issue 1: It Is All About Relationships and Reputation

The simple fact is, your customers have lots of reasons to leave you in the dust if they want to:

➤ They have other options, and those range from buying a competitive brand to deciding not to buy your type of product at all.

➤ They have so much information at their fingertips that they can end up delaying the decision to buy while they research even more. Or, possibly, they can force you into cutting prices or adding special services just to win their purchase.

➤ They are bombarded with so many advertising and promotion messages that they are not really sure what your value is.

My best guess is that the hyperactive nature of today's marketplace will result in a backlash fairly soon. Our customers will let out a collective shout of "Enough already!" and will start seeking out simplicity and clarity in place of information overload. And this is very good news for branded businesses.

The old concept of "word of mouth" advertising and personal referrals is starting to make its way into our new economy model. This very personal notion, that a friend tells you what she thinks of something that she tried, is simple and much less intrusive than most advertising. You ask for an opinion, and you get it. You ask what someone thinks about a brand or a company, and that person tells you.

How is this being played out today in the broader context of a wired community? Let's look at four different means of providing word of mouth, or personal, referrals:

1. **Customer review or rating.** If you have visited one of the book or music Web sites, you probably know that the sites encourage people to write their comments on items that they have used. If you harbor any desire to be a book or music critic, here is your chance. Similarly, Web sites such as eBay want users to rate the experience of purchasing through their system and from the individual seller.

2. **Independent survey system.** Have you purchased something online and, at the close of the transaction, been asked if you would take one minute more to rate the business experience? When you click "yes," you are taken to a survey form from a service such as BizRate.com. The company uses a standard questionnaire that probes your satisfaction level with the Web site itself as well as the products. It checks back after you receive the product to see how you feel at that point. You can see how this builds up a lot of information across a wide group of users.

3. **Opinion-gathering Web sites.** Epinions.com is the new-age version of the magazine articles that rate various products. Rather than expert testers reporting on a product's merits or faults, average citizens tell their opinions. There is an important difference here in that the former is a more disciplined, far less biased approach; the latter is much more colorful because it is *opinion,* not fact-based. But this may become a very powerful tool over time for its ability to create a neighborly, over-the-back-fence atmosphere.

4. **Subject-specific message boards.** Do you want to air your opinions on whether vitamin C cures colds or what the stock market is likely to do next quarter? Well, somewhere out there is a message board waiting for you to tap in and talk. This is another form of community, similar to the opinion sites.

### Mentoring Memo

A new term that you should become familiar with is "reputation manager." I have seen it in print a few times now in discussions about Web site development, and I expect it to become much more widespread soon. The idea is that a Web site needs to learn about the customer's experience and satisfaction, and it does this by actively seeking opinions. This concept underscores the importance of knowing what the customer thinks before he walks away from you.

If you want to offer your thoughts on a product or service, you have plenty of opportunity to speak up. If you want some notion of the reputation of a product or service, you can probably find some people out there who have posted their opinions on the matter.

How does an opinion become a reputation? When it gets multiplied. How do you sort out which opinions are meaningful? That gets much harder to do. Do you want to know what 100 people think of a certain brand of lawnmower? That would be interesting to check out before you buy. Do you want to know if 100 people think you should have open-heart surgery? Maybe if they are all heart surgeons. Maybe if they are all people who've had the surgery already. But if they are 100 average Joe's, who cares what they think? Maybe you and I don't, but I'll put $10 down right now on a bet that says you could build a chat room around people just talking about what they think about heart surgery, with little or no experience beyond what they heard about their neighbor Harry.

What are the implications for you as a brand manager?

➤ Individual opinions coalesce into reputations, and when the reputation of your brand or company can be broadcast for a worldwide audience, each individual opinion-maker becomes very, very important. You will probably never see 100 percent approval ratings for your brand, so there can always be a dissatisfied renegade out there with a negative opinion. But how many wonderfully satisfied customers do you have? Customer service becomes a core strategy pretty quickly in this environment.

➤ There is an old axiom that reputations are built over time, and I think that is a truism. The only catch is that nobody ever defined how much time. And realistically, the only reason that it took "time" is that reputation is entirely dependent on communication; it is the sum total of individual opinions. How fast can word get around? When I can tap into a database of opinions and see what 50 or 100 people think of your products, the concept of time becomes irrelevant. Your product may be a music CD launched yesterday, but 100 teenagers may have already logged on to talk about their favorite tracks.

➤ Go back through Chapter 19, "Careful Communication: What's Right and Great About the Brand," where we talked about careful communication about your brand. Rethink what various people in the company say about the brand and how they communicate. Do you need to spend some time in training your customer service people on some of the subtleties of listening skills? Do your salespeople even begin to understand what your brand profile is all about?

➤ Could your reputation actually become a *barrier to entry* for others looking to steal some of your thunder? This is an enviable position, but one that warrants consideration as a long-term strategy and goal.

### Talk the Talk

A **barrier to entry** is something that makes it more difficult for a new competitor to get established. It can take many forms: In the ice cream business, it could be the ability to store and transport product at −20°; in the insurance business, it could be an outstanding reputation for treating client claims quickly. The barrier is whatever element of doing business forces a new entrant to think long and hard, or to invest very deeply.

# Issue 2: Assume That Change Is a Constant

As I write this, Napster.com, the music-sharing Web site that I mentioned briefly back in Chapter 1, "Living in a Branded World," has received a court order to shut down—and then another order just days later to stay open until further notice. This one Web site in particular has become a lightning rod for old economy/new economy arguments, as well as some very important legal issues. A one-sentence background for those of you not familiar with this case is that Napster.com allows individuals to swap copies of musical recordings over the Internet, ignoring the copyright that belongs to the recording artists.

Taken to its logical conclusion, it means—well, nobody is sure what it means. One side says that the artists are losing sales because one copy of a CD could end up being used by a hundred different people. The other side says this is just a new-fangled version of product sampling and will lead to greater sales.

This one situation is a good example of many of the types of change that may affect your business in the next few years.

➤ Napster.com is a classic example of disruptive technology. It doesn't *alter* the competitive landscape for record labels—it puts crater-size holes and landslides into it.

➤ This isn't simply a new competitor, but instead *it is a new business that has changed all the rules in another business*. In Chapter 17, "Who Is Your Competition? Are You Sure About That?" we looked at the idea of "stealth bomber" competition. I strongly encourage you to do some brainstorming around this concept. Use the question "What new business could put us out of business?" as a way to get people involved. This is a classic question to put to people all over the company, and it is a place where your product development people may be most valuable.

➤ Napster.com throws a financial cloud over the music business as well, so the management teams of those companies are made to fight fires on several fronts all at once. Where do revenues come from if product sales are drastically cut? What kind of product could put your company into a financial tailspin?

Now that we have you on the lookout for guerillas threatening disruptive change, let's calm

**Heads Up**

The Napster.com example is one of extreme change, and it promises to stay a good-size issue for some time to come. *It pits the freedom to innovate against the safeguards of ownership.* Both of those are volatile, emotional, and very pragmatic issues. Are there implications here for your brand?

things down and look at change from the complete opposite end of the spectrum. This time the question is this: Does one change inevitably lead to more, or can we human beings ever leave well enough alone? Is there any such thing as "well enough" anymore?

It was just one little company selling out to a large corporation, but the sale of Kiehl's Pharmacy in New York City has generated a lot of press. The pharmacy had been in business 149 years and was owned by one family for the last 79 years. Kiehl's held on to the old idea of a neighborhood pharmacist as someone who compounded what you needed right there in the store. Products such as shampoo and hand cream were created right along with medications and prescriptions.

This pharmacy—in New York, one of the most competitive retail markets in the world—created an upscale consumer brand. Kiehl's packaging is very simple: black-and-white labels crowded with type and hard to read. The brand was built on personal selling and very generous sampling. Kiehl's is the envy of many big businesses who spent a lot more money and got a lot less exclusivity.

The brand achieved a kind of cult image; these were products so basic and pure that they were obviously special, and therefore not meant for the masses. This inside-out logic made sense to the makeup artists and beauty professionals who passed along the message of "specialness" to models and actors. The fashion magazines started mentioning the brand as a favorite of the "in crowd," and the brand's image soared higher.

Kiehl's got distribution in high-end stores such as Neiman Marcus decades ago, adding places like Barney's and Saks Fifth Avenue in more recent years. The company built a mail-order business as well. Kiehl's became a moneymaking marvel by breaking a lot of the rules of mass marketing. That's because the company never did mass marketing.

I have never been to the store in New York myself, and I don't spend a lot of time hanging around with fashion models, but even I can tell you that Kiehl's claim to fame was its generosity with free samples. These people absolutely believed that if you tried one of their products, you would be happy and would come back to buy more. And, at a reported $40 million a year in sales—and, it has been hinted, 85 percent profit margin (which I assume is really 85 percent gross margin—remember Chapter 18, "'What's the Price?' Has No Easy Answer," on pricing?)—Kiehl's has built an empire to be envied.

The owner decided early in 2000 to sell the Kiehl's business to L'Oreal, an international giant in the cosmetics business. A very good background article on the Kiehl's company and its sale can be found in the July/August 2000 issue of *FSB/Fortune Small Business* magazine. All the articles I have read about this sale say that the current owner, the granddaughter of the man who bought the pharmacy back in 1921, felt that it was time to get out. The business had grown to capacity and beyond, and was now on the verge of having significant problems that could hurt the brand.

So, can a giant corporation with lots of expertise in building and marketing large consumer brands leave well enough alone? If you suddenly owned Kiehl's, could you? I can almost guarantee—and, in fact, would put money down on a bet—that three things will happen:

➤ There is a brand profile-type document somewhere in the L'Oreal offices right now being studied and committed to memory so that no one misses the special-ness of the brand.

➤ The brand equity in the Kiehl's name is being professionally researched as we speak.

➤ By early 2001, the business press will revisit the Kiehl's sale for a what-happened-to analysis, and you will see articles in *The Wall Street Journal* and other places eager to analyze L'Oreal's actions.

Keep an eye on this one. I am sure you will see it covered in the business press. Can anyone leave well enough alone? That's a tough one for any of us.

# Issue 3: Open Mind, Insert Ideas— Staying Relevant

The issue of relevancy has to be looked at from two sides: Your brand has to stay rele-vant to a strong target audience, and you need to stay relevant to a rapidly changing business environment.

Let's talk about how brands stay relevant. For our examples, we will revisit the com-panies profiled in the "Branding Inspiration" chapters: Welch's, Media Metrix, and KISS 108. Because you now have so much background on each of them, it is easier to see some of their decisions from the perspective of "staying relevant." If you haven't yet read Chapters 11, "Branding Inspiration: Information and Education Go Branded," 12, "Branding Inspiration: Product, Service, and Science Brands," and 13, "Branding Inspiration: People and Entertainment as Brands," you may want to go back and read them now because I will only summarize the steps that they took, not explain each one again. Each of them has done different things.

Welch's® is a long-established product-manufacturing business. For this company, staying relevant has meant three things:

➤ Adding new products in line with changing tastes
➤ Introducing packaging changes in line with changing lifestyles
➤ Making some changes in how the company communicates with the consumer

What about Media Metrix? This is a young company in a young and very much still evolving industry. In its short life span, Media Metrix has already done several things:

➤ Acquired a company (Relevant Knowledge) that gives Media Metrix the ability to offer insight and measurement products for Internet advertising.

➤ Acquired a second company (Jupiter Communications, Inc.) that now broadens the Media Metrix product line even further with Internet business analysis and insights.

➤ Provides a new communications medium, based on this second acquisition. Jupiter Forums runs Internet economy conferences that draw in a wide cross-section of attendees and, at the same time, create content that turns around and builds the company profile.

KISS 108 Radio started out in 1979 as the disco station reincarnation of a small "beautiful music" station. How has this station managed to stay relevant in such a competitive and always-evolving industry?

➤ The concept of "take the station to the street" that was created back in 1979 has never been forgotten. This is personality-driven radio.

➤ Look again at the list of KISS Concert performers and how it has evolved, always reflecting the hottest, latest trends.

➤ Look again at the promotions and how the on-air personalities are so closely linked to the station's activities. This is a *very personal* business.

Three very different companies, each doing things to stay fresh in the customers' eyes. But more than anything else, when you look over what they have done, you will see all of them *building a tighter relationship with their customers*. None of these three companies leaves customer relationships to the whims of the marketplace. None of them trusts in the randomness of chance. Each is having fun and making money the old-fashioned way: pleasing its customers. And each of them has more customers as each year goes by. Whether your brand is 4 years old, 20 years old, or more than 100 years old, this is good, disciplined thinking.

Before we leave the subject of keeping your brand relevant, I want to encourage you to go back and spend some very serious time working with Part 4, "Building Your Brand Perspective." The more you study successful brands, the more you will see that the people who manage them have a deep respect for and understanding of what the brand is about. That is why I am such a strong proponent of doing the work of building a written brand profile. It is a living document, so it can certainly be changed over time. However, one of its greatest strengths is its permanence—not literally (I just said that it can be changed), but in that it captures important elements of the brand's identity. It provides the proverbial calm port in a storm when you need to make changes. The stress at that point is the need to make *smart* decisions about which changes to make.

Now, what about keeping the Brand Called You relevant? You have got to read, to listen, and to join, and you can do all of these from the comfort of your own home or in the midst of 24/7 social whirlwind—whichever suits your style best.

# Issue 4: It's All About Interaction, Not Just the Internet

This may seem self-evident, but some days I wonder: The Internet is only one type of interaction. There is so much focus, so much exhilaration, and so much fear about what the Internet is doing in our lives that too many people seem to have lost their perspective.

Brand management is about building strong customer relationships with the brand, and the "right" way to do that needs to be carefully decided. If ever there was a business where one size does not fit all, this is it.

Back in Chapter 4, "E-Commerce Makes Branding Hotter Than Ever," we talked about the importance to your brand of choosing the correct strategic role for the Internet. There are tremendous—and often very expensive—differences between using the Internet as one piece of your overall communications strategy and using it as the place where you will make all your money.

For many of you, the Internet is a marketing device. It is about communications and customer service, and frankly, some of your companies have built a Web site under the "just in case" rule, which can be explained like this: "Just in case somebody checks it out, of course we have a Web site—doesn't everyone these days?"

If your brand is well-suited to handling online transactions, whether the Internet will be your primary sales location or a convenient new outlet, watch out. This is a very big decision, and for many of us consumers, it is rapidly turning into a deal maker or a deal breaker. If you have ever had the unpleasant experience of trying to buy something from a Web site that was anything less than 1,000 percent committed to being a superior transactional environment, you know what I mean.

The goal of all your marketing and sales activities is productive communication with the customer. The social—and, therefore, business—environment that we live in demands a fluid interactivity. Our customers expect information and service when they want it, and they have been taught by technological innovation that they can have it—even when that interaction does not involve any technology on their part.

What do these four old-fashioned, stand-in-line activities have in common?

➤ Returning something to a department store

➤ Placing an order over the telephone for something in a catalog

➤ Renewing a driver's license

➤ Mailing a package at the post office

In all four, the customer needs no technology. He just needs to communicate what he wants and provide select pieces of information. So why do people get so crazy and frustrated if it takes more than a few minutes to accomplish one of these things? And why does each of these activities generate so many complaints? Our expectation is that the *other person* in the transaction *does* have technology on her side, and should therefore have all the information and ability to make things move as fast as our expectations.

The bottom line is to use technology to help with interaction. Technology on its own is often just a carrier, not the message itself. No matter how gee-whiz your technology is, it can never substitute for the content of the message. One of the most interesting things to watch in this regard will be the evolution of online advertising. We have banner ads and e-mail ads galore right now. Many of us have taught ourselves to simply not see banner ads, much like we have adapted to print and television ads. We quickly learn to be very selective. What will come next?

# Issue 5: Brand Champions Will Change Customer Service

One of the greatest challenges that brand champions will face in the coming decade is learning how to create a core strategy around customer service.

Whose job is it to build a core competency in customer service? Usually, it isn't the brand manager's, that's for sure. But today—well, it now has to be one of the key elements of brand management. Add this to your list of responsibilities. You don't need to design and run the department, but you need to care deeply about the training of the people, how familiar they are with the brand profile, and how free they are to ask you tough questions and get straight answers.

Think of customer service as an element of your one-to-one marketing campaign, and maybe you will see this differently. You wouldn't let something as intricate and intimate as your ability to get to know the customer better simply fall by the wayside. You would be right on the front lines, learning all about it and influencing the decisions on how the communication will be done and how the information will be used.

Customer service is moving up to that level of importance, and as the brand champion, you need to make sure it gets the attention it deserves.

**The Least You Need to Know**

➤ The relationship that a customer has with a brand shapes his entire opinion; when you put together a lot of individual opinions, the brand has a reputation. Word spreads fast.

➤ The rapid-fire pace of change forces us to make a lot of decisions faster than we would like. Be careful that all those decisions to change really are meaningful and that some are not decisions to *not* change at all.

➤ Customer service and customer care need to become core pieces of your brand strategy. They may not be familiar to most brand managers today, but that is about to change.

# Glossary of Terms

**all-digital media**   All providers on the Web, including Web sites (WWW addresses), proprietary online services (such as AOL), and applications such as instant messaging and e-mail.

**barrier to entry**   Something that makes it more difficult for a competitor to get established in a market.

**best shoppers**   Those individuals who are most valuable to a company through a combination of their profitability and loyalty.

**brand**   An identifiable entity that makes specific promises of value.

**brand awareness**   A measurement of how aware a person is of the brand name. It is measured for both top-of-mind awareness or when aided by a prompt of some type, for example, "Are you aware of Nancy's Napkins?"

**brand equity**   The sum total of all the different values that people attach to the brand name.

**brand group**   Those people directly involved with the day-to-day management of a brand.

**branding**   The process of choosing which promises to make, what kind of value to assign, and what will be identifiable about an entity.

**bricks and clicks**   A reference to companies that have operations both at retail stores and on the Web.

**bricks and mortar**   A way to refer to retail stores (here on Earth, not on the Web) and other buildings.

**cannibalize**   What happens when a product gets its sales by taking a customer away from another like product. The inverse of this is **incremental sales**.

**category management**   A process of analyzing consumer preferences to identify the best mix of products that will satisfy consumer desire for variety and a retailer's desire for profitability.

**channel conflict**   When channels of distribution for a product overlap too closely, the customer may feel threatened, for example when exclusive designer labels, usually sold only in boutiques, open their own factory outlet stores.

**channels of distribution**   The various classes of trade (though sometimes also used to mean the specific chain of stores) where a product can be found.

**class of trade**   Used to distinguish one type of outlet from another. Drugstores are a separate class of trade from warehouse club stores.

**competitive set**   The group of brands or product types that the end user can choose between.

**content**   In the Internet world, the matter contained within the Web site, which may be reports, items to purchase, horoscopes, and so on.

**cybersquatting**   Getting and holding ownership of a domain name that you believe is valuable to another.

**decision tree**   A commonly used tool in problem-solving systems to help sort out the options at each decision point.

**demographic data**   The facts and figures about a population in terms of age, income, household size, and other factors.

**direct to consumer**   DTC for short. When a company takes its message directly to the consumer. In this book, it is used to discuss pharmaceutical companies advertising their prescription products to the consumer.

**distribution chain**   The series of stops that a product makes getting from its origin to the end user. Also sometimes used to refer to the collection of points where the product is available (for example, all hardware and home improvement stores), although this is really more properly referred to as the channels of distribution.

**domain name**   The set of words, letters, or numbers that identifies a Web address.

**efficient consumer response (ECR)**   The re-engineering of the consumer packaged goods industry.

**elasticity**   The amount of stretch in a brand equity or a price that is still acceptable to the target audience.

**end user**   The final point in the sales cycle; the person or organization that will actually use the product.

**Five P's**   The five classic elements of a brand marketing program: product, what we are selling; price, how much it can sell for; place, where it will be sold; promotion, how we will motivate a purchase; and person, who will want it.

**genericized**   When a brand name is used to mean a whole class of products, as in Kleenex for facial tissue.

**grandmother research**   Casual market research that has no predictive value.

**home/work**   In the context used in this book, the combined Web activity from both home and office locations.

**incremental sales**   New sales that add up to a bigger total revenue, rather than sales taken away from another of your brands. *See* **cannibalize** for the inverse of this.

**infotainment**   The move toward making information more fun and easier to grasp.

**implied endorsement**   When someone hears an advertisement and assumes that the person featured believes that the item is good.

**licensing agreement**   Granting the brand rights owned by one company to another company for the express purpose of making or marketing something under that brand name.

**line extension**   A product that is added onto an existing product line in a slightly different form (or flavor, color, and so on).

**link**   A software device that takes the user directly to a specific place on a Web site.

**logo**   A symbol that identifies an entity. This may be a graphic or a set of words.

**margin**   The difference between the base price and the new selling price, expressed either in dollars or in percent.

**marketing mix**   Shorthand expression for the basic components of how a brand will be marketed.

**markup**   A percentage added onto a base price.

**mission statement**   A declaration of the goals of the organization.

**national brands**   In distribution across virtually the entire country.

**order bias**   The order in which elements being researched are shown to the participants.

**original selling price and resale price**   The starting price for an item the first time it is sold versus anytime after that, when cost or profit is added on top before being sold again.

**positioning statement**   A set of words that captures the essential message of the brand.

**private label**   Also sometimes called store brand, these are products marketed under the store's own name.

**promotion**   An incentive to purchase a product.

**promotional advertising**  Utilizing the power of an advertising medium to deliver a message designed to encourage immediate purchase.

**psychographic data**  Often referred to as lifestyle data, reflecting attitudes, beliefs, and personal choices more so than age or other variables.

**question sequence**  The order in which questions are asked in a market research study.

**reach**  The percent of total potential market that is reached.

**regional brands**  Not available nationally, but rather in some smaller section of the country.

**scanning**  Using an optical reading device to identify an item by the set of black lines in a barcode. Note that the barcode contains the UPC, defined later.

**store brands**  Also called private-label brands, these are products marketed under the brand name of the retailer.

**transactional data**  The record of what was purchased, by whom, where, and when.

**transactional database**  The record of a large group of transactions that can be analyzed by customer, store, time of day, and other variables.

**unique identifier**  A set of numbers in a unique sequence that identifies one object or person from another.

**unique visitors**  The estimated number of total users of a Web site who visited once in the time period.

**Universal Product Code (UPC)**  The numbers, in a unique sequence, that identify many products. They are included in a barcode along with the set of lines that are read by a scanner.

**virtual**  Something that cannot be seen in its entirety or touched, and yet that exists, like a Web site.

**virtual void**  A sarcastic expression for the nothingness of the Web.

**virtual world**  The collection of all that is on the Web.

**vision statement**  A declaration of what the organization is focused on being.

# Resources and Revelations Guide

This guide is broken into three sections that contain the following information:

➤ List of trademarks used and their owners

➤ List of sources for your reference

➤ Exclusive bonus: Internet Movers and Shakers Guide

## Trademark Information

Many brands have been mentioned throughout the chapters. I have tried to list all of them here, with their owners, for your reference. If a brand was mentioned more than once, I am listing the trademark information in only one location.

### Chapter 1

1. babyGap is a registered trademark of Gap, Inc., San Bruno, California.

2. Fidelity® and Magellan® are registered trademarks of FMR Corp., Boston, Massachusetts.

3. Coke® is a registered trademark of the Coca Cola Bottling Co., Atlanta, Georgia.

4. Sony® is a registered trademark of Sony Corp., Tokyo, Japan.

5. MP3 is a service mark of MP3 Holdings, Inc., New York, New York.

6. The Napster.com Web site is operated by Napster, Inc., San Mateo, California.

7. Nike® is a registered trademark of Nike, Inc., Beaverton, Oregon.

8. Titleist® is a registered trademark of Acushnet Company, New Bedford, Massachusetts.

9. Pepsi® is a registered trademark of Pepsico, Inc., Purchase, New York.

10. Claritin® is a registered trademark of Schering Corporation, Kenilworth, New Jersey.

11. *Merriam-Webster's® Online Dictionary* is a registered trademark of Merriam-Webster, Inc., Springfield, Massachusetts.

# Chapter 2

1. Clearasil®, Topex®, Oil of Olay®, Fasteeth®, and Fixodent® are all registered trademarks of the Procter & Gamble Company, Cincinnati, Ohio.

2. Lavoris® is now a registered trademark of Dep Corporation, Rancho Dominguez, California.

3. Welch's® is a registered trademark of Welch Foods, Inc., Concord, Massachusetts.

# Chapter 4

1. The Internet Economy Indicators™ is a trademark of the Center for Research in Electronic Commerce, Graduate School of Business, University of Texas at Austin. © 2000.

# Chapter 6

1. Tylenol® is a registered trademark of McNeil Consumer Brands, Inc., New Brunswick, New Jersey.

2. King Arthur Flour® is a registered trademark of Sands, Taylor and Wood Co., Norwich, Vermont.

3. Saturn® is a registered trademark of Saturn Corp., Spring Hill, Tennessee.

4. Rubbermaid® is a registered trademark of Rubbermaid Home Products, Inc., Wooster, Ohio.

5. Arm & Hammer® is a registered trademark of Arm & Hammer Division of Church & Dwight Co., Princeton, New Jersey.

6. Chrysler PT Cruiser® is a registered trademark of Daimler Chrysler Corporation, Auburn Hills, Michigan.

7. Clorox® is a registered trademark of The Clorox Company, Oakland, California.

8. Barbie® is a registered trademark of Mattel, Inc., El Segundo, California.

9. Hasbro® is a registered trademark of Hasbro Industries, Inc., Pawtucket, Rhode Island.

10. The Disney Store is a service mark of Walt Disney Company, Burbank, California.

11. The Lion King® is a registered trademark of Walt Disney Company, Burbank, California.

## Chapter 7

1. KISS 108-FM™ is a trademark of AMFM, Inc.

## Chapter 9

1. The GE medallion and GE® are registered trademarks of General Electric Company, Schenectady, New York.

2. CREAM OF WHEAT® is a registered trademark of Nabisco, Inc., East Hanover, New Jersey.

3. Carnation® brand condensed milk is a registered trademark of Carnation Co., Los Angeles, California.

4. Best Buy is a service mark of Best Buy Concepts, Inc., Eden Prairie, Minnesota.

5. Toys 'R' Us and is a registered trademark of Geoffrey, Inc., Wilmington, Delaware.

6. Kids 'R' Us is a registered trademark of Geoffrey, Inc., Wilmington, Delaware.

7. Smarterkids.com is a service mark of SmarterKids.com, Inc., Needham, Massachusetts.

8. *The Complete Idiot's Guide*™ is a registered trademark of Macmillan USA, Inc., Indianapolis, Indiana.

9. *Chicken Soup for the Soul*® is a registered trademark of John Canfield and Mark Victor Hansen, Santa Barbara, California.

10. IWon.com is a trademark of IWon, Inc.

11. Grandmother's® is a registered trademark of Whipple Company, Natick, Massachusetts.

12. Dell® is a registered trademark of Dell Computer Corporation, Austin, Texas.

13. 6FigureJobs.com is a service mark of 6FigureJobs.com LLC Corp., New Canaan, Delaware.

14. Business Week® is a registered trademark of McGraw-Hill, Inc., New York, New York.

15. ColgateTotal® is a registered trademark of Colgate Palmolive Corporation, New York, New York.

16. FreeInternet.com is a service mark of Freei.net, Corp., Federal Way, Washington.

17. Streamline.com is a service mark of Streamline.com, Inc., Westwood, Massachusetts.

18. MasterCard is a service mark of MasterCard International, New York, New York.

19. Tiffany is a service mark and trademark of Tiffany & Co., New York, New York.

20. Fast Company® is a registered trademark of Fast Company Inc., Boston, Massachusetts.

21. KFC® is a registered trademark of KFC Corporation, Louisville, Kentucky.

22. *The Wall Street Journal*® is a registered trademark of Dow Jones & Co., Inc., New York, New York.

23. Hewlett-Packard® is a registered trademark of Hewlett-Packard Co., Palo Alto, California.

24. DeBeers is no longer a registered trademark.

25. Band-Aid® and Band-Aid Brand® are registered trademarks of Johnson & Johnson, New Brunswick, New Jersey.

# Chapter 10

1. Maxwell House® is a registered trademark of Kraft General Foods, Glenview, Illinois.

2. Timex® is a registered trademark of Timex Corp., Middletown, Connecticut.

3. Mitsubishi® is a registered trademark of Mitsubishi Shgi Kaisha Ltd., Tokyo, Japan.

4. Lexus® is a registered trademark of Toyota Motor Corp., Aichi-ken, Japan.

5. Sprint® is a trademark of Sprint Communications Company L.P., Kansas City, Missouri.

6. McDonald's® is a trademark of McDonald's Corp., Oak Brook Park, Illinois.

7. Apple Computer® is a registered trademark of Apple Computer Inc., Cupertino, California.

8. Salesforce.com is a service mark of salesforce.com Inc, San Francisco, California.

9. Sprint PCS® is a trademark of Sprint Communications Company L.P., Kansas City, Missouri.

10. Honda® and Thinking™ are trademarks of Honda Motor Co., Tokyo, Japan.

11. Lipitor® is a registered trademark of Warner Lambert Company, Morris Plains, New Jersey.

12. Sun® Microsystems and We're the dot in .com™ are trademarks of Sun Microsystems Inc., Palo Alto, California.

13. Nortel Networks™ and How the World Shares Ideas™ are trademarks of Northern Telecom Ltd., Montreal, Quebec, Canada.

14. Hewlett-Packard® is a registered trademark of Hewlett-Packard Co., Palo Alto, California.

15. Office Depot™ is a service mark of Office Depot Inc., Boca Raton, Florida.

16. United States Postal Service® and Fly Like an Eagle™ are trademarks of United States Postal Service, Washington, D.C.

17. Aleve® is a registered trademark of Bayer-Roche LLC, Elkhart, IN, and All Day Long. All Day Strong.™ is a trademark of Procter & Gamble Co., Cincinnati, Ohio.

# Chapter 13

1. Emeril's® and Emerilware® are trademarks of Emeril's Food of Love Productions, Inc., New Orleans, Louisiana.

2. Universal Orlando® is a registered trademark of Universal City Studios Inc., Universal City, California.

3. Network 40™ is a trademark of Network Magazine Group, New York, New York.

# Chapter 16

1. Macy's® is a registered trademark of Federated Department Stores, Cincinnati, Ohio.

2. Volkswagen New Beetle® is a registered trademark of Volkswagen Corporation, Wolfsburg, Germany.

3. Liz Claiborne® is a registered trademark of Liz Claiborne Inc., New York, New York.

# Chapter 18

1. Skippy® Peanut Butter is a registered trademark of Bestfoods, Englewood Cliffs, New Jersey.

# Chapter 21

1. Fidelity Investments® is a registered trademark of FMR Corp., Boston, Massachusetts.

2. AT&T™ is a service mark of AT&T Corp., New York, New York.

3. CREAM OF WHEAT® is a registered trademark of Nabisco Brands Company, Wilmington, Delaware.

4. General Electric® is a trademark of General Electric Company, Schenectady, New York.

# Sources Referenced

Throughout the book, I referenced a number of publications or associations. Many of them are listed here for you.

## Chapter 1

1. *Fast Company Magazine* is owned by Fast Company Media Group LLC, Boston, Massachusetts.

2. Tom Peters, *The Brand You 50,* Alfred A. Knopf publisher.

3. Del Jones, *Author Says: Workers, Brand Yourself* © 2000 *USA Today.*

4. The Private Label information from Tom Aquilina is based on a Gallup Poll in 1996 that was updated by independent research in 1999.

## Chapter 3

1. Nelson, Emily. "Reunion at P&G University," June 7, 2000. © 2000 *The Wall Street Journal.*

## Chapter 4

1. Media Metrix reports used:

   ➤ Digital Media Report, March 2000 and April 2000. © 2000 Media Metrix, Inc.

   ➤ Multi-Country Home Usage Report, April 2000. © 2000, Media Metrix, Inc.

   ➤ Media Metrix/NPD Toy e-Visory, Holiday 1999. © 1999 Media Metrix, Inc.

2. The Internet Economy Indicators © 2000 University of Texas.

3. Indrajitt Sinha. *Cost Transparency*: *The Net's Real Threat to Prices and Brands*; *Harvard Business Review.* March–April 2000. © 2000 *Harvard Business Review.*

## Chapter 16

1. Daniel Fisher. "Luxe.com." *Forbes.* May 1, 2000. © 2000 *Forbes Magazine.*

# Exclusive Bonus for You
## Internet Movers and Shakers Report
**Source:** Media Metrix        **Reporting Period:** July 2000

**Top Ten Sites in Twenty Popular Categories**

## What kind of activity does it take to create a successful Web site?

Now you can see Web activity for 200 Web sites right here in *The Complete Idiot's Guide to Brand Management.* Media Metrix Inc, the pioneer and leader in Internet measurement, provides this valuable guide for you to study.

### What can you learn from these charts?

1. Which categories are of higher interest to consumers?
2. Which Web sites are generating the highest numbers of Unique Visitors?
3. What percent of Web users are these sites reaching?
4. Which Web sites should you consider buying advertising from?
5. The Web sites you should be studying in depth for insights into why they are so successful.
   What are they doing differently? What can you learn from their marketing techniques?

## Definitions and Tips for Reading the Charts

### Unique Visitors Home/Work (000s):
The actual number of total users who visited the reported Web site or online property
at least once in the given month. All unique visitors are unduplicated (only counted once).

### Digital Media Home/Work % Reach:
The percentage of projected individuals within a designated demographic or market break
category that accessed the Web content of a specific site or categoy among the total number
of projected individuals using the Web during the month.

### Sample Size:
Approximately 55,000 individuals throughout the U.S. participate in the Media Metrix sample.

### Category Reference Points:
At the top of each chart you will see a line that looks like this:

**Total Health Universe**                   **21,945**            **27.4%**

This tells you the total number of Unique Visitors to that category of Web sites (for example,
(all health-related) and the % Reach for the category. In this example, health-related Web sites
had almost 22 million Unique Visitors during the month of July, 2000 and that corresponds
to over one quarter of all Web users during the period.

# How the Movers and Shakers Report Can Help You and Your Brand

Are you thinking about starting a Web site? Do you wish you knew more about what the competition really looks like? You can go online and spend hours moving from one Web site to another, going in and out of various search engines to see what links show up and still be left wondering about some very important issues:

➤ Which Web sites in your categories are generating the highest number of visitors?

➤ Which Web sites are pretty close together in visitor count, and which ones are half their size or less?

➤ Which Web sites should you consider running banner ads on?

➤ If you knew which Web sites were doing the best job of attracting visitors, then you could focus your analysis a lot more clearly.

➤ If you knew the top Web sites in a number of categories, not just your own, then you could start to build a framework for Web success: What do the most popular Web sites have in common?

➤ What do the most popular transactional Web sites have in common?

➤ What do the most popular informational Web sites have in common?

➤ If you could just get your hands on some of this high-level data, you could push your own Internet strategy further toward reality.

If you have ever wished that you could get your hands on data like this, then today is your lucky day. If you have ever tried to buy data like this, then you know that it is virtually impossible for the average person to access and too costly for most smaller businesses to afford. It is an expensive process to collect and manage the billions of data points involved, so it is not likely that most of us will get regular access any time soon.

I am very happy to be able to provide you with Internet measurement data for 200 of the top Web sites in the world, courtesy of Media Metrix, Inc. The charts you will see on the next few pages provide you with the number of unique visitors and the percent of the Web population they reach. We chose the time period of July 2000 as a good midpoint to study, for two reasons:

➤ It is midway between the big holiday shopping seasons of 1999 and 2000.

➤ The Internet shakeout and consolidation has been underway for the last six months or so. This will be a good baseline for you to have as news reports over the next year or two tell us what is changing and who is "winning."

In conjunction with Media Metrix, I have chosen 20 categories for you to review in this special section:

| Health | Department stores | Entertainment/Kids | Sports |
| Retailer | Consumer goods | Business finance news/ research | Apparel |

| Community | Entertainment/Music | Consumer Electronics | General news |
|---|---|---|---|
| Gaming | Travel information | Services/Discussion/ Chat | Automotive |
| Career | Online trading | Travel transactions | Hobbies/ Lifestyle |

## Can You Get More Information? Yes!

I strongly encourage you to go to the Media Metrix Web site, www.mediametrix.com, once a month to check on the latest press releases and studies. The site posts tremendous articles and analyses that you can read for free.

You will also find a treasure chest of press releases from the Media Metrix archives. I considered reprinting some of my favorite pieces here but decided that it would be much easier for you to get the whole story online.

Here are 10 of the many press releases that I think you need to know about. The ones I have chosen represent a good cross-section of important insight (note the demographic analysis that is fifth on the list—it is excellent material) and a window into the emerging cultural impact of the Web (look at the Napster and political convention articles, for instance).

9/12/00: Teens Spend Less Than Half as Much Time Online as Adults

9/11/00: Napster Application Quadruples to Nearly Five Million U.S. Home Users, According to Media Metrix

8/24/00: Political Web Site Usage Comparable to Budweiser.com, Pepcidac.com, Powerade.com Traffic During Convention Weeks

8/22/00: Media Metrix Releases U.S. Top 50 Web and Digital Media Properties for July 2000 and Reveals Top-Gaining Web Categories

8/21/00: The Dollar Divide: Demographic Segmentation and Web Usage Patterns by Household Income

8/17/00: B-to-B, Fastest Growing Online Ad Segment, to Reach $3 Billion by 2005

8/10/00: Entertainment Genre Dominates Year 2000 Top Newcomer List

8/09/00: Women Outpace Men Online In Number and Growth Rate

7/20/00: Media Metrix Releases Internet Measurement Results for Australia, Canada, France, Germany, Japan, United Kingdom, and the United States

One read through this list signals that there is tremendous value in bookmarking the Media Metrix site.

As I give one final thank-you to the people at Media Metrix for their generous contributions to this book, I hope you will find this data exciting and filled with learning opportunities.

# Top Ten Health Sites

July 2000
**Source: Media Metrix**

| Sites | Unique Visitors Home/Work (000s) | Digital Media Home/Work % Reach |
|---|---|---|
| **Total Health Universe** | **21,945** | **27.4%** |
| 1 ONHEALTH.COM | 5,234 | 6.5% |
| 2 WEBMD.COM | 4,250 | 5.3% |
| 3 EDIETS.COM | 2,284 | 2.9% |
| 4 DRKOOP.COM | 1,712 | 2.1% |
| 5 PLANETRX.COM | 1,623 | 2.0% |
| 6 DRUGSTORE.COM | 1,500 | 1.9% |
| 7 THRIVEONLINE.COM | 1,217 | 1.5% |
| 8 INTELIHEALTH.COM | 1,117 | 1.4% |
| 9 PREVENTION.COM | 1,089 | 1.4% |
| 10 MAYOHEALTH.ORG | 1,052 | 1.3% |

Note: Category universe does not include channel data

# Top Ten Gaming Sites

July 2000
**Source: Media Metrix**

| Sites | Unique Visitors Home/Work (000s) | Digital Media Home/Work % Reach |
|---|---|---|
| **Total Gaming Universe** | **34,737** | **43.4%** |
| 1 SPEEDYCLICK.COM | 6,534 | 8.2% |
| 2 FREELOTTO.COM | 6,179 | 7.7% |
| 3 SHOCKWAVE.COM | 5,738 | 7.2% |
| 4 WEBSTAKES.COM | 5,314 | 6.6% |
| 5 LUCKYSURF.COM | 5,048 | 6.3% |
| 6 UPROAR.COM | 4,717 | 5.9% |
| 7 IWIN.COM | 4,717 | 5.9% |
| 8 GAMESVILLE* | 3,979 | 5.0% |
| 9 PRIZECENTRAL.COM | 3,345 | 4.2% |
| 10 TREELOOT.COM | 3,180 | 4.0% |

Note: Category universe does not include channel data

# Top Ten Automotive Sites

July 2000
**Source: Media Metrix**

| Sites | Unique Visitors Home/Work (000s) | Digital Media Home/Work % Reach |
|---|---|---|
| **Total Automotive Universe** | **18,637** | **23.3%** |
| 1 CARPOINT.COM | 3,077 | 3.8% |
| 2 KBB.COM | 2,795 | 3.5% |
| 3 CARCLUB.COM | 1,647 | 2.1% |
| 4 CARS.COM | 1,519 | 1.9% |
| 5 EDMUNDS.COM | 1,446 | 1.8% |
| 6 AUTOBYTEL.COM | 1,417 | 1.8% |
| 7 AUTOWEB.COM | 1,338 | 1.7% |
| 8 AUTOTRADER.COM | 1,314 | 1.6% |
| 9 SWITCHOUSE.COM | 1,228 | 1.5% |
| 10 EBAYMOTORS.COM | 989 | 1.2% |

Note: Category universe does not include channel data

# Top Ten Sports Sites

July 2000
**Source: Media Metrix**

| Sites | Unique Visitors Home/Work (000s) | Digital Media Home/Work % Reach |
|---|---|---|
| **Total Sports Universe** | **20,247** | **25.3%** |
| 1 ESPN* | 5,306 | 6.6% |
| 2 SPORTSLINE.COM SITES* | 4,468 | 5.6% |
| 3 CNNSI.COM | 2,161 | 2.7% |
| 4 NASCAR.COM | 1,785 | 2.2% |
| 5 SANDBOX.COM | 1,751 | 2.2% |
| 6 MAJORLEAGUEBASEBALL.COM | 1,696 | 2.1% |
| 7 NFL.COM | 1,182 | 1.5% |
| 8 SPORTINGNEWS.COM | 1,010 | 1.3% |
| 9 FOXSPORTS.COM | 914 | 1.1% |
| 10 NBA.COM | 845 | 1.1% |

Note: Category universe does not include channel data

# Top Ten Music-Retailer Sites

July 2000
**Source: Media Metrix**

| Sites | Unique Visitors Home/Work (000s) | Digital Media Home/Work % Reach |
|---|---|---|
| **Total Music-Retailer Universe** | **14,192** | **17.7%** |
| 1 BARNESANDNOBLE.COM | 5,281 | 6.6% |
| 2 CDNOW.COM | 3,857 | 4.8% |
| 3 BMGMUSICSERVICE.COM | 3,199 | 4.0% |
| 4 COLUMBIAHOUSE.COM | 2,244 | 2.8% |
| 5 NETRADIO.COM | 861 | 1.1% |
| 6 BMG.COM | 595 | 0.7% |
| 7 TOWERRECORDS.COM | 380 | 0.5% |
| 8 CDUNIVERSE.COM | 325 | 0.4% |
| 9 JANDR.COM | 276 | 0.3% |
| 10 MUSICMAKER.COM | 223 | 0.3% |

Note: Category universe does not include channel data

# Top Ten Career Sites

July 2000
**Source: Media Metrix**

| Sites | Unique Visitors Home/Work (000s) | Digital Media Home/Work % Reach |
|---|---|---|
| **Total Career Universe** | **13,343** | **16.7%** |
| 1 JOBSONLINE.COM | 5,003 | 6.2% |
| 2 MONSTER.COM | 4,303 | 5.4% |
| 3 HOTJOBS.COM | 1,814 | 2.3% |
| 4 CAREERBUILDER.COM | 1,568 | 2.0% |
| 5 HEADHUNTER.NET | 1,262 | 1.6% |
| 6 CAREERPATH.COM | 1,072 | 1.3% |
| 7 JOBS.COM | 585 | 0.7% |
| 8 CAREERMOSAIC.COM | 519 | 0.6% |
| 9 CAREERMAG.COM | 411 | 0.5% |
| 10 DICE.COM | 388 | 0.5% |

Note: Category universe does not include channel data

# Top Ten Business Finance-News/Research Sites

July 2000
**Source: Media Metrix**

| Sites | Unique Visitors Home/Work (000s) | Digital Media Home/Work % Reach |
|---|---|---|
| **Total Business Finance-News/Research Universe** | **18,508** | **23.1%** |
| 1 TIME.COM | 4,170 | 5.2% |
| 2 MARKETWATCH.COM | 3,606 | 4.5% |
| 3 ONMONEY.COM | 1,568 | 2.0% |
| 4 YOUWINMAIL.COM | 1,450 | 1.8% |
| 5 CNNFN.COM | 1,389 | 1.7% |
| 6 BIZLAND.COM | 1,160 | 1.4% |
| 7 CNBC.COM | 1,150 | 1.4% |
| 8 THESTREET.COM | 1,149 | 1.4% |
| 9 WSJ.COM | 1,017 | 1.3% |
| 10 BLOOMBERG.COM | 987 | 1.2% |

Note: Category universe does not include channel data

# Top Ten Apparel Sites

July 2000
**Source: Media Metrix**

| Sites | Unique Visitors Home/Work (000s) | Digital Media Home/Work % Reach |
|---|---|---|
| **Total Apparel Universe** | **10,948** | **13.7%** |
| 1 GAP.COM | 1,378 | 1.7% |
| 2 ALLOY.COM | 1,278 | 1.6% |
| 3 VICTORIASSECRET.COM | 1,115 | 1.4% |
| 4 LANDSEND.COM | 964 | 1.2% |
| 5 OLDNAVY.COM | 933 | 1.2% |
| 6 EDDIEBAUER.COM | 795 | 1.0% |
| 7 LLBEAN.COM | 725 | 0.9% |
| 8 NORDSTROM.COM | 591 | 0.7% |
| 9 JCREW.COM | 547 | 0.7% |
| 10 ONEHANESPLACE.COM | 465 | 0.6% |

Note: Category universe does not include channel data

311

# Top Ten General News Sites

July 2000
**Source: Media Metrix**

| Sites | Unique Visitors Home/Work (000s) | Digital Media Home/Work % Reach |
|---|---|---|
| **Total General News Universe** | **29,298** | **36.6%** |
| 1 MSNBC.COM | 10,041 | 12.5% |
| 2 CNN.COM | 5,117 | 6.4% |
| 3 TIME.COM | 4,170 | 5.2% |
| 4 NYTIMES.COM | 3,015 | 3.8% |
| 5 ABC NEWS* | 3,006 | 3.8% |
| 6 USATODAY.COM | 2,517 | 3.1% |
| 7 WASHINGTONPOST.COM | 2,166 | 2.7% |
| 8 SLATE.COM | 1,911 | 2.4% |
| 9 FOXNEWS.COM | 1,390 | 1.7% |
| 10 LA TIMES* | 1,273 | 1.6% |

Note: Category universe does not include channel data

# Top Ten Entertainment-Music Sites

July 2000
**Source: Media Metrix**

| Sites | Unique Visitors Home/Work (000s) | Digital Media Home/Work % Reach |
|---|---|---|
| **Total Entertainment-Music Univ** | **26,044** | **32.5%** |
| 1 WINDOWSMEDIA.COM | 6,348 | 7.9% |
| 2 CDNOW.COM | 3,857 | 4.8% |
| 3 MTV.COM | 2,815 | 3.5% |
| 4 MP3.COM | 2,800 | 3.5% |
| 5 PLANETOFMUSIC.COM | 2,599 | 3.2% |
| 6 MP3S.COM | 1,708 | 2.1% |
| 7 SONICNET.COM | 1,672 | 2.1% |
| 8 AUDIOHIGHWAY.COM | 1,501 | 1.9% |
| 9 LAUNCH.COM | 1,238 | 1.5% |
| 10 ARTISTDIRECT.COM | 1,235 | 1.5% |

Note: Category universe does not include channel data

# Top Ten Consumer Electronics Sites

July 2000
**Source: Media Metrix**

| Sites | Unique Visitors Home/Work (000s) | Digital Media Home/Work % Reach |
|---|---|---|
| **Total Consumer Electronics Universe** | **15,101** | **18.9%** |
| 1 BESTBUY.COM | 1,691 | 2.1% |
| 2 NETMARKET.COM SITES* | 1,190 | 1.5% |
| 3 SPRINTPCS.COM | 1,119 | 1.4% |
| 4 3COM.COM | 1,081 | 1.3% |
| 5 CIRCUITCITY.COM | 1,017 | 1.3% |
| 6 NINTENDO.COM | 974 | 1.2% |
| 7 800.COM | 887 | 1.1% |
| 8 ATTWS.COM | 868 | 1.1% |
| 9 PRICEWATCH.COM | 868 | 1.1% |
| 10 RADIOSHACK.COM | 723 | 0.9% |

* An aggregation of commonly owned/branded domain names

# Top Ten Department Stores- Retail Sites

July 2000
**Source: Media Metrix**

| Sites | Unique Visitors Home/Work (000s) | Digital Media Home/Work % Reach |
|---|---|---|
| **Total Department Stores- Retail Universe** | **9,057** | **11.3%** |
| 1 SEARS.COM | 2,475 | 3.1% |
| 2 JCPENNEY.COM | 2,242 | 2.8% |
| 3 WALMART.COM | 1,477 | 1.8% |
| 4 NETMARKET.COM SITES* | 1,190 | 1.5% |
| 5 TARGET.COM | 1,139 | 1.4% |
| 6 COSTCO.COM | 856 | 1.1% |
| 7 MACYS.COM | 450 | 0.6% |
| 8 SERVICEMERCHANDISE.COM | 417 | 0.5% |
| 9 VALUEAMERICA.COM | 395 | 0.5% |
| 10 SHOPDISCOVERY.COM | 250 | 0.3% |

* An aggregation of commonly owned/branded domain names.

# Top Ten Consumer Goods Retail Sites

July 2000
**Source: Media Metrix**

| Sites | Unique Visitors Home/Work (000s) | Digital Media Home/Work % Reach |
|---|---|---|
| **Total Consumer Goods Retail Universe** | **9,128** | **11.4%** |
| 1 FREESHOP.COM | 2,531 | 3.2% |
| 2 STAPLES.COM | 1,596 | 2.0% |
| 3 OFFICEDEPOT.COM | 1,301 | 1.6% |
| 4 OFFICEMAX.COM | 1,100 | 1.4% |
| 5 ATYOUROFFICE.COM | 559 | 0.7% |
| 6 CHECKSUNLIMITED.COM | 547 | 0.7% |
| 7 POPULARLINK.COM | 439 | 0.5% |
| 8 CHEFSCATALOG.COM | 417 | 0.5% |
| 9 WWFSHOPZONE.COM | 388 | 0.5% |
| 10 ARRID.COM | 315 | 0.4% |

# Top Ten Travel Information Sites

July 2000
**Source: Media Metrix**

| Sites | Unique Visitors Home/Work (000s) | Digital Media Home/Work % Reach |
|---|---|---|
| Total Travel Information Universe | **19,720** | 24.6% |
| 1 EXPEDIA.COM TRAVEL* | 6682 | 8.3% |
| 2 MAPQUEST.COM | 6621 | 8.3% |
| 3 MAPBLAST.COM | 1206 | 1.5% |
| 4 BASSHOTELS.COM | 1115 | 1.4% |
| 5 MAPSONUS.COM | 1101 | 1.4% |
| 6 MARRIOTT.COM | 1048 | 1.3% |
| 7 IFLYSWA.COM | 995 | 1.2% |
| 8 SMARTERLIVING.COM | 602 | 0.8% |
| 9 BID4VACATIONS.COM | 523 | 0.7% |
| 10 MARRIOTTREWARDS.COM | 510 | 0.6% |

# Top Ten Travel Transactions Sites

July 2000
**Source: Media Metrix**

| Sites | Unique Visitors Home/Work (000s) | Digital Media Home/Work % Reach |
|---|---|---|
| **Total Travel Transactions Universe** | **21,595** | **27.0%** |
| 1 PRICELINE.COM | 6,815 | 8.5% |
| 2 EXPEDIA.COM TRAVEL* | 6,682 | 8.3% |
| 3 ITN.NET | 2,547 | 3.2% |
| 4 SOUTHWEST.COM | 2,391 | 3.0% |
| 5 LOWESTFARE.COM | 1,873 | 2.3% |
| 6 DELTA-AIR.COM | 1,855 | 2.3% |
| 7 AA.COM | 1,839 | 2.3% |
| 8 USAIRWAYS.COM | 1,690 | 2.1% |
| 9 NWA.COM | 1,477 | 1.8% |
| 10 CHEAPTICKETS.COM | 1,241 | 1.5% |

* An aggregation of commonly owned/branded domain names.

# Top Ten Online Trading Sites

July 2000
**Source: Media Metrix**

| Sites | Unique Visitors Home/Work (000s) | Digital Media Home/Work % Reach |
|---|---|---|
| **Total Online Trading Universe** | **8,129** | **10.1%** |
| 1 ETRADE.COM | 2,097 | 2.6% |
| 2 FIDELITY.COM | 1,669 | 2.1% |
| 3 SCHWAB.COM | 937 | 1.2% |
| 4 AMERITRADE.COM | 727 | 0.9% |
| 5 DLJDIRECT.COM | 547 | 0.7% |
| 6 DATEK.COM | 461 | 0.6% |
| 7 TDWATERHOUSE.COM | 374 | 0.5% |
| 8 STOCKMASTER.COM | 326 | 0.4% |
| 9 BUYANDHOLD.COM | 325 | 0.4% |
| 10 TROWEPRICE.COM | 274 | 0.3% |

# Top Ten Community Sites

July 2000
**Source: Media Metrix**

| Sites | Unique Visitors Home/Work (000s) | Digital Media Home/Work % Reach |
|---|---|---|
| **Total Community Universe** | **8,129** | **10.1%** |
| 1 IVILLAGE SITES* | 6,736 | 8.4% |
| 2 ONHEALTH.COM | 5,234 | 6.5% |
| 3 WOMEN.COM | 4,466 | 5.6% |
| 4 THEGLOBE.COM | 3,536 | 4.4% |
| 5 TALKCITY.COM | 2,240 | 2.8% |
| 6 MYFAMILY.COM | 1,997 | 2.5% |
| 7 OXYGEN.COM | 1,876 | 2.3% |
| 8 THIRDAGE.COM | 1,753 | 2.2% |
| 9 HOMEARTS.COM | 1,509 | 1.9% |
| 10 ALLOY.COM | 1,278 | 1.6% |

* An aggregation of commonly owned/branded domain names

# Top Ten Services-Discussion/Chat Sites

July 2000
**Source: Media Metrix**

| Sites | Unique Visitors Home/Work (000s) | Digital Media Home/Work % Reach |
|---|---|---|
| **Total Community Universe** | **14,891** | **18.6%** |
| 1 ICQ.COM | 4,373 | 5.5% |
| 2 DELPHI.COM | 3,649 | 4.6% |
| 3 EGROUPS.COM | 2,946 | 3.7% |
| 4 INSIDETHEWEB.COM | 1,457 | 1.8% |
| 5 ASKME.COM | 1,075 | 1.3% |
| 6 INFOROCKET.COM | 639 | 0.8% |
| 7 ECIRCLES.COM | 359 | 0.4% |
| 8 PLANETFEEDBACK.COM | 300 | 0.4% |
| 9 COOLBOARD.COM | 264 | 0.3% |
| 10 CHAT.RU | 234 | 0.3% |

# Top Ten Entertainment-Kid Sites

July 2000
**Source: Media Metrix**

| Sites | Unique Visitors Home/Work (000s) | Digital Media Home/Work % Reach |
|---|---|---|
| **Total Entertainment - Kids Universe** | **17,918** | **22.4%** |
| 1 DISNEY ONLINE* | 7,251 | 9.1% |
| 2 CARTOONNETWORK.COM | 2,165 | 2.7% |
| 3 NICK.COM | 2,122 | 2.6% |
| 4 MAMAMEDIA.COM | 1,174 | 1.5% |
| 5 FOXKIDS.COM | 1,078 | 1.3% |
| 6 CUPCAKEPARTY.COM | 1,074 | 1.3% |
| 7 NICKJR.COM | 895 | 1.1% |
| 8 POKEMON.COM | 863 | 1.1% |
| 9 KBKIDS.COM | 762 | 1.0% |
| 10 YAHOOLIGANS.COM | 582 | 0.7% |

\* An aggregation of commonly owned/branded domain names.

# Top Ten Hobbies/Lifestyle Sites

July 2000
**Source: Media Metrix**

| Sites | Unique Visitors Home/Work (000s) | Digital Media Home/Work % Reach |
|---|---|---|
| **Total Hobbies/Lifestyle Universe** | **17,776** | **22.2%** |
| 1 OURHOUSE.COM | 2,462 | 3.1% |
| 2 ANCESTRY.COM | 1,826 | 2.3% |
| 3 HOMESTORE.COM | 1,511 | 1.9% |
| 4 FOODTV.COM | 1,333 | 1.7% |
| 5 ROOTSWEB.COM | 1,188 | 1.5% |
| 6 GARDEN.COM | 1,186 | 1.5% |
| 7 BHG.COM | 813 | 1.0% |
| 8 FAMILYTREEMAKER.COM | 778 | 1.0% |
| 9 GENEALOGY.COM | 732 | 0.9% |
| 10 HGTV.COM | 688 | 0.9% |

# Index

## Q

## R

**THE COMPLETE IDIOT'S GUIDE TO**

| Arts & Sciences | Business & Personal Finance | Computers & the Internet | Family & Home | Hobbies & Crafts | Language Reference | Health & Fitness | Personal Enrichment | Sports & Recreation | Teens |

# IDIOTSGUIDES.COM

## Introducing a new
## and different Web site

Millions of people love to learn through *The Complete Idiot's Guide*® books. Discover the same pleasure online in **idiotsguides.com**–part of The Learning Network.

**Idiotsguides.com** is a new and different Web site, where you can:

- Explore and download more than 150 fascinating and useful mini-guides—FREE! Print out or send to a friend.

- Share your own knowledge and experience as a mini-guide contributor.

- Join discussions with authors and exchange ideas with other lifelong learners.

- Read sample chapters from a vast library of *Complete Idiot's Guide*® books.

- Find out how to become an author.

- Check out upcoming book promotions and author signings.

- Purchase books through your favorite online retailer.

# Learning for Fun. Learning for Life.

# IDIOTSGUIDES.COM • LEARNINGNETWORK.COM

Copyright © 2000 Macmillan USA, Inc.